PENGUIN BOOKS

BICYCLE DIARIES

A cofounder of the musical group Talking Heads, David Byrne has also released several solo albums, most recently *Here Lies Love* with Fatboy Slim, in addition to collaborating with such noted artists as Twyla Tharp, Robert Wilson, and Brian Eno. His art includes photography and installation works and has been published in five books. He lives in New York and he recently added some new bike racks of his own design around town. His Web site is www.davidbyrne.com.

Bicycle Diaries

David Byrne

Penguin Books

PENGUIN BOOKS
Published by the Penguin Group
Penguin Group (USA) Inc., 375 Hudson Street, New York, New York 10014, U.S.A. ·
Penguin Group (Canada), 90 Eglinton Avenue East, Suite 700, Toronto, Ontario, Canada
M4P 2Y3 (a division of Pearson Penguin Canada Inc.) · Penguin Books Ltd, 80 Strand,
London WC2R 0RL, England · Penguin Ireland, 25 St Stephen's Green, Dublin 2, Ireland
(a division of Penguin Books Ltd) · Penguin Group (Australia), 250 Camberwell Road,
Camberwell, Victoria 3124, Australia (a division of Pearson Australia Group Pty Ltd) ·
Penguin Books India Pvt Ltd, 11 Community Centre, Panchsheel Park, New Delhi–110 017,
India · Penguin Group (NZ), 67 Apollo Drive, Rosedale, North Shore 0632, New Zealand
(a division of Pearson New Zealand Ltd) · Penguin Books (South Africa) (Pty) Ltd, 24 Sturdee
Avenue, Rosebank, Johannesburg 2196, South Africa

Penguin Books Ltd, Registered Offices: 80 Strand, London WC2R 0RL, England

First published in the United States of America by Viking Penguin,
a member of Penguin Group (USA) Inc. 2009
This edition with a new preface published in Penguin Books 2010

11   13   15   17   19   20   18   16   14   12

Cover illustration: **David Byrne**
Cover design: **Paul Buckley**
Interior design: **Daniel Lagin**

Photographs by the author unless otherwise stated.

THE LIBRARY OF CONGRESS HAS CATALOGED THE HARDCOVER EDITION AS FOLLOWS:
Byrne, David, 1952–
Bicycle diaries / David Byrne.
p.   cm.
ISBN 978-0-670-02114-7 (hc.)
ISBN 978-0-14-311796-4 (pbk.)
1. Bicycle touring.   2. Byrne, David, 1952– —Diaries.
3. Byrne, David, 1952– —Travel.   I. Title.
GV1044.B97 2009
796.6'4—dc22   2009009390

Printed in the United States of America
Set in Celeste with Apollo

*Penguin is committed to publishing works of quality and integrity.
In that spirit, we are proud to offer this book to our readers;
however, the story, the experiences, and the words
are the author's alone.*

For Malu—who doesn't ride a bike…yet

Preface to
the Paperback Edition

When the hardcover and e-Book editions of this book came out in 2009, I decided that rather than do readings as a form of promotion I would instead participate in small events in various towns. These presentations and discussions focused not just on bicycles, but also on the past and future of our cities. (This book, I hope the reader will discover, is not really about bicycles either.) I went to San Francisco, Portland, Los Angeles, Seattle, Austin, Minneapolis, Chicago, Toronto, Ottawa, Philadelphia, Washington, D.C., Providence, Boston, and Atlanta. At each location there were four of us on stage: a representative from the city government, an advocate (usually for urban cycling, but sometimes for public transportation too), a theorist or historian of cities, and me. We each talked for less than twenty minutes, showed slides, and took questions at the end. These events were modest in scale—usually the theaters held less than one thousand people—but in most cases they seemed to have left a lasting impression, both with me and with the locals. In each city I met a gaggle of people who, in various ways, are grappling with many of the ideas, impressions, and issues about cities that I present in this book. Quite a few of these ideas are not original. Others have said the same things and sometimes better; certainly in more detail. My ideas come partially from books, but just as often from riding around the aforementioned cities on a bicycle.

The folks who presented at and attended these panels are the ones who are doing the actual work to transform our cities. One of the things I took away from these events was a sense that there is a groundswell of interest in making our cities less car-centric and generally more livable. These town meetings sometimes became a focal point for those feelings, a place where they could be aired, which was exciting. I got the impression that given a little more momentum, changes were not just possible, but inevitable.

How did this happen? In part these widely felt urges aren't inspired by speeches by academics or politicians but are due to the fact that cities have become attractive again as places to live, work, and raise children—more so than they have been in a while. As cities become more attractive the inhabitants naturally take a different view of their immediate surroundings; they're more engaged if it's not just a place just to work in the daytime or occasionally take in a show or a meal. There's a healthy self-interest involved in the movement to make cities more livable. For urban residents, their home lives and their careers, the way they get from home to work and back, and what that feels like are all connected. One's life isn't quite as compartmentalized— where one lives, works, and plays are often within, well, biking distance. Having all these things intersect and overlap rather than being completely separated and isolated from one another can make for a pretty nice life. No "duty now for the future," as the band DEVO once paraphrased our religious tendency to postpone living and enjoyment—as if we were meant to put up with substandard circumstances because we'll be rewarded later. With what, a house in the suburbs? That's the reward? Lots of people realize that isn't exactly the gold ring it has been made out to be.

Once the compartmentalization of one's life starts to break down, the impulse is to try to make *all* of it better, not just to focus on having nicer lawns, shady streets, and country clubs in the suburbs that are miles from where one works . . . or to focus on a bigger office and an assigned parking space when in town. In these town meetings I sensed that people are beginning to view their cities not just as a temporary stopping-off point in one's career or one's life journey—a city is no longer viewed as a place to escape from as soon as one has made enough money—but as an end in itself. As more people share this attitude, the creative capital in cities begins to outweigh the perceived advantage of the lawns and ease of parking in the suburbs. Cities have always been places where one can continually reinvent oneself personally, psychologically, and creatively. It's become accepted that we may as well make them livable too.

It's become clear that we'll have to undo a lot of what was done in the last seventy years. Like the Russians emerging from the Soviet system, we are beginning to emerge from the era of the dominance of the automobile. We've got ingrained patterns and ways of thinking (and not thinking) to deal with, just like they do.

The insights I took away from these events have been very heartening—despite the current lack of initiative on dealing with a host of other issues, from global warming and the economic collapse to the behavior of the banks (still unregulated as I write this!). One could get pretty cynical. Maybe I was lucky, but these events showed me that there is cause for optimism. In general the city representatives who participated are on the same side as the advocates. They both agree that structuring our towns to make them more and more car-friendly has led to—*ummm*—a dead end. The end of that highway isn't a town at all, but an intersection next to a parking lot. I've been to those towns—or what's left of them.

It was interesting that in our pre-event meetings, many of the participants assumed I'd be the focus of attention. But that's not what happened. The audiences came because they were energized and excited by the issues being aired—it's their lives, after all—so they usually focused their questions on the city representative. I was happy to be merely the catalyst or the excuse for putting the whole thing together, but the nuts-and-bolts details of upcoming projects and proposals were thankfully the real interest. These attendees want their cities improved, and they knew I was not the one who was going to make that happen. Sometimes this focus on the local city rep degenerated into calls for "I need a bike lane on my street" or a complaint about inconsiderate drivers, but folks mostly sensed that their towns were changing for the better and that change is incremental.

Sometimes the local politicians waffled and hedged their statements, with no concrete plans to present in response to the public's questions. But quite a few of them presented real initiatives and proposals and were able to cite improvements that were currently under way.

The theorists and historians at these events tended to be the wild cards. Don Shoup joined us in L.A., where he is regarded as the "parking guru"—a subject dear to the hearts of Angelinos. He did a presentation detailing the behavior of drivers looking for parking places. How long will they circle a block, how wide a radius of blocks would they circle? If there is the possibility of free parking in the vicinity, do the streets inevitably get filled and clogged with hopeful circlers? (Yes, an amazing percentage of traffic is actually caused by people who are looking for cheap parking.) In New York, Mitchell Joachim proposed that homes could be literally grown—made out of plants trained and bred to be our nests, thus being "green" in more ways than one. He made another proposal, which was for houses made of lab-grown meat! The round window, which could be opened and closed like a lens, looked like a giant anus! Ugh. Historian Samuel Zipp, from Brown University in Providence, Rhode Island, showed the evolution and transformations of that town exclusively using lovely historical postcards. Beginning with images of streets filled with trolleys and almost no cars stretching until the early 1970s, when I went to school there, when the river that runs through town was paved over to transform the center of town into a massive auto interchange. (It has since been uncovered, and downtown is much improved.) Mistakes aren't always forever.

As entrenched as our thinking about cities has been, recent events indicate that things might be changing. Detroit is, we hear, turning its derelict empty urban center back into farmland. Bike-share programs are starting up in Ottawa, Denver, Minneapolis, Washington, D.C., and Toronto. San Francisco has emerged from years of bureaucratic tangles and has added a protected bike lane on Market Street.

In Brazil, São Paulo and Rio de Janeiro are initiating bike programs. L.A. has rebranded their buses and created high-speed lanes (as will New York next year); the use of public transportation has increased significantly there—something mind-boggling for that city. There's a lot of momentum.

Here in New York the commissioner of the Department of Transportation, Janette Sadik-Kahn, continues to make changes

New bike lane on Market Street, San Francisco. Frank Chan, San Francisco Bike Coalition

that would have been unthinkable years ago. Broadway between Forty-eighth and Thirty-fourth streets is now part pedestrian zone and public plaza, part bike lane. Thirty-fourth Street will get high-speed crosstown buses and more pedestrian space; the public space around Union Square will be expanded with traffic eliminated from its northern side. Bike lanes on the east side of Manhattan are coming. I can imagine some of our formerly unfriendly streets becoming New World versions of, for example, La Rambla in Barcelona: great boulevards that have room for cars, but are primarily a place for walking, for seeing and being seen, and for getting from one place to another in a pleasant way.

I tried the Vélib' public bicycle-rental program in Paris. To release the bike is a little bit confusing at first, with all the swiping and button pushing, but then it's easy. I went for a ride down along the Seine, over a pedestrian bridge by the Eiffel Tower, and circled back to my hotel. It costs one euro for a twenty-four-hour period (or you can buy a monthly or yearly pass), and within that period there is unlimited use as long as each individual ride doesn't exceed thirty minutes. This means you can get groceries, go to the movies, meet friends for dinner, or commute to work if it's not too far. As there are Vélib' stations all over town, you reinsert the bike in the nearest station-locking port to your destination, and the clock stops ticking. Then, at no additional charge, you can pick up another one to get back home or to your next stop and the clock resets at zero again.

One bike at the station had a flat tire, and its port flashed red, indicating it was not available for use. I was also advised to check the brakes and chains before removing a bike, as sometimes they're not well maintained. When I asked about the recent U.S. news stories that the Vélib' bikes were getting vandalized and trashed, purportedly by the immigrant population of the Parisian suburbs, I was told that such reports seemed like hearsay, that the theft and vandalism rate is much lower than reported. I'd also heard that the system has been

Vélib' bike share program, Paris. Matthew Rankin

extremely lucrative for the city, and maybe the reported costs of upkeep are an effort by street furniture/ad platform company JC Decaux to renegotiate their deal with the city. Whatever the truth is, the French seem proud of their system.

That said, we in North America still have a long way to go. The U.S. government's new gas-mileage goal for cars is 35.5 mpg—which is, face it, pathetic. We have the ability right now to build cars that get 100 mpg, but of course that would put all the SUVs and Hummers off the road, so I guess that's not acceptable, not just yet. I just read that GM is optimistic about their new car—a new Cherokee Jeep model! Talk about ingrained thinking! Where my parents live, in bucolic Columbia, Maryland, there is one bus in and out of town per day. As they no longer drive, they are effectively trapped, held prisoner in a well-manicured suburb. Lots of other elderly folks who moved to the suburbs everywhere are finding themselves in similar situations or will in the near future.

Bicycle manufacturers are responding to urban developments as well. Many more models of city bikes are available now than just a year or two ago. These bikes—many loosely modeled on Dutch-style bikes or the old-school bikes some of us had as kids—aren't for racing or for doing tricks, but for getting around elegantly and cleanly. They often have carriers to put our shopping bags, and guards so our clothes don't get soiled. There are electric bikes out now too, so one could conceivably commute to work over greater distances without even breaking a sweat. I just saw two electric-bike wheels being developed at MIT that, besides giving you a boost, automatically log onto a Web site that one day might register your carbon credits for cycling to work. This kind of monetary incentive would make cycling extremely seductive and popular.

Where is this all going? I'm optimistic these days. I envision transformed cities, often with more people on the streets, people who aren't made to feel that they are intruders, secondary to cars. I note a resurgence in neighborhood unity and have a sense that many of us are learning to slow down and enjoy life a little more. It's not just about bikes, either. Quite a few U.S. cities, including Cincinnati, Dallas, and L.A., have plans to bury some of their freeways and put parkland on top.

In Boston they have already done this and it's wonderful. It reconnects the riverfront with the rest of the city; people are just, well, happier. The Hudson River Park's bikeway on the west side of Manhattan is glorious—I use it to get uptown and downtown safely and quickly almost every day—but it's right next to a highway, separated from the city as whole. I dream of the day when the highway might be buried and the present park might expand and integrate with the streets of Manhattan. I don't live near the east side's big, bad old FDR

Plan for park over a highway, Dallas. © Mei-Chun Jau

Drive, but as far as I'm concerned, that could go underground as well.

These changes have payoffs. Raising the quality of city life results in increased productivity, prosperity, and health, both mental and physical. Employees have fewer sick days and the health care system is less burdened—the load we all have to carry becomes lighter. These changes are of course greener as well, though being green because it's good for one's future is a weak carrot. What I've noticed is that if something makes one feel better that's a stronger incentive. That kind of immediate positive feedback is what has created this momentum, and legislative and structural changes will keep it on the rails.

I never intended to become an activist on these subjects—and I'm not. I feel like more an observer, someone reporting my own subjective take on things. Our cities are alive, like us; they have both a deep intelligence that guides them and a physical presence. They're both a brain and a body. They are our neural networks writ large, our psychological drives made physical, and by changing and fixing our cities we are reflecting similar changes going on inside. When our built world does not accurately correspond to our vision, to our physiology, and to our innate psychology, we suffer, and feel alienated, as if we are inhabiting the wrong body or mind. When our surroundings are more aligned with us, we fit better, more comfortably. The rewards are immense and wide-ranging.

But mostly it's just more fun.

David Byrne,
New York City,
May 2010

Acknowledgments

Scott Moyers, my agent at the Wylie Agency, suggested some time ago that there might be a book here, with the thread of my bike explorations of various cities as a linking device. His reference was W. G. Sebald, specifically his book *The Rings of Saturn*, which uses a rambling walk in the English countryside as a means of connecting a lot of thoughts, musings, and anecdotes. I can't pretend to have come anywhere close to Sebald as a writer, but setting the bar that high gave me something to shoot for. I may also have mentioned to Scott *Tropical Truth*, Caetano Veloso's account of the Tropicália years in Brazil, in which he uses his memory of that time as a springboard to discuss a host of issues and events. Both books go off on a lot of tangents, which, for them at least, works fine. I could see that it was possible to make the form work.

Though I'd been keeping a travel and tour diary for decades, Danielle Spencer in my studio helped encourage and facilitate moving that online. Blogging it's called. I'm still finding my way to where I fit in the blogosphere—I realized early that I didn't want to produce either an exclusively metablog (a series of links to interesting things seen or read online) or an exclusively personal diary—I don't think my personal life is very interesting or unique. However, I did find that the journal/blog was a great way of trying to express and articulate thoughts, feelings, and ideas—many of which occurred to me while traveling, which often meant biking around various towns. And the blog allows links, photos, videos, audio, and all sorts of things to be part of the reading experience—an experience I hope digital readers will be able to render eventually.

Thanks to editors Paul Slovak and Walter Donohue for notes and comments—we all realized that a blog is not a book. Thanks to my girlfriend, Cindy, for comments and companionship on some of these rides. And thanks to Emma and Tom, my parents, for getting me my first bike.

Contents

Introduction

A bike is the world's most used form of transportation.

I've been riding a bicycle as my principal means of transportation in New York since the early 1980s. I tentatively first gave it a try, and it felt good even here in New York. I felt energized and liberated. I had an old three-speed leftover from my childhood in the Baltimore suburbs, and for New York City that's pretty much all you need. My life at that time was more or less restricted to downtown Manhattan—the East Village and SoHo—and it soon became apparent to me that biking was an easy way to run errands in the daytime or efficiently hit a few clubs, art openings, or nightspots in the evening without searching for a cab or the nearest subway. I know, one doesn't usually think of nightclubbing and bike riding as being soul mates, but there is so much to see and hear in New York, and I discovered that zipping from one place to another by bike was amazingly fast and efficient. So I stuck with it, despite the aura of uncoolness and the danger, as there weren't many people riding in the city back then. Car drivers at that time weren't expecting to share the road with cyclists, so they would cut you off or squeeze you into parked cars even more than they do now. As I got a little older I also may have felt that cycling was a convenient way of getting some exercise, but at first I wasn't thinking of that. It just felt good to cruise down the dirty potholed streets. It was exhilarating.

By the late '80s I'd discovered folding bikes, and as my work and curiosity took me to various parts of the world, I usually took one along. That same sense of liberation I experienced in New York recurred as I pedaled around many of the world's principal cities. I felt more connected to the life on the streets than I would have inside a car or in some form of public transport: I could stop whenever I wanted to; it was often (very often) faster than a car or taxi for getting from point A to point B; and I didn't have to follow any set route. The same exhilaration, as the air and street life whizzed by, happened again in each town. It was, for me, addictive.

This point of view—faster than a walk, slower than a train, often slightly higher than a person—became my panoramic window on much of the world over the last thirty years—and it still is. It's a big window and it looks out on a mainly urban landscape. (I'm not a racer or sports cyclist.) Through this window I catch glimpses of the mind of my fellow man, as expressed in the cities he lives in. Cities, it occurred to me, are physical manifestations of our deepest beliefs and our often unconscious thoughts, not so much as individuals, but as the social animals we are. A cognitive scientist need only look at what we have made—the hives we have created—to know what we think and what we believe to be important, as well as how we structure those thoughts and beliefs. It's all there, in plain view, right out in the open; you don't need CAT scans and cultural anthropologists to show you what's going on inside the human mind; its inner workings are manifested in three dimensions, all around us. Our values and hopes are sometimes awfully embarrassingly easy to read. They're right there—in the storefronts, museums, temples, shops, and office buildings and in how these structures interrelate, or sometimes don't. They say, in their unique visual language, "This is what we think matters, this is how we live and how we play." Riding a bike through all this is like navigating the collective neural pathways of some vast global mind. It really is a trip inside the collective psyche of a compacted group of people. A *Fantastic*

Voyage, but without the cheesy special effects. One can sense the collective brain—happy, cruel, deceitful, and generous—at work and at play. Endless variations on familiar themes repeat and recur: triumphant or melancholic, hopeful or resigned, the permutations keep unfolding and multiplying.

Yes, in most of these cities I was usually just passing through. And one might say that what I could see would therefore by definition be shallow, limited, and particular. That's true, and many of the things I've written about cities might be viewed as a kind of self-examination, with the city functioning as a mirror. But I also believe that a visitor staying briefly can read the details, the specifics made visible, and then the larger picture and the city's hidden agendas emerge almost by themselves. Economics is revealed in shop fronts and history in door frames. Oddly, as the microscope moves in for a closer look, the perspective widens at the same time.

Each chapter in this book focuses on a particular city, though there are many more I could have included. Not surprisingly, different cites have their own unique faces and ways of expressing what they feel is important. Sometimes one's questions and trains of thought almost seem predetermined by each urban landscape. So, for example, some chapters ended up focusing more on history in the urban landscape while others look at music or art—each depending on the particular city.

Naturally, some cities are more accommodating to a cyclist than others. Not just geographically or because of the climate, though that makes a difference, but because of the kinds of behavior that are encouraged and the way some cities are organized, or not organized. Surprisingly, the least accommodating are sometimes the most interesting. Rome, for example, is amazing on a bike. The car traffic in central Italian cities is notoriously snarled, so one can make good time on a bike, and, if the famous hills in that town are avoided, one can glide from one amazing vista to the next. It's not a bike-friendly city by any means—the every-man-for-himself vibe hasn't encouraged the creation of secure bike lanes in these big towns—but if one accepts that reality, at least temporarily, and is careful, the experience is something to be recommended.

These diaries go back at least a dozen years. Many were written during work-related visits to various towns—for a performance or an exhibit, in my case. Lots of folks have jobs that take them all over the world. I found that biking around for just a few hours a day—or even just to and from work—helps keep me sane. People can lose their bearings when they travel, unmoored from their familiar physical surroundings, and that somehow loosens some psychic connections as well. Sometimes that's a good thing—it can open the mind, offer new insights—but frequently it's also traumatic in a not-so-good way. Some people retreat into themselves or their hotel rooms if a place is unfamiliar, or lash out in an attempt to gain some control. I myself find that the physical sensation of self-powered transport coupled with the feeling of self-control endemic to this two-wheeled situation is nicely empowering and reassuring, even if temporary, and it is enough to center me for the rest of the day.

It sounds like some form of meditation, and in a way it is. Performing a familiar task, like driving a car or riding a bicycle, puts one into a zone that is not too deep or involving. The activity is repetitive, mechanical, and it distracts and occupies the conscious mind, or at least part of it, in a way that is just engaging enough but not too much—it doesn't cause you to be caught off guard. It facilitates a state of mind that allows some but not too much of the unconscious to bubble up. As someone who believes that much of the source of his work and creativity is to be gleaned from those bubbles, it's a reliable place to find that connection. In the same way that perplexing problems sometimes get resolved in one's sleep, when the conscious mind is distracted the unconscious works things out.

During the time these diaries were written I have seen some cities, like New York, become more bike-friendly in radical new ways, while in others the changes have been slow and incremental—they have yet to reach a tipping point as far as accepting cycling as a practical and valid means of transportation. Some cities have managed to find a way to make themselves more livable, and have even reaped some financial rewards as a result, while others have sunk deeper into the pits they started digging for themselves decades ago. I discuss these developments, urban planning, and policy in the New York City chapter, as well as describe my limited involvement in local politics (and entertainment) as it pertains to making my city more bike-friendly, and, I think, a more human place to live.

American Cities

Most U.S. cities are not very bike-friendly. They're not very pedestrian-friendly either. They're car-friendly—or at least they try very hard to be. In most of these cities one could say that the machines have won. Lives, city planning, budgets, and time are all focused around the automobile. It's long-term unsustainable and short-term lousy living. How did it get this way? Maybe we can blame Le Corbusier for his "visionary" Radiant City proposals in the early part of the last century:

Le Corbusier, "Radiant City" (plans). Banque d'Images/Art Resource, NY. © 2009 Artists Rights Society (ARS), New York / ADAGP, Paris / FLC

His utopian proposals—cities (just towers really) enmeshed in a net of multilane roads—were perfectly in synch with what the car and oil companies wanted. Given that four of the five biggest corporations in the world still are oil and gas companies, it's not surprising how those weird and car-friendly visions have lingered. In the postwar period General Motors was the largest company in the whole world. Its president, Charlie Wilson said, "What's good for GM is good for the country." Does anyone still believe that GM ever had the country's best interests at heart?

Maybe we can also blame Robert Moses, who was so successful at slicing up New York City with elevated expressways and concrete canyons. His force of will and proselytizing had wide-ranging effects. Other cities copied his example. Or maybe we can blame Hitler, who built the autobahns in order to allow German troops and supplies fast, efficient, and reliable access to all points along the fronts during World War II.

I try to explore some of these towns—Dallas, Detroit, Phoenix, Atlanta—by bike, and it's frustrating. The various parts of town are often "connected"—if one can call it that—mainly by freeways, massive awe-inspiring concrete ribbons that usually kill the neighborhoods they pass through, and often the ones they are supposed to connect as well. The areas bordering expressways inevitably become dead zones. There may be, near the edges of town, an exit ramp leading to a KFC or a Red Lobster, but that's not a neighborhood. What remains of these severed communities is eventually replaced by shopping malls and big-box stores isolated in vast deserts of parking. These are strung along the highways that have killed the towns that the highways were meant to connect. The roads, housing developments with no focus, and shopping centers eventually sprawl as far as the eye can see as the highways inch farther and farther out. Monotonous, tedious, exhausting . . . and soon to be gone, I suspect.

I grew up in the suburbs of Baltimore. One of the houses we lived in there had a housing development to the right and some older houses behind it—with woods and a working farm in front. We lived right where suburban development had (temporarily) stopped—at the point where it met the farmland. Like a lot of people, I grew to disdain the suburbs, their artificialness and sterility. But I could never shake them entirely. There was some kind of weird fascination and attraction that I (and I think many others) can't quite get out of my system.

I must have gotten hooked on cycling early on: in high school I used to pedal over to my girlfriend's house in the evenings, which was at least four miles away, so I could hang out and smooch after I'd finished my homework. We almost did it right by the adjoining city dump once—no intruders there.

My generation makes fun of the suburbs and the shopping malls, the TV commercials and the sitcoms that we grew up with—but they're part of us too. So our ironic view is leavened with something like love. Though we couldn't wait to get out of these places they are something like comfort food for us. Having come from those completely uncool places we are not and can never be the urban sophisticates we read about, and neither are we rural specimens—stoic, self-sufficient, and relaxed— at ease and comfortable in the wild. These suburbs, where so many of us spent our formative years, still push emotional buttons for us; they're both attractive and deeply disturbing.

In Baltimore when I was in high school I used to go downtown by bus and wander around the shopping districts. It was exciting. Malls didn't exist yet! There were lots of people, hustle and bustle. Riding an escalator at Hutzler's or Hecht's (downtown department stores) was a thrill! Bad girls went there to shoplift cool clothes. But white flight was already in progress and soon, amazingly quickly, the center of Baltimore was abandoned except to those who couldn't afford to leave it. Many streets soon featured boarded-up row houses. And in the late 1960s there were race riots in the aftermath of which more whites left and the corner bars adopted what was called riot architecture. They don't teach this kind of architecture at Yale.

It consists of filling in the windows of your establishment with painted cinder blocks and leaving a couple of glass bricks in the center. On the other side of the tracks from the downtown shopping zone whole blocks were simply razed. Like the legendary South Bronx it looked like a war zone—and in a way it is. An undeclared civil war in which the car is winning. The losers are our cities and in most cases African Americans and Latinos.

There once existed natural geographical reasons for most towns to come into being: a meeting of rivers, as in Pittsburgh; a river meeting a lake, as in Cleveland or Chicago; a canal meeting a lake, as in Buffalo; a secure and sheltered harbor, as in Baltimore, Houston, and Galveston. Eventually, what was originally a geographical justification for choosing one place over another to settle got cemented down as rail lines reached across the open spaces and connected these cities. As more and more people were attracted to these towns, the density of habitation and attendant business opportunities became additional reasons for even more people to make their homes there. They were drawn to live in proximity to other people, as social animals will tend to do. In many cases the rivers or lakes eventually became irrelevant, and shipping moved elsewhere or shipping by water was replaced by rail and eventually by trucks. As a result the rivers and waterfronts soon became derelict and the industry built alongside them became ugly inconveniences. Nice people shunned those neighborhoods. I sound a bit didactic in this recapitulation of history—bear with me, it's a way of trying to figure out for myself how we got here.

There is often a highway along the waterfront in many towns. Before these highways were built, the waterfronts, already dead zones, were seen as the most logical places from which to usurp land for conversion into a concrete artery. Inevitably, little by little, the citizens of these towns become walled off from their own waterfronts, and the waterfronts became dead zones of yet a different kind—concrete dead zones of clean, swooping flyovers and access ramps that soon were filled with whizzing cars. Under these were abandoned shopping carts, homeless people, and piles of toxic waste. Often you couldn't even access the water as a pedestrian unless you climbed a few fences.

Most of the time it turns out the cars are merely using these highways not to have easier access to businesses and residences in the nearby city, as might have been originally proposed, but to bypass that city entirely. The highways allowed people to flee the cities and to isolate themselves in bedroom communities, which must have seemed to many like a good thing—one's own domain, a yard for the kids, safe schools, backyard barbeques, ample parking.

Years ago it was thought that our cities were not sufficiently car-friendly. People who wanted to move about in a car quickly found the streets frustratingly congested and crowded. So planners suggested that massive freeways and concrete arteries would solve the congestion problem. They didn't. They quickly filled up with even more cars—maybe because more people thought they could get to and fro faster on an expressway. So even more highways were built.

In some cases ring roads were added, encircling cities, to enable the motorist to get from one side of town to the other, or from one suburb to another, without even entering the city. When I bike around these places I discover that sometimes the only way to get from point A to point B is via a highway. The smaller roads have atrophied or sometimes they just aren't there anymore. Often they've been cut in two or sliced and diced by the larger arteries so you can't get from one place to another on surface streets even if you want to. As a cyclist or a pedestrian it makes one feel unwanted, like an interloper, and you end up sort of pissed off. Needless to say, riding a bike along the shoulder of an expressway is no fun. There's nothing romantic about it either—you're not a cool outlaw, you're simply somewhere you don't belong.

Niagara Falls

I wake up in America. The sun is blasting and I am in a tour bus in a huge parking lot in Buffalo—somewhere near the Canadian border. A highway passes alongside the parking lot and cars whoosh by.

I am in the middle of nowhere. In the middle distance there is an office building and to my left a hotel. Inside the hotel, women in identical suits sit watching a PowerPoint presentation in a glassed-in room. A man is walking to and fro in the lobby loudly explaining a marketing scheme into his cell phone headset. Americans are focused, intent, bent on self-improvement and enlarging their market share. The newspapers in the lobby show the U.S. Army attacking a mosque and the magazines show hooded Iraqis being tortured and abused by U.S. soldiers. The Salvation Army is setting up tables by the conference rooms. The ladies all have giant Burger King cups.

I have a few hours free so I head off on my bike toward Niagara Falls, which is not that far from Buffalo, though it ends up being farther than I thought. I ride on the shoulder of a road that is lined with chain stores, none of them specific to this area. Everyone who works in them is therefore an employee hired by some anonymous distant corporation. They probably are only allowed to make small decisions and they have almost no stake or investment in the place where they work. Marx called this alienation. Communism may have been a sick dream, but he was right about this aspect. Of course, I can't see any of the people who work in these places along the shoulder of the highway. There are no people visible anywhere, just cars pulling in and out of parking lots. I pass Hooters, Denny's, Ponderosa, Fuddruckers, Tops, Red Lobster, the Marriott Hotel, the Red Roof Inn, Wendy's, IHOP, Olive Garden . . . and roads with names like Commerce, Sweet Home, and Corporate Parkway.

Now I pass some Niagara Falls information joints. I must be getting closer! Then, farther on, there is motel after motel. Years

ago, this area used to be a prime honeymoon spot—though now it's a little hard to imagine anyone honeymooning here except in an ironic way. An ironic honeymoon? Anyway, who would want to honeymoon on a stretch of highway that looks like it could be anywhere in America?

Farther down the road—and I've gone at least ten miles now—there is evidence of the massive electrical power generated by the still-invisible falls. The sun is beating down and I'm feeling weird, hot, and a little tired . . . this landscape tells a strange story. Somewhere, off in the distance, is an amazing and awe-inspiring natural phenomenon, yet I pass by land that is unfit even to be industrialized, and has therefore been abandoned—an egret stands in a muddy stream among old tires and bits of busted signage. The mostly closed Lockheed plant on a rise looks disturbingly like a contemporary jail.

I arrive at the town of Niagara itself, which is a peculiar ghetto of black and Italian immigrants. I pass Italian grocery stores, hair salons, and liquor stores. I stop for a sausage sandwich and a Gatorade. A pale woman of maybe seventy sits in front of an ashtray overflowing with butts, leafing through a *Country Weekly* magazine. I suggest she might get sunburned on a hot day like today. She sniffs and ignores that warning and instead shows me a photo of Alan Jackson in her magazine. He's her favorite—"this year"—she says.

The falls are truly amazing. Out of nowhere, one emerges from this crappy town to signs pointing to the bridge to Canada, border guards, and the park. As one approaches the falls one can see a strange mist rising in the distance and the air is now cool, as if one had entered a giant air-conditioned room. I stand at a rail and stare at this mighty weirdness, looking, looking, as

if prolonged looking will cement this thing in my brain, and then I turn around and head back.

The Struggle, the Show

I saw an amazing video called *The Backyard*. It's about backyard wrestling—kids imitating WWF hijinks and then pushing them a bit further, a little more extreme. They use bats covered in barbed wire, jump into pits filled with fluorescent lightbulbs, set one another on fire, and of course hit one another with chairs and ladders, just like they've seen on TV, but it's all more DIY.

It's jaw-dropping—hilarious and sometimes horrific. It's hard to look as a kid slices himself with a razor to make the blood flow so it will all look more real.

In some cases their parents cheer them on.

Much of it is all about putting on a good but harmless show, as it is with the WWF, but a good show also seems to demand a certain amount of real blood, genuine risk, and danger. And sometimes these performers seem to get just a little carried away and the border between show and real life starts to get awfully fuzzy.

I ask myself, are these kids who—to borrow from the Trent Reznor song—need to hurt themselves to see if they can feel? Are they so feeling-deprived that any sensation, including pain, will do? Pain is a pretty easy feeling to achieve. Those on the receiving end of the punishment at these events often seem to stand there passively, waiting patiently to be smashed over the head with a fluorescent tube or trash can. The "punishment" appears to be accepted and unavoidable, almost wished for. Is it really punishment if one desires it?

Here then is what's going on behind the placid suburban houses I'm biking by: wildly over-the-top shows, dangerous dramas, torture, pain, and shrieks of loopy excitement. My friends and I liked to play army in our suburban neighborhood growing up, but we weren't nearly as creative as this lot—and there was almost never any physical contact.

Kodak Moments

I am in Rochester, New York, for an exhibition of my work and a talk at Eastman House, the former home of George Eastman, the founder of Kodak.

Mr. Eastman, as they refer to him here, never married, lived with his mother, and eventually killed himself with a gun. He left a one-line suicide note, which is on display: "To my friends: My work is done. Why wait?" He did the deed almost immediately after signing an updated will. Ever considerate, efficient, and

Hulton Archive / Getty Images

maybe just a little obsessively neat, he placed a damp cloth across his chest to minimize any splatter before he pulled the trigger. George was physically ill and wanted to avoid further suffering.

There are clocks placed inconspicuously all over the residence. Most of them are hidden in corners of rooms and alongside paintings so Mr. Eastman could keep his servants punctual. They knew that he could always tell what time it was because, though he might appear to be looking at them, there was likely to be a timepiece somewhere right behind them. Every object and piece of furniture owned by him had an engraved tag (Prop of G Eastman) screwed into it on some hidden surface.

His mother's bedroom, which was directly across from his, has two small beds in it placed side by side. George's bedroom is now empty—only the fireplace remains. It was the scene of the suicide. I sort of suspect that George and his mom actually slept side by side, but maybe I have an overactive imagination.

In the center of Rochester there is a wonderful waterfall, a smaller but still spectacular Niagara where the Genesee River plummets into a deep gorge.

© 2009 Rudy Rucker

I biked by this cataract last time I performed here, sort of stumbling upon it by accident. The falls are pretty spectacular, and why the city hasn't made them more of a focus is at first a puzzle. The writer Rudy Rucker says that thirty years ago one couldn't even see the falls as they were so obscured by industrial pollution, so I guess that sort of answers that question.

I look around the gorge. Dominating one side is the almost abandoned Kodak plant, which doubtless used the river as both a source of power and as a dumping place for lots of photo chemicals. On the other side of the river are more factories and the remnants of a hydroelectric plant. It seems that this boomtown (the first boom was when the Erie Canal connected here, allowing shipping from the Great Lakes and Chicago up and down the Genesee and on down to New York City) happily made industry a priority and it soon dominated the waterfront on all sides. The river was almost hidden from public view throughout most of the town in those days. The mansions of the wealthy were situated well outside that industrial zone. George even had his own cows on his property, as he liked fresh milk.

A man driving me to Eastman House says that housing projects built in the 1960s now dominate part of the riverfront, that they were built there because it was not prime real estate at that time. Soon the projects became run down, and now developers are hoping to oust the remaining folks who live there, as the riverfront is gradually becoming cool, desirable, and lucrative.

This area is home not only to Kodak, but also to Xerox, Bausch & Lomb, and, in a nearby small town . . . Jell-O. All of these industries seem to me to be evocative of the last century. Kodak has made some serious layoffs lately, and, curiously, they seem optimistic about their future, as who really believes that film will remain a large industry for long? And who uses a Xerox machine anymore? There's always room for Jell-O though.

Biking around one can see that the city is beautifully situated—but the past is holding on for dear life with a viselike grip, a grip that strangles too many of these towns. Not that old buildings and neighborhoods should be torn down, just the opposite, but they probably need to have new functions.

"He Got What He Wanted but Lost What He Had"

I arrive in Valencia, a "town" near L.A., in the early evening. I wash up and walk around outside to get my bearings. I seem to be nowhere or maybe on a movie set—there isn't a soul on the sidewalks and the buildings nearby are all relatively new condos in fake this or that style. Across the street are indoor-outdoor malls that architecturally imitate streets, but their "streets" have no people on them.

A bronze statue of a couple carrying bags—a mother and daughter, caught in mid–shopping spree—is anchored to the sidewalk. A monument to shopping, or a memorial? I walk

on and feel a chill—I am more scared here than in a bad New York neighborhood. It's as if a neutron bomb exploded here just before I arrived, or as if there was once a bustling civilization here that has just abandoned the place. Am I about to find out why they left so quickly? Everywhere there is lush vegetation fed by hidden sprinklers, and everything is clean. It seems to be a physical manifestation of the Little Richard quote "He got what he wanted but lost what he had." This place is obviously a dream come true—visually at least. It seems to be everything we say we want—but sometimes when we get what we want it turns out to be a nightmare.

In the morning I am driven to the combined offices and set of the HBO series *Big Love*, and I get a short tour of the interior sets of this TV show—sets that represent the homes of the show's three Mormon wives. I love these artificial places. You're on the set and it's completely believable as a suburban home—there are

books and magazines lying around that the characters would plausibly read, and here are some of their clothes they've apparently tossed aside. And then you look up and there is no ceiling above you and huge air-conditioning ducts loom overhead. Outside the "window" is a massive photo backdrop of the mountains that ring suburban Salt Lake City, where the show is set.

These jarring juxtapositions are beautiful—in some ways they make our own homes, offices, and bars seem just as hollow and superficial as the sets. What we call home is just a set too. We think of the familiar intimate details in our own spaces—those magazines and books, the tossed-aside articles of clothing—as unique, integral to our lives. In a sense, though, all they are is set dressing for our own narratives. We think of our personal spaces as "real," and we feel they are filled with the stuff of our lives that's different than everyone else's. But especially out here, in Valencia, the "real" built landscape, those places I walk around, are made of structures that are no more real than this movie set. The mental dislocation is a wonderful feeling. The disconnect is somehow thrilling.

My Hometown

We travel great distances to gawk at the ruins of once-great civilizations, but where are the contemporary ruins? Where in our world are the ruins in progress? Where are the once-great cities that are now gradually being abandoned and are slowly crumbling, leaving hints of what people from the future will dig up and find a thousand years from now?

I am on a train passing through Baltimore, where I grew up. I can see vacant lots, charred remains of burned buildings surrounded by rubbish, billboards advertising churches, and other billboards for DNA testing of children's paternity. Johns Hopkins Hospital looms out of the squalor. The hospital is on an isolated island situated slightly east of downtown. The downtown area is separated from the hospital complex by a sea of run-down homes, a freeway, and a massive prison complex. Eastern Europe and the Soviet bloc come to mind. Failed industry and failed housing schemes and forced relocation disguised as urban renewal.

I hear the faint cacophony of many distant cell-phone rings in the train car—snippets of Mozart and hip-hop, old-school ring tones, and pop-song fragments—all emanating out of miniscule phone speakers. All tinkling away here and there. All incredibly poor reproductions of other music. These ring tones are "signs" for "real" music. This is music not meant to be actually listened to as music, but to remind you of and refer to other, real, music. These are audio road signs that proclaim "I am a Mozart person" or, more often, "I can't even be bothered to select a ring tone." A modern symphony of music that is not music but asks that you remember music.

Two men in the woods by the side of the train tracks are crouching by a small fire on a piece of overgrown, unused land. They share a forty ounce. Urban camping, of a sort. Behind them, beyond the thinning fall foliage, one can see a busy street. Here they are. Huck Finn and Jim. Hidden in plain sight. A parallel invisible world.

Baltimore, I read this weekend, has five times the homicide rate of New York City. Five times! No wonder the HBO show *The Wire* took place in Baltimore. They adopted the name Charm City the week that the garbagemen went on strike.

Much of nearby Washington, DC, is like this too, although there are isolated swaths of wealthy enclaves there. Baltimore lost its steel industry, its shipbuilding, its port industry and associated shipping, and much of its aerospace industry (which was located in the suburbs anyway). I'm not nostalgic for steel mills and coal mines, not even for GM plants, where they refuse— still!—to make anything but gas guzzlers, as they have for decades. Hell, fuck 'em—they've got it coming (as I revise this in April 2009 they are looking for a government bailout). They deserve to go down for such greedy, shortsighted behavior. Sad thing is, it's the little guy who will lose his job because of the big guys' stupidity. The big guys will get rewarded with another high-paying job. Those GM bosses should all get replaced by new folks, maybe by Japanese or Koreans, who at least know to make economical, fuel-efficient cars.

We encounter this kind of decay and devastation in Eastern Europe and in the former Soviet republics, but we've been taught to expect to see it there. We in the West have been told that those societies were under the boot of an evil, inefficient empire—where the will and gumption of the people was squashed—and that such desolation is the result. But would the will of the people, if they had been able to express it in that land, have arrived at something different? Haven't we, in our presumed democracy, arrived at the same end?

The reality in front of me clashes with what I was taught in school. The reality I see says that there isn't really any difference, that no matter what the ideology the end result is pretty much the same. I'm exaggerating: from a train window or from a bicycle on surface streets I sometimes only see the backsides of everything, which might be unfair.

The train heads out of town. One sees the hind parts of factories. Kudzu. Honeysuckle. Sumac with its fuzzy branches. Chain-link fences. Garbage. Old tires and rusty truck parts. Identical streets of identical row houses—workers' housing like in a Dickens novel. A billboard announcing "I Love You Baby Doll." Parking lots and truck yards. Then, suddenly, we're out of town. Herons skim wetlands and wade in brackish water. East Coast second-growth forests appear—skinny little trees, densely packed.

Detroit

I bike from the center of town out to the suburbs. It's an amazing ride—a time line through a city's history, its glory and betrayal. Detroit is not that different from many other cities across the

United States, just more dramatic in its ups and downs. In the center of town there is the convention center and the sports arena. There is a shopping district downtown that, like Baltimore's, has seen much better days—it's now mostly dirty discount stores selling wigs and cheap imports. There's a strip of Greek restaurants in an area called Greektown. They smash plates in some of these places, which is fun. Once I leave the central district I begin to encounter some true devastation. As in many similar towns, there are vaguely concentric rings of office zones, industrial zones, low-income housing, businesses, and eventually suburbs. As I leave downtown I find myself riding first through what seems to be the remains of a ghetto, now overgrown and returning to the earth: vast vacant lots, covered over with grasses and some filled with rubble. If you have seen pictures of Berlin after the war, then that's what this area looks like—desolate, uninhabited. Once in a

Brush Park, Michigan. © Yves Marchand and Romain Meffre

while there is evidence of some habitation, but mostly it's a posta-pocalyptic landscape at its finest.

As I ride on I enter a zone of light industry, or former light industry, as most of this area has been abandoned as well. Future condos or artists' lofts, one might imagine—were this London or Berlin. But poor Detroit seems to have been hit repeatedly, and the likelihood of its recovery seems like a long shot. Though if someone had told me that the most expensive apartment building in New York City would now be a stone's throw from the Bowery I would have said, "You're dreaming, and try not to step on that homeless guy sprawled there."

Miles later—through some funky but at least inhabited neighborhoods—I emerge into the suburbs. There are little "villages" and houses with manicured lawns. I gather that beyond

Michigan Central Station © Yves Marchand and Romain Meffre

this circle, somewhere near Eminem's now famous Eight Mile Road, the film begins to run backward; the desolation reappears, though this time the funkiness is more rural—trailer parks and little houses.

In a way, this was one of the best and most memorable bike rides I've ever taken. In a car one would have sought out a freeway, one of the notorious concrete arteries, and would never have seen any of this stuff. Riding for hours right next to it was visceral and heartbreaking—in ways that looking at ancient ruins aren't. I recommend it.

Sweetwater, Texas

I eat at a restaurant across the highway from the hotel where I'm staying. My steak is delicious—as it should be here. The decor in the restaurant is all red—chairs, tables, and trim—in honor of the local high school football team, the Mustangs. There is a very large painting of the football coach covering the wall behind me. I watch a man across from me shoot up his insulin at his table after he and his wife finish their meal. He does it deftly, as casually as one would look at one's watch. It's beautiful.

The restaurant (the only one within walking distance of the hotel, which doesn't have one) doesn't serve alcohol. I'm not that surprised. Between the early—for a New Yorker—dinner hours and the many dry counties around here I know we're not in New York anymore. I enjoy not being in New York. I am under no illusion that my world is in any way better than this world, but still I wonder at how some of these Puritanical restrictions have lingered—the encouragement to go to bed early and the injunction against enjoying a drink with one's meal. I suspect that drinking, even a glass of wine or two with dinner, is, like drug use, probably considered a sign of moral weakness. The assumption is that there lurks within us a secret desire for pure, sensuous, all-hell-breaking-loose pleasure, which is something to be nipped in the bud, for pragmatic reasons. In a sense maybe loosening up was, for the early settlers, not something to be encouraged, as the farmers and ranchers who settled here had to survive by the skin of their teeth. You never know what will come out of that bottle once you open it. If life is hard, if you're just getting by, then slipping off that straight and narrow path could have serious consequences. Drinking, therefore, like drug use, becomes relegated to "bad" places—to honkytonks and dark, sad bars. Either way both druggies and drinkers tend to create their own countercultures. Being ostracized then creates the "bad" scenes that the punishment had hoped to eradicate.

In the local paper a debate is taking place over whether high school students should be subjected to a curfew. It's not clear what hour is being proposed, but some of the students who aspire to have after-school jobs would certainly not be able to take those jobs if the work hours extended past this proposed curfew. Other students who have after-school sports or other activities would likewise be hamstrung. Many of these students would have to walk home from these jobs or activities, as they are not yet old enough to drive or don't have their own cars. They would therefore risk being picked up as curfew breakers.

One student quoted in the paper offered that since the local skating rink and some other activities have been closed there is nothing to do in town, so kids, bored out of their minds, will inevitably find something to do, and sometimes it might be disruptive—all that young energy has to go somewhere.

Some students, though, are all in favor of the curfew, as are the local football coaches, who seem to function as the resident wise men around here. I suspect that this proposed curfew could be an unspoken and underhanded way to facilitate and legitimize the rounding up of "loitering" Mexican kids—who are no doubt seen as the principal troublemakers here.

I ride around the older part of town. A motel that was once on the main highway reiterates the moral message: if Jesus never fails, then by implication the problem must be with you.

I wonder if this frontier Puritan fundamentalism, combined with economic pragmatism, is what makes buildings like this minimal one so common, unremarkable, and acceptable out here.

They are beautifully Spartan and purely functional—in their austerity they are in perfect keeping with nineteenth-century architect Louis Sullivan's dictum "form follows function." He claimed, "It is the pervading law of all things organic and inorganic, of all things physical and metaphysical." The implication was that this was not just a style or aesthetic guideline. This was a moral code. This was how God, the supreme architect, works. This humble structure—and many others around here—has followed that dictum to the very end of the line! These structures take the prize: they make the twentieth-century modernists all over the world look positively baroque—and therefore less moral.

There are people selling watermelons in a shopping-center parking lot, next to a U.S. flag made of plastic cups jammed into a fence.

Down the road is an abandoned drive-in and a church in a prefab metal building with a sign urging visitors to Come Be Apart.

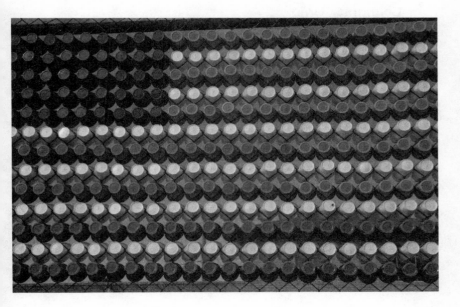

Columbus, Ohio

I bike across a suburban industrial park, which brings me to the backside of a complex that includes a shopping mall and a simulated street filled with restaurants and some condos. Night is just beginning to fall, the sodium vapor lamps are beginning to flicker on, and their orange chemical glow fills the parking lot. The landscaped and perfectly smooth grassy areas have turned a strange color in this odd light. It's an otherworldly experience gliding through these zones. I'm reminded of a movie in which the pleasant landscaping and the gently curving drives outlined by white curbs hide violent and perverted crimes and secret research taking place within the ubiquitous anonymous modern buildings. No one would take much notice of weird behavior around here. Nothing would look suspicious or out of place. I glimpse an interstate highway briefly through a planted grove of trees. It leads to Cleveland and Cincinnati. The whoosh of the cars and semis passing on it is like distant industrial Muzak, the sound of a mechanical wave machine, or a whispered conversation heard through dense foliage.

This perfect landscape has retained its surface familiarity, virtually, but the deep reasons for its existence—the social and sensual—have been eliminated. Immaculate green shapes fill the dividers on the access roads. The placement of a carefully pruned grove of leafy trees softens the edges of a mirror-walled research facility. Hidden cameras are mounted on posts among the branches, and discreetly posted signs warn of the presence of guard dogs—the only things that betray the seriousness and gravity of whatever goes on inside. Decor and manicured landscaping allude to some memory of landscape—they are a visual "description" of a place, but they are not that place. The sculpted grassy areas and bushes are allusions that "point at" and reference an archetypical bucolic scene. All the proper elements that are needed to constitute a lovely landscape are here, but reduced to signs and symbols. This is an imitation of a planet, with a well-developed culture, where these things originally evolved.

I sense that the same impulse that keeps a bottle of beer or a glass of wine out of a restaurant and that sees radically Spartan architecture as eminently wise has been at work in the landscaping here. The wacky religious fundamentalism that drives much of the United States makes for places that on the surface don't betray any religious foundation at all. But it's there, a deep invisible base implicit in the landscaped industrial parks and weird nonspaces that evoke nostalgia for the nonexistent.

A soap opera character on the bar TV says, "You killed him, you smothered him with doughnuts!" Another character, another scene—she is sitting in a room with a man and an elderly woman—the lead character wonders if she's dead. The man says, "No, you're alive," and the other woman hands her a plate of doughnuts.

A commercial comes on. A couple are on a date and the woman's voice-over articulates interior thoughts of what a wonderful guy her friend has set her up with: "He's so cute, and his IQ is higher than my bank balance . . . but she didn't tell me he has . . . Tourette's syndrome."

New Orleans—an Alternative

Pre-Katrina I biked around New Orleans many times. The city is pretty flat, which makes it easy on the knees. On one trip I discovered a bike path along the top of some of the earthen levees. It was delightful; one could see the river on one side and the city spread out on the other.

Here there are few of the usual interstates that divide and wound cities. There's mostly just I-10, on its massive concrete pilings, which snakes into the center of town, desperately trying to stay above most of the funk and humanity below. New Orleans was, and I suspect still is, one of a few large cities across the U.S.A. with character and personality, with its own food, culture, language, and music. It never fails to inspire, though it

has clearly flourished despite much neglect and years of abuse that were revealed to the world when the hurricane struck.

I bike along Magazine Street and then on St. Charles where what at first glance appears to be Spanish moss in the trees turns out to be Mardi Gras beads, hanging from the weird branches, block after block—and it's not even Mardi Gras season.

The vibe here is open—people look at you, talk to you, and are incredibly friendly. It's a bit like Brazil that way, a bit more African, in how people acknowledge one another, certainly more so than Denver or San Diego, where people avert their eyes and are suspicious if you say hello. Though it might seem strange to propose this here in the Deep South, this also seems like one of the least racist cities, in certain respects. I know that can't be strictly true, but I sense there are more black-owned businesses, cultural projects, and enterprises here—mixed in with the usual white financial hegemony—than in many American cities. I sense a little less of the anger, fear, and suspicion that often permeate American cities—though I'm aware that this is for many also a desperately and inescapably poor city. Hopelessness and violent crime live here too.

I would like to think that some of the positive aspects of this town might be due to its African American heritage, but then I think again of my former hometown—Baltimore—which is largely black, or of Washington, DC, aka Chocolate City, which, when I was growing up, was 70 percent black. Those places, their urban centers, are, outside the government buildings and white enclaves, depressing, sad, and dangerous. There must be other factors at work in this town that have stopped it from going down that same road. Maybe the French Roman Catholic attitude toward sin and pleasure that got mixed in helps make the African sensuality more acceptable down here. My guess is based on its similarities to Latin American cities like Havana, Lima, Cartagena, and Salvador, where the mix of Africa and Roman Catholicism have also produced vibrant music and culture.

I also sense less alienation among people doing their jobs

here. Maybe it's because more businesses are locally owned or maybe people just relate to one another differently. Whatever it is, it's one of the few U.S. cities that is about living, though the life here is far from easy and much of that life was taken away and the infrastructure destroyed by Katrina and the lack of response. Sad that one of the few large U.S. cities with a unique character was abandoned and left to be washed away.

For many years I found it surreal, amusing, and just downright weird to bike through dead zones, barren suburbs, or downtowns on the verge of becoming ruins. Such strange landscapes have their attraction. But the novelty has worn off a little, and now I'm more drawn to destinations where I can bike on paths in parklands bordering rivers and lakes rather than on the shoulders along expressways, sucking in fumes and risking my life.

The Return of Pittsburgh

I meet my friend John Chernoff, the teacher, writer, and drummer, at the Mattress Factory, an art space on the north side of town. He talks to me about city finances and the transformations this city has gone through. Some old-timers still remember when Pittsburgh was booming and smoky. Between the smoke from the foundries, the coal dust, and the exhaust from the coal heat in the houses, the sky was often dark at noon. Black clouds covered the city for much of the year. It's hard to imagine such an apocalyptic landscape being real, but it was. There are probably quite a few cities in China just like that now.

The last steel mill closed only recently. They tear them down and the areas that remain are called brownfields—especially if they are being rehabilitated. John says, "The new developments along the river are all brownfields. There are a lot of sites that are now under major reconstruction, such as the old Homestead foundry site that is now a development called Waterfront. Along the South Side, the site of the old Jones and Laughlin steel plant, redevelopment is under way. What makes it a 'brownfield site'

W. Eugene Smith / Black Star

is that it has been cleared in preparation for rehabilitation or redevelopment."

In their heyday these foundries were vast—the largest one stretched for miles along the riverbank. The little valleys that branch out from the river each were home to their own mines, and little towns of workers' housing and churches would be squished into the remaining spaces in these furrows. A law, still on the books, says that if coal is found under your house you have to allow it to be dug out.

Now, of course, with the passing of all this industry, many of those little towns are boarded up, as were large sections of Pittsburgh's neighborhoods. But other parts are now, in 2005, emerging, beginning to revive, in one form or another. In 2000 Pittsburgh had more unemployment than Detroit or Cleveland—things were looking pretty dismal. People who used to get twenty-three dollars an hour in a steel foundry were having to take jobs in restaurants. Many left town; those who stayed hoped the steel industry would come back. It didn't, but many eventually found jobs in the health-care industry or technology, jobs that didn't pay quite as much—but with some restructuring they were able to get by.

The city is pretty much bankrupt, especially after having built two incredible stadiums right next to one another. The voters said no to the stadium expenditures, but a revamped initiative snuck through, and now the bills have come due, and, as there was no increase in taxes to pay for them, the debts are devastating. The Republican legislature squashed any tax increases, especially in the wealthier suburbs, so other services have been cut instead of the stadiums: city pools were closed, the police force cut. The financial and tax burden has fallen on those, mostly poor, who still live in the city itself.

Luckily some of the oligarchs—the Heinzes, the Mellons, and a few others—continue to live in the city and don't want their town to go straight to hell, so they are working to reinvigorate the city center, block by block, inch by inch, and to figure out some means of obtaining funds from the wealthier property owners. The largest tenants in the city now, post-heavy industry, are schools and hospitals, which unfortunately don't pay taxes, so something else has to be done to raise money. Money either has to be found or those institutions will have to close up shop. But John and others seem optimistic. John elaborates: "The city is not bankrupt just because of the stadiums. There are a lot of factors at work, such as the shrinking population. Like many other cities, this one lacks sufficient federal and state funding support. There are people working to turn places around in addition to the oligarchs—grassroots community groups and small businesses all over the place. The bakery we visited in Millvale is an example of a business locating itself in an old neighborhood, which helps bring life back to those areas."

Various disastrous urban renewal schemes of the 1960s and '70s have yet to be undone. A beautiful freeway cuts the North Side in two, insulating the stadiums and all their attendant businesses from the local neighborhoods. John: "There are grassroots efforts being made to work on such matters as the North Side neighborhoods around the stadium. The renovated houses we saw on the North Side, around central North Side and the Mexican War streets, are worth a lot of money now."

Housing projects created high-crime zones. The neighborhoods that were deemed beyond help—that didn't get that "gift" of urban renewal back in the day, the neighborhoods of immigrant worker housing scattered here and there—are the ones that are reviving now. Some of them look beautiful. They still have local bars, mom-and-pop stores, and pedestrian traffic. I saw the same thing happening in Milwaukee.

After lunch we visit a church in Millvale that had been recommended as having interesting murals. Millvale is a few miles up the river, a former mining village nestled in one of those little valleys. Lots of boarded-up stores line the streets, but a great French bakery, as John mentioned, has courageously made a stand. I buy a cake, as it's my birthday.

The church in this little town is Croatian, and the murals, by Maxo Vanka, are spectacular. The Diego Rivera of Pittsburgh, I would say. The murals were done during eight weeks in 1937, and they cover the interior of the church. Of course there is one of the Virgin holding a child, but below her, for example, on either side of what is now the altar, are images of the Croatian people: on the left is a crowd of them from the old world, and on the right from the new; a steel foundry can be seen belching smoke behind this grouping.

More unusual for a church are the political and antiwar aspects of the murals that echo the Crucifixion—widows mourn over a soldier in a coffin containing a bleeding corpse, and crosses cover the hillside behind them. Another wall depicts corrupt justice: a figure in a gas mask holds scales on which the gold outweighs bread. Clearly World War I had a big effect on Maxo.

In one image the Virgin, on the verge of being bayoneted herself, separates two soldiers.

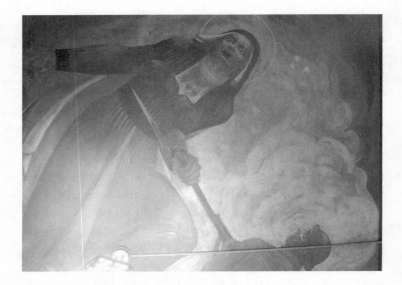

In another mural an oligarch done up as Death reads the stock reports while being served a chicken dinner by two black servants. Finally, we see Jesus being stabbed by a bayonet, in a kind of second Crucifixion.

Bold and brave stuff to confront the Sunday parishioners with. The murals are all badly in need of renovation—years of coal dust have darkened them. But one can hope that these amazing things will survive and be cleaned soon.

On a more recent visit I ride around through the hills that are everywhere here except by the waterfront and that make cycling a challenge. I can see changes since my visit just four years earlier. It seems that Pittsburgh is more than just standing—the cultural district downtown is jumping on the weekend, the little neighborhoods are thriving with their corner bars and grocery stores, the strip district still has its booming markets and, I am told, folks are moving back into the city. This latter change is essential to turning a town around, as it will provide the tax base, and the humanity, that will enable this kick start that the Heinzes and others have initiated to keep things running on their own steam.

Sometimes a rebirth can be started in one neighborhood and then it spreads to the surrounding areas—if they're not cut off or isolated. Artists move into a former factory district and soon cafés and grocery stores follow. A music club opens, a gallery and a bookstore. Developers turn the warehouses into luxury condos and the process begins again, somewhere else. Or, as in some downtowns like Kansas City's, a local impresario might decide to put shows in someplace like the Uptown Theater, a venue in a sketchy part of town that was on the verge of being torn down. A business opportunity and a show of faith. A bar opens close by, a record store, and before too long the area has begun to be more livable. One significant investment can sometimes trigger a chain of events. The Heinzes have done something like that in downtown Pittsburgh, renovating theaters and arts centers, which have attracted other businesses. It's working.

Though I have tended to paint a bleak picture, not every city in the U.S.A. is going to hell in a handbasket because of dying industry, stupid planning decisions, or racially motivated white flight. It doesn't have to be that way. San Francisco, Portland, much of Seattle, much of Chicago, Minneapolis, Savannah, and many more are vibrant and full of life. These are places where things are turning around, where the quality of life has completely returned, or where it was never allowed to be destroyed. Strangely, the recent economic downturn might be a great opportunity. Sustainability, public transport, and bike lanes aren't scoffed at anymore. Congressman Earl Blumenauer, a longtime advocate for biking as a means of public transportation, thinks now is the time.

Some of these other cities I visited might come back too. Often it only takes some political will and one or two significant changes and then things begin to change by themselves. Cities as a rule use less energy per capita than do suburban communities where people are living spread out, so as the cost of energy spirals up, those grimy urban streets start to look like they might have possibilities. The economy has tanked, the United States can lose its place as number one world power, but that doesn't mean that many of these cities can't still become more livable. Life can still be good—not only good, it can be better than what most of us can imagine. A working-class neighborhood can be full of life. A neighborhood that has many different kinds of people and businesses in it is usually a good place to live. If there were some legislation that ensured that a mixed-use and mixed-income neighborhood would emerge when developers move in, it would be wise, because those are the liveliest and healthiest kinds of communities.

Berlin

Nostalgia for the Mud

Flying into Tegel Airport in Berlin I look down at the neatly ordered fields and roads—even in the surrounding forests the trees are in neat rows—and I think to myself how this entire country, the landscape, everything as far as one can see, has been ordered. There is no wildness, chaos, or funkiness, not here or much of anywhere in industrialized Europe. Man is in charge and has, over many centuries, put nature in its place. In many countries there is an ethos that complements this gardener point of view—an ethos that values wildness. So as a result there are isolated parks and protected areas—like green zoos—here and there.

I remember in 1988 scouting the German countryside for film locations for a movie called *The Forest* that the theater director Bob Wilson and I had hoped to make. At that time the Wall was still up, but I managed to scout locations in the East as well, which made the scouting job fun and challenging. Given the title of the piece, inevitably there were to be scenes in a virgin forest, so I went looking for one. In all of Germany we found one piece of virgin forest—a preserved one-kilometer-square roadside tract.

It was indeed different, very different, from all the other forests we had seen. None of the trees were straight; they were gnarled, twisted, and had evidently led interesting lives. The forest floor was littered with massive dead and rotting trunks—twisted corpses, the ancestors of those giants still standing. It was just like the forests described in fairy tales or seen in certain movies—chaotic but almost comforting, creepy but beautifully alluring. One felt that one was inside of a creature and outside of it at the same time. As if one were walking around the innards of a huge being. A bit sad, I think, that my visual reference for an unmediated forest derives from images in fiction and movies. Sad too that the forest in this preserved area was once quite common, but now lives on mainly in our collective imaginations—an image burned into our psyches over millennia, indelible, but now having little relationship to the real world. This little parcel was the only one left—except for a rumored larger forest in Poland, but going there to shoot would have been impractical.

Europe is manicured. The whole continent, except for some semi-accessible places in the Alps, northern Scotland, and Scandinavia, has been groomed and tended by the hand of man. It's a vast millennial project, this custodial effort, requiring the cooperation, over centuries, of scores of nations and peoples, all speaking different languages and with different cultures. The greatest physical human enterprise of all.

America has nothing like it. There is no historically manicured landscape except maybe in the aptly named New England, or perhaps parts of the Great Plains, where the steppes of North America have been organized by agribusiness. America still has, lurking around its edges in tattered remnants, bits of unkempt wildness and danger. Even in places where that wildness is illusory it still exists within living memory, at least for now—people therefore internalize its existence and act as if it is still there, and behave accordingly. The seductive and dangerously chaotic and capricious unknown lies just beyond the farmland in many places—or is at least remembered as being there not so long ago.

Europeans' attitude toward their landscape is to cultivate the continent as if it were a vast garden, while Americans prefer to subdue the landscape by force, paving over vast areas, or plant-ing miles of a single crop—like corn—that stretch to the horizon. In the New World it is assumed that there will always be more land over the horizon, so sustainable cultivation and conservation are often viewed as namby-pamby. I suppose a lot of Russia and the former Soviet republics are like this too, which might explain a thing or two. Maybe that's why lots of North Americans feel that the whole world has to be tamed and brought under control while Europeans, having more or less achieved that control in their own lands, feel a duty to nurture and manage rather than simply subdue. Industrialization and agricultural subjugation throughout most of Europe is now a thing of the past—its legacy a nasty memory of polluted rivers and blackened skies, many of which are now being cleaned up, sort of.

I ride my bike along the bike lanes here in Berlin and it all seems very civilized, pleasant, and enlightened. No cars park or

drive in the bike lanes, and the cyclists don't ride on the streets or on the sidewalks either. There are little stoplights just for the bikers, even turn signals! (Cyclists often get to turn a few seconds before the rest of the traffic, to allow them to get out of the way.) Needless to say, most cyclists here do stop for these lights. Pedestrians don't wander into the bike lanes either! I'm kind of in shock—it all works so well. Why can't it be like this where I live?

Here even the bikes themselves are practical. They are usually black, with only a few gears, mudguards, and often a basket—something no sport cyclist would ever even dream of adding to a mountain bike in North America. In Holland they go even further, with special carts for kids and groceries and bike windshields (!) for your child. Granted, riding in the streets of New York City, with the recurring potholes, bumps, and yearly resurfacings, is closer to an extreme sport than riding is here, where somehow, despite the harsh winters, the streets are mostly smooth and obstacle free. Hmmm. The biggest bumps here are on the occasional cobblestone streets or bits of pavement. How do they do it? Or rather, how is it that the richest country in the world doesn't seem to be able to do it?

In making smooth streets some may say that the Germans have ironed out the psychological bumps in their daily lives. If the New York City streets are wilder and funkier (at least outside of "Mall Manhattan"), then these German streets are on Prozac—civilized but slightly less exciting. But should we in the United States be forced to ride on "exciting" streets?

Modern northern European society is fairly homogenized. There are immigrants, but they still don't make up a huge percentage of the population. There are also fewer economic differences and gulfs between the classes here than there are in the United States, except among those same immigrants—the Turkish in Germany, Indonesians in Holland, Africans in Belgium, and North Africans and Arabs in France. For the white folks, the locals, it is certainly a more egalitarian life than in the U.S.A., at least as far as social services are concerned. These same white folks are now aware that people from their former colonies now wonder why they also can't get the free medical care and schools. Even if people can vote in a country, as they certainly can in most of the United States, if there are incredibly wide economic differences and inequalities in education and health care, then the majority's interests and the public good cannot prevail. A minority's will is trumping that of the majority. Then true equal representation doesn't exist.

I've been in Germany many times over the years. At first, in the late '70s, Berlin seemed exotic and exciting, a cold war icon. I remember traveling the well-guarded corridor leading to Berlin from Hamburg—a kind of gauntlet through part of East Germany, it seemed to us then—and past Checkpoint Charlie, the U.S.-controlled gate in the Berlin Wall, with its associated tales and propaganda exhibits of desperate and failed escapes from the East. There was at the same time the degeneracy evidenced in the various punk clubs and discos in West Berlin. You always remembered that you were confined here, a prisoner on an island of luxury, culture, and pleasure—plopped inside the drab, serious, high-minded East. The city as a tease, a temptation. I imagine that made living there a little more exciting and a little crazier as well.

For the walled city with no room to expand that it was in the '60s, '70s, and '80s Berlin had a surprising number of parks and greenways. Being almost flat, it was, and still is, a perfect place for getting around on a bike, though the winters can be bitterly cold with the winds sweeping down from the north. It has a great film festival, which often features movies from the East and from countries not known in the West for their cinema. I once saw a wonderful Turkish film in which a respected theater director takes a quick job acting in a shampoo commercial, only to find himself stuck living in the imaginary world of the characters in the advertisement. His new family knows him only as the character in the ad, and they know what he does for a living, etc., but he, the actor, has no idea. After some initial befuddlement, he gives in and attempts to adjust to his new life.

Prisoner Number Seven

When Rudolf Hess died—the last Nazi prisoner held in Spandau Prison—reportedly by strangling himself with an electrical cord, the whole building in that western suburb of the city was said to have been dismantled, brick by brick. The bricks were carted off in the night by the British, whose sector the prison was in, and then ground into powder and thrown into the sea—as if the prison, or even its bricks, might have attracted neo-Nazi sympathizers if left intact. Did they think the sympathizers believed some of Hess's energy might have rubbed off on the bricks? Anyway, one day it was there and the next day it was gone; all that remained was a sandlot.

For twenty years he was the only prisoner in the whole complex, "the loneliest man in the world" according to one book. What a beautiful image. Apparently he could wander more or less at will around the vast prison, but no one was allowed to touch him or to shake his hand. (Again, like the bricks, it seems it was assumed he possessed some magical Nazi touch juju.) He had famously flown to Scotland in 1941 in hopes of negotiating a peace deal. He parachuted onto a laird's property south of Glasgow and was allegedly arrested by a man wielding a pitchfork.

Trade-off

I arrive in town from the airport. The taxi is slowly prowling around in the early morning looking for my destination, and it is gray and no one is about. But there, on the other side of the street, a man is walking in a bright red outfit; he is a round German dressed as an American Indian chief, feathers in his headdress, winter moccasins and all. He is all alone—the street is deserted. At first I think to myself, Oh, the nutters here are really inventive! but then I realize it's Carnival week and he's probably stumbling home after a long night. There is a whole Wild West phenomenon here sparked by the novelist Karl May. His series of popular Western novels features the Indians as the heroes.

The German national colors, not the colors of the flag but the colors one sees most often, are yellow, mostly of a dull sulfur hue; green, leaning toward a dull forest tone; and brown, ranging from a muddy beige to a rich brown earth tone. These warm earth colors and their combinations are the most popular ones for buildings, clothes, and accessories. To me they signify Germanness—the national and cultural identity. This is national stereotyping for sure, but it makes me wonder: does every culture have its palette? Certainly buildings used to be made of local materials and as a result London's buildings are often redbrick while those in Dallas are beige.

In the hotel elevator there are glass walls that allow a view of the highway just outside the hotel, and simultaneously on the opposite side, a view of the elevator shaft and its workings. The cables and mechanical devices are all immaculate—spotless, almost dust free. In New York these shafts would be filthy, every surface caked with dirt and decades worth of old grease, and the floor at the bottom of the shaft would be littered with discarded coffee cups and rat pellets. When I mentioned this to a North American friend he responded, "Yes, but we Americans have better music."

Whoa! You may not care for techno, a musical mainstay of a lot of the discos here, but a lot of people would claim that Ludwig van, Bach, and Wagner alone could hold their own against whatever North American crap you care to name. So yes, that statement is ridiculous, but what does it mean? What was implied? Besides being unprovable, is there an underlying assumption that cultural and social qualities are finite? That a surplus of one necessarily means a deficit of another? That cleanliness and order will necessarily sap some other qualities? (This has a corollary that if someone is beautiful he must be stupid.) That whole nations and people have psychic things in common that only take effect when you cross passport control? Is this idea like the one expressed in Will Self's wacky short story "The Quantity Theory of Insanity," where there is only so much sanity to go around? The implication is that every psychological thing, every part of our mental makeup and character is a trade-off against some other, unexpressed, form of social behavior. If you're happier than average, you have, in this view, forfeited something else—intelligence, for example.

Are our brains weirdly finite? Do we intuit this odd tit-for-tat idea? We're familiar with blind people whose brains have changed, with new neural connections being established in the areas formerly allocated for sight. Is the same true with other psychic parts of ourselves? Do any of those psychological/mental clichés hold true? Do great creative geniuses necessarily have less common or business sense? Do extremely rational minds inevitably miss out on some wild, creative intuitions? Are sensuous people hopelessly disorganized? As one improves oneself in one area does another area necessarily shrink and suffer as a result? Is there a chart with sliding scales we can look at so we can be aware of how we're doing on the psychic tally board?

Music Stripped Bare

Berlin is now hailed as the cultural center of Europe. Well, by some. In the afternoon I go gallery hopping with artist/designer Stefan Sagmeister. Everyone in the galleries is superfriendly and helpful without being at all pushy or solicitous, which is a real change from the chilly vibe one often gets in New York galleries. A lot of the galleries here are located in older buildings that have a curious structure. The city blocks are quite large, so often the buildings—offices, apartments, and now galleries—are in edifices that form the perimeter of the entire block, like a giant rectangular doughnut—a shape that leaves a massive empty space in the middle, hidden from street traffic and approachable from the street only via periodic tunnels in the doughnut.

These interior courtyards are massive. Some are so big that there is often another whole apartment structure built inside the first one, and sometimes yet another structure might nestle inside that one—like Russian dolls as an architectural model. Some of the interior buildings were formerly small factories, but now they are transformed into charming cafés with outdoor seating and spaces where the clientele leave their bicycles—often unlocked. The entrances to the new art galleries are often within these courtyards. The interiors of these galleries are not usually as massive as some elsewhere in the world, as they are in restored and reworked former offices rather than former industrial spaces.

Stefan and I talk about the fate of the CD, and of recorded music in general. Stefan has just been to South Korea, which he

© 2006 Aerowest / Google Inc.

describes as being a few years ahead of us in some respects—he says no one there buys CDs anymore. In fact, when he wanted to buy a CD copy of something he'd heard he had to go to a specialty shop to obtain it—as one would in Europe or North or South America to buy a recording on vinyl.

We wonder about the fate of the images and design associated with LPs and CDs—something he's been involved with quite a few times. He reminds me that the linking of image and music is a result of the fact that vinyl scratches easily, so it needed sturdy board packaging. And until relatively recently even those packages didn't come with images, credits, liner notes, etc.—music packaging originally was generic. People happily enjoyed music for centuries before that without any accompanying visual aids or attractive packaging. However, I found out that when Alex Steinweiss designed an early album sleeve for Beethoven's Eroica symphony, the package caused sales to increase 800 percent. So design is nothing to sneeze at. The music package has evolved into an embodiment of a worldview represented not just by the music but also by the package, the performer, the band, the show, the costumes, the videos, and all the other peripheral materials. But it might soon be back to just the audio without all the rest of it thanks to the digital world, where many folks buy digital versions of just the one song they like, and the surrounding and accompanying materials and images are left behind or ignored. The era of the data cloud surrounding pop music as representative of a weltanschauung might be over. Stefan doesn't seem nostalgic about it.

Political Art

We have dinner with Matthias Arndt, a local gallerist, and his girlfriend, an art historian. Matthias has moved his gallery from Mitte, where he first opened, to a big new space near the former Checkpoint Charlie, where there are clusters of new galleries. He says most of his sales are to collectors who live outside

Berlin—and most of those are to collectors outside Germany. Despite the glut of galleries and artists here, the local community of potential buyers and curators doesn't support the local artists much. They're appreciated—at least in the sense of being collected—elsewhere.

The artists here do have it pretty good in another sense. Many incredible studios and living spaces are available here for much less money than in Williamsburg or East London. And they're in the center of town too.

In Matthias's gallery there is a piece I like by Thomas Hirschhorn of mannequin hands holding aloft a mixture of literary tomes and ordinary tools—it makes for a sort of hilarious intellectual "workers arise!" image. An idealized revolution—symbolically embodied on a (large) tabletop. In another era I could imagine this piece being an actual proposal for a large-scale monument that might have been made in the former East. Maybe this proposal for a monument might have been done

Thomas Hirschhorn, "Exhibition Photograph, Matthias Gallery Show" © 2009 Artists Rights Society (ARS), New York / ADAGP, Paris

by a high school senior using available materials: paperbacks rather than more visually impressive antique bound volumes, and puny screwdrivers and measuring tapes rather than larger hammers and sickles. And of course, like a junior high school science project, Hirschhorn's piece is held together with packing tape.

The "Problem" of Beauty

Matthias mentions a young Leipzig-schooled painter who has now become very popular—an artist who Matthias passed on representing some years ago. "Too beautiful" was what he thought of the work then. He says he has a problem with beauty—and realizes that this prejudice is not always in his best interests. Stefan quotes the late Tibor Kalman—the designer for whom Stefan worked and who also often worked with me—as saying, "I have no problem with beauty, but it isn't very interesting."

Matthias says beauty, being ephemeral, evanescent, and impermanent, reminds us of death. I would have never put an equal sign between the two myself—this statement seems overly romantic à la Rilke, but I see his point. The morbidity of beauty. Huh. I suppose when one is referring to a person—a strikingly beautiful young man or woman, for example—it rings true, as their beauty will inevitably fade, and will eventually be gone completely. So, by that reasoning, leafing through a fashion magazine is essentially a tragic and melancholy experience. Well, it might be anyway, but for other reasons. But what about people who age gracefully—who become more interesting, or nontraditionally beautiful, with age? A trip to the Louvre in Matthias's view would be downright depressing. I often think of beauty in a song (a thing that disappears as soon as you hear it) or in a fleeting view of a landscape, which renews itself (we hope), or of the kinds of objects that sometimes become even more beautiful as they age and begin to show signs of wear and tear. My friend C says the same thing sometimes happens with people—some of them grow into their faces, for example, looking merely childlike when young, and not that interesting, but becoming more themselves as they begin to show some age. They're not really beautiful when young, at least not deeply.

Some people find beauty hard to define—often things we at first find ugly or strange grow on us and we discover a depth and beauty that can be more profound than mere prettiness. The definition is complex and slippery and it changes over time. It's not absolute and can't be fixed. If that's true, then no one can point to a thing or person and ever say unequivocally, "That's beautiful."

In a kind of defense of the notion of some kind of absolute beauty I've read that there are evolutionary and biological reasons that explain our criteria for ascribing physical beauty and attractiveness to people. People and animals have built-in visual preferences that we use to judge attractiveness and fitness. It's said that symmetry, for example, is evidence of smooth physiological development—that symmetrical facial features are a sign of probable genetic health and fitness. The implication is that we may be biologically programmed to view certain things—in this case some other people—as beautiful. The accompanying implication is that we find them beautiful because they are suitable and desirable as mates. We call them beautiful but we're thinking about something else.

I suspect that if that is true then it may extend to other aesthetic areas—landscapes and rooms, for example. Why not? Don't some landscapes, with their unique light and setting, imply somewhat timeless criteria that would signal to our ancestors that this spot is a good place to nest, a good place to hunt, a good place to grow food, a good place to meet a mate?

The talk turns to beauty's opposite, in a sense—to the artists of the Vienna actionist movement of the 1960s, in particular Otto Muehl, who went to jail for allegedly having sex with everything and everybody in his commune—children included.

Here are the text/instructions for one of his "actions": "I spread artificial honey on an old grandmother and then allow her to be attacked by 5 kg of flies that I had previously starved for 7 days in a box. I then kill the flies on her wrinkled skin with a fly-swatter." Poor granny.

And another (from http://www.brightlightsfilm.com/38 /muhl3.htm#12):

The action is divided into various phases. First comes the still life. It begins very economically. You start with warm water on the bodies of the models, which runs—it doesn't do any damage. Then comes oil, various soups with dumplings, meat and vegetables, perhaps even a bunch of grapes. Than [sic] comes color: ketchup, marmalade, red beet juice flows down. The skin is still visible. Then it gets going and the heavy artillery is brought out. I often made dough, which stretched down ponderously, or an egg, flour, or cabbage. Finally I poured on bed feathers. There was a certain structure there, how the materials were used one after the other. It was almost like cooking. I also once made, "The Breading of the Buttocks." First milk, then flour, egg, and breadcrumbs. I didn't take the entire body—only the ass, very provocative. The woman knelt in an armchair, her ass turned to the audience. First I sprayed the buttocks with milk. Then I dusted it with flour, as if breading a Wienerschnitzel. The flour stuck. Then I spread the egg yolk over that and at last the bread-crumbs. That looked really great!

And one for which he was arrested:

The Christmas action "O Tannenbaum." I lay naked in bed with a woman under a Christmas tree. I had hired a butcher. He killed a pig with a slaughtering-gun. He tore the heart out and hurled it onto us. The heart was still twitching. Blood spattered. Breathless silence reigned in the room.

I slowly climbed up a ladder and urinated on the woman and the pig's heart in the bed below. At that point, a women's libber lost control. She rushed the ladder on which I stood and screamed: "You pig, you filthy swine!" I had 1 kg. of flour and dusted her down with it. A white fog. She screamed again, "You swine!" and she was gone, vanished. In the meantime, someone attempted to pelt me with potatoes. He came closer and closer and it was dangerous. I had another 1 kg. of flour and dashed it against him. The flour dusted his face and his suit. He stood there white as a snowman.

Otto Muehl, shot from "Can Anyone Explain" © 2009 Artists Rights Society (ARS), New York / ADAGP, Paris

He said, "My life should be perfect, have direction, be an artwork." Otto took this wish seriously, and soon he abandoned the arty actions and happenings created for a rarefied art-world audience and decided that they were actually a kind of therapy in themselves—they didn't require the audience. So these activities could be beneficially incorporated and integrated into one's life outside of the museum and gallery context. He would finally rip art out of its "frame," as he had long dreamed.

"The action also has a frame, a stage, and people stand around. It is not serious. It is artificially produced. I want to rid myself of the word artificial."

He founded a commune influenced by the psychosexual theories of Wilhelm Reich. It was a kind of action-group-

Otto Muehl, *Untitled,* CNAC / MNAM / Dist. Réunion des Musées Nationaux / Art Resource, NY. © 2009 Artists Rights Society (ARS), New York / ADAGP, Paris

psychoanalysis. Members were encouraged to act out—physically—their sexual and psychological issues. We can only imagine, based on Muehl's earlier actions, what these might have been. Marriage in the commune was prohibited. There was a jazz band too, as Muehl was a big fan of Charlie Parker. Rumor is that the commune turned into his personal fiefdom, a real grotesque hippy artist cult nightmare.

Now, being somewhat rehabilitated in the perception of the art world, Muehl has, in recent years, been accorded big retrospectives in prestigious museums.

Stasiland

Berlin is lovely in the summer. In the morning I attempt to go for a ride in Tiergarten, the massive central park here, but Colin Powell, he of the Evil Empire (the Bush administration is still in power on this trip), is staying at the Intercontinental Hotel, so many of Berlin's roads are closed and armed riot police are everywhere. They are bored, most of them, and they lounge around taking the sun, reading newspapers, and drinking coffees.

The presence in town of the Empire means I have to ride a very circuitous route wherever I venture near the central city—avoiding roadblocks and redirected traffic—but the weather is perfect, so it's okay.

I'd heard that there is a Stasi museum in Berlin. I have recently read the book *Stasiland*, which details that life in which Big Brother encouraged everyone to spy on everyone else, so the museum sounds intriguing. It is some distance from the center of town—almost out in the suburbs—in a massive complex that served as the East German security services' headquarters. It's not listed in most of the museum guides—and Berlin has a lot of museums—so it requires a little bit of research to locate. I bike out, appropriately enough, along the amazing Karl-Marx-Allee, a sort of Soviet-inspired version of the Champs Élysées or

Avenida 9 de Julio in Buenos Aires or maybe New York's Park Avenue. But this boulevard is even wider and grander than many of those. The vaguely Moscow-style grand apartment buildings that line this boulevard outdo those in Moscow and rival the apartments on large avenues in other cities, except these are more orderly and repetitive, echoing each other, going on and on as far as one can see. The scale of both the street and these buildings is not quite human, and the images that come to mind and the accompanying sensations imply to me an idealistic utopian infinite heaven. Ideals and ideologies do not have boundaries, after all. This particular heaven, to me, is not like the typical ugly, bland modernist projects. That was a utopia of another sort. These have almost northern Italian detailing, and though they're frightening in their somewhat inhuman scale and surreal repetition, they are far more appealing than typical North American housing projects or even a lot of Western modernist buildings where lack of decor came to be held up as a moral virtue. Here's an infrared digital image:

On one side of the boulevard the ground floors are sad and forlorn—former cinemas, hardware stores, and medical supply stores—most of which are either shut, decrepit, or reconfigured as DVD shops or similar fast-buck enterprises. The other side has charming outdoor cafés with tables arrayed in the shade of trees. The stores in general in this part of town seem to have lagged behind the gentrification that is now endemic in the center of town since the Wall came down. The luxury shops and goods that flooded into the former center of East Berlin haven't gotten here yet. There is a window display in a medical supply shop that to me harks back to an earlier time:

A thing of beauty. What *kind* of thing, though? The basic food groups? Not exactly the basic food groups as *we* know them, but maybe that was the idea.

The hard times in some of the Eastern bloc Communist countries after World War II ensured that some of the existing architecture was left alone. Yes, it's a cliché that neglect equals preservation, but there's some truth there as well. At least the buildings that weren't bombed in successive wars weren't torn down and replaced with bland new edifices, housing projects, or highway overpasses. The Easties couldn't afford it. Instead, the buildings were often given new purposes, as it was cheaper to do a slight refurbishment than to build a whole new structure. There was little money for wholesale urban redevelopment here, unlike in many Western European and North American cities, and besides, the Allied bombing had cleared much of the city anyway. While Robert Moses had to raze whole neighborhoods in New York to make space for his highways and housing developments, here the demolition part of the job had already been accomplished. Some buildings that in the West would have been torn down were left standing as they were the few that remained, and those are now extremely desirable. One blatant exception is the former Communist Party headquarters on Alexanderplatz in the former East Berlin, a giant postwar modernist monument, copper-mirrored and toxic—both psychologically and chemically—which is being slowly and very carefully dismantled due to the amount of asbestos inside. The removal of this psychic eyesore is controversial, as it symbolically erases a prominent reminder of the former regime and of the country's recent history—just as the Nazis took over and repurposed formerly Jewish-owned offices and buildings and then the Communists later reworked and renamed the Nazi buildings to their own ends. Eliminating this eyesore is wiping away part of the collective memory.

I passed through and worked in West Berlin fairly often in the '80s, when the Wall was still up. West Berlin then was an artificially pumped-up, arty capitalist showcase, the better to show those commies on the other side of the fence what high life and culture they were missing. East Berlin was full of incredible historical buildings and shabby apartments, and there were no amenities. It really was gray and depressing—at least to a visitor. And it smelled—many houses and businesses were heated by coal fires, a smell I recognized, and loved, from visiting my grandma in Glasgow as a child. Even the sky seemed grayer to Western visitors then.

I suspect that many of the folks who lived in the East felt otherwise and may have viewed the half of the city on the Western side as a decadent cesspool of junkies and hookers (which it partly was) while they alone were maintaining the traditionally high German intellectual, cultural, and moral values and standards. Someone, they might have reasoned, had to preserve civilization while the Yankees turned West Berlin into a soldier's playground and a haven for crazy artists, playwrights, drug addicts, and musicians of questionable talent.

In West Berlin at that time the young Germans who didn't mind living inside a walled island were compensated—they could escape compulsory military service, rents were relatively cheap, and parking laws were almost nonexistent. (Cars would park on the sidewalks, at any angle, and never get towed.) Kreuzberg, the Lower East Side of West Berlin, was one of the most decadent low-life places I've ever seen. Lots of black leather, heroin, and late-night punk clubs—a sort of government-sponsored bohemian world just out of reach, but significantly visible to the Easties just over the Wall. The rest of luxurious Western decadence—the plentiful food, crazy fashions, and expensive cars—the Easties could see on bootleg films and TV, and they could probably smell wafting across no-man's-land the currywursts and kebabs that fueled the nightlife just across the Wall.

After the Wall came down all that changed. There was no further need to artificially entice people to live in an isolated island city anymore. Now the decadence here is of another sort, and it has migrated to various neighborhoods in the center of the former East. Friedrichstrasse and the surrounding boulevards are filled with luxury-goods boutiques, designer labels, and swanky hotels. There was a brief time right after the Wall came down when the historic buildings of Mitte were selling for peanuts, and many of them quickly became squats and cheap housing for artists, but that was a relatively short-lived period. Now there are a few coffee shops and some graffiti remaining as reminders of those post-Wall days, but the fancy-goods stores and developers are moving in fast and the rents are going up. More mentally disrupting, for me at least, is that the entire center of town has moved. When the Wall was up, what we in the West considered the center of West Berlin was somewhere around the tower of the bombed Kaiser Wilhelm Gedächtniskirche, and Kurfürstendamm and Kantstrasse radiated outward, but now the center has shifted back to more or less where it was before, pre–cold war—to Friedrichstrasse, Alexanderplatz, and Potsdamer Platz. It's as if my memory were playing tricks on me.

Big old Karl-Marx-Allee has yet to catch the wave of gentrification, though the apartment buildings have been cleaned up and I hear the former apartments of party members and Stasi higher-ups are lovely. So, this route is a fitting prelude to the Stasi Museum visit.

Stasiland, the book by Anna Funder, an Australian journalist stationed in the former East Germany, investigates personal stories involving that notorious state security agency. Funder's perceptions are wonderful. She spots the bizarre and oppressive not only in the detaining and spying on citizens and the unexplained deaths, but also in things like a weird sexless popular dance (the Lipsi) that the government attempted to insert into popular culture as a kind of immunization against Elvis's rock-and-roll gyrations.

The Stasi kept massive "files" of all types: Some consisted of jars of smells of suspected subversives—jars that were filled

Arnd Wiegmann / Reuters

with scraps of clothing, or preferably underwear, secretly pro-
cured from some poor soul suspected of a lack of patriotism.
In some cases if actual clothing belonging to the suspect could
not be found then an agent would surreptitiously wipe where
that suspect had been seated and then quickly preserve the rag,
labeling it by name of suspect and how long he or she had been
seated on said chair. These rags were filed away just in case
that person should disappear, and then at some future date a
dog could sniff the rag and presumably discover the culprit's
hiding place.

It goes on. . . . In the book there's a beautiful Kafkaesque scene where a woman, denied employment for suspect activities, is called in for questioning:

"Why don't you have a job?"
"You tell me."
"You're a smart woman, surely you can find employment."
"No, I am unemployed."
"That can't be, there is no unemployment in the People's Republic."

We like to think such stories are typical of middle European paranoia and behavior under repressive Socialist regimes. But imagine someone being questioned by Homeland Security saying, "But I was tortured, the information was obtained under duress."

"The United States does not torture people, so that can't be true."

These days many people know of the Stasi from the recent movie *The Lives of Others.* The combination of psychological and Orwellian horror is hellish and weirdly seductive. The agency was known for turning citizens against their neighbors by subtle pressure, implied threats, or economic incentives. It seems it's something that many national security agencies do from time to time. ("If you see something, say something.") Turning the citizenry into rats makes the entire populace scared and docile, and after a while no one knows who's informing on whom. *Anyone* could be an informer or an agent. The world becomes a Philip K. Dick novel—although in his version everyone would also be informing on themselves.

The Stasi Museum is a massive compound that encloses a whole city block. I ride my bike into the inner courtyard and lock it up. Since both the parking and the main entrances to the various buildings are located inside the compound, when it was functioning no one outside could see who was coming or going—exits and entrances from the building all took place within the large interior courtyard. I am told that the whole complex is now for sale! For one euro! Well, there are conditions. The city is actually trying to sell it to Germany, on the condition that they will turn it into a proper museum.

As it now exists, the museum is rudimentary. One floor of former offices displays clunky spy devices: cameras in logs, behind large coat buttons, and in fake rocks. Here's one in a birdhouse—a little obvious, I think:

Maybe the intent was actually not to hide this surveillance gear too well. Maybe it was deemed more important to make people aware that they were being looked at and listened to rather than having the public just suspect that the spying was going on. A camera this blatant would confirm the rumors. If you're not aware you're being observed, if there isn't occasional proof, then you won't live in fear, so then what's the point? The best surveillance is when everyone suspects that they're being watched all the time. The government then doesn't even have to watch the cameras—they need only let people *believe* someone might be watching. Sometimes buildings here in the United States put up fake surveillance cameras in the hopes of discouraging perps. Of course, it wasn't all just charmingly nutty surveillance stuff here at Stasi headquarters—not everything is clunky tech that we now find oddly amusing. People's lives were ruined, devastated, destroyed; their careers came to a dead end at the least suspicion. There were prison terms and torture without stated reason (where have I heard that one before?), and information and culture was heavily censored. And the food in the East wasn't that great, either.

On a higher floor were the preserved offices of the head of Stasi, Erich Mielke. His offices weren't very grand by Western standards, but he did have a little apartment attached, which was pretty cute. One can now look at this style of furnishing as an example of a very peculiar design aesthetic. I'm sure for some the mere sight of these curtains and old phones would make them shudder, but for many now they embody a kind of totalitarian kitsch.

The style is hardly luxurious—but then maybe these higher-ups saw themselves as modest functionaries who were just doing the noble work of the state, of the masses, rather than surrounding themselves with luxury as would quasi-oligarchs or entitled royalty. I remember visiting Pravda headquarters in Moscow in the '90s, and the decorator must have been the

same guy. In that room there were also no decadent touches—which in a power nexus like that was a little surprising. There is almost an absence of power symbols—no marble staircases, giant chandeliers, or even soft leather chairs. Maybe this austerity was meant to be representative of the higher calling being represented, but in this context that pretension coupled with absolute power became all the more chilling. There was one odd decorative item in the Pravda director's office—a very long bookshelf that held only the collected works of Lenin. (When did Lenin have time to write all those volumes?)

As the Berlin Wall was coming down the shredding machines in this place went into overdrive. Imagine what an instantaneous change of worldview that must have been—one minute you're the proud controller of destinies and the next you're a disgusting worm intent on erasing your own life's work. I guess the folks who erased the CIA torture tapes and Nixon's eighteen minutes must have felt the same way. Maybe they all didn't exactly feel guilty, but they at least knew they and their bosses would be up shit creek if they were caught. Most of the Stasi shredding machines were overwhelmed and got clogged and they had to call for reinforcements. A huge number of documents were destroyed, but there were far too many to shred in just a few days, so there are organizations now that will allow you to locate your file, if it is readable. There is also a group that is attempting to reconstitute documents from the shredded strips of paper—very labor intensive. Here, from our side of the pond, in New York City, is a page from John Lennon's FBI file. On this particular page none of it is "uncensored"—it appears sort of like a piece of conceptual art.

courtesy Federal Bureau of Investigation

What Is the Time Limit on Justice?

Should the people whose lives were ruined by the Stasi, or by any similar governmental agency anywhere, be due financial reparations? Should their real estate be returned to them or to their heirs? Should there at least have been a truth and reconciliation committee here, as there was in South Africa, to clear the air and allow the country and individuals to move on? (In their version, there are no punishments or reparations, but only if indeed the entire truth is aired.)

The people of Zimbabwe, formerly Rhodesia, have been attempting in recent years to reclaim the farming lands taken from their ancestors many years ago by the white settlers. The whites have sometimes lived on these appropriated farms for three generations or more, and naturally they now think of them as theirs; they view the land as their homeland now too. The whites accept—so we are told—that the nation should not and cannot be ruled by outsiders anymore, or even by a small white minority, but they see these homes and farms as their own. They have raised children, built infrastructure, and improved the fields. But not just on their own farm. To some extent they have put into place the infrastructure that allowed the whole country to function. But, as the political tide has recently turned and the whites are no longer the political bosses, their right to hold on to 80 percent of the country's arable land just because their ancestors stole it seems less a viable argument and less likely to continue. Mugabe, who may have come into power showing promise that a self-governed African country rich in resources and with functioning systems might flourish, has sadly devolved into a corrupt and violent despot desperate to hold on to power at any cost. The descendants of the original inhabitants from the precolonial era, along with Mugabe's greedy and opportunistic self-appointed representatives, have begun to reappropriate the farms by force.

Is this fair? Not exactly, but neither was the appropriation of the land years ago by the whites. Justice, some might say, was simply delayed. If I can steal from you, and you are powerless to reclaim your property or land, even for generations, does it then at some point legally and morally become mine? At some point does the passage of time itself transfer ownership? What point might that be? Ten years? A hundred? A thousand?

Most likely any ultimate attempt at justice will be skewed. Maybe absolute justice, like absolute anything, rarely exists except in mathematics. In Zimbabwe whites will be forcibly removed, improved land will sometimes sadly go unused, and some reclaimed land will inevitably be wasted by the new owners, unaccustomed as they might be to managing such a resource. There will most likely be unscrupulous landgrabs and struggles for property among the new owners. But maybe, after some time, if things don't get completely out of hand, a kind of balance will be achieved. Some will argue that not even a single white person belongs on this land, and they have a point. But with some compassion and forgiveness perhaps a few of the descendants of the thieves might find a place and a home and even some honor and respect. Almost all of us, of every race, have something to be ashamed of in our history. Sometimes it is close by, within memory, a constant reminder. Sometimes it happened generations ago, and we feel no personal sense of guilt or obligation, but then things change and what was forgotten or buried comes back to life.

I would argue that it is increasingly hard for anyone anywhere to say, "I belong here and you don't." Human migrations have never stopped, they're endless, and mingling is tough, but it can often be fruitful—a source of innovation and creativity.

Will there be a bloody scramble for those beautiful '50s modernist homes in the Vedado district of Havana at some point? Israel, Palestine, South Dakota, Tibet—all involve some appropriation of land by one group from another. Does one theft of land or property inevitably prophesize a reciprocal theft? Is delayed justice inevitable? Is it even justice?

When does the clock for justice and reparation run out, if ever? Can the victims of the Stasi demand some compensation? Can German Jews reclaim their houses in Leipzig and in Berlin (those that are still standing)? Can the descendants of Russians exiled since the revolution return and claim their beautiful homes in St. Petersburg? The Chinese multitudes, tossed out of their family homes during the cultural revolution by Red Guard hoodlums—compounds where they'd lived for generations—can they now return? Can everyone simply make history go backward when it's their time in power, and does the associated violence constitute justice?

Is anyone native to anywhere? I think, in most cases, not. And maybe, somehow, that might be where the answer lies.

Parallels

Here is a frame from *Hitler's Secretary*, a documentary that is pretty much one long contemporary interview with that woman. It is a wonderful example of how we humans can deceive ourselves, delude ourselves, and blinker ourselves.

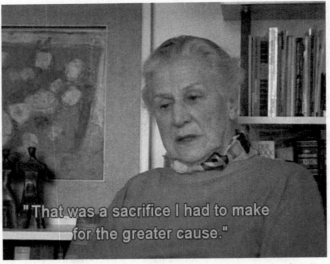

Blind Spot—Hitler's Secretary. A film by André Heller and Othmar Schmiderer (Dor Film production). Dor Film / Heller Werkstatt

Now, of course, she realizes what she had willed herself not to see or admit, just as today many people (fewer now than previously) refuse to admit that what the Bush administration was doing was unethical, unconstitutional, maybe even illegal because their buttons were pushed with words like *national security, patriotism, terrorism, democracy, small government, free market* . . .

Our ability to live in denial and hide from the facts in front of our faces is obvious. I can't possibly believe that people can perpetrate the horrors they do without justifying them to themselves, or better yet denying their existence entirely—or, as Hitler's secretary does, claiming that some eggs inevitably get broken to make an omelet. I think someone in the Bush administration may have used the same metaphor. It seems to me that this capacity for denial must have evolved out of a survival mechanism—some mental ability that helps one to focus and to exclude unhelpful news and distracting or diverting information when on the hunt or when courting. The skill and complexity of denial behaviors may have become absolutely necessary, at least at the time that they are needed—though sometimes later another point of view can be entertained and the truth confronted.

Far from being a fault, a deficiency, this capacity for denial was, and still is, a much-needed survival mechanism—one that, perversely, makes us human. Do animals practice denial? Would a dog say, "Who, me, shit on the rug, are you kidding?" and, more important, would a dog be able to convince himself that he didn't shit on the rug? I think animals can indeed be tricky and deceitful, but whether they can deceive themselves . . . well, we'll probably never know. Maybe it is this mental skill set that allows us to be as single-minded, and therefore as successful, as we often are.

The fact that demagogues, advertisers, marketing experts, and religious leaders have learned to tap into these powerful innate instincts and behaviors is often unfortunate, but maybe inevitable. Their exploitation of our abilities is regrettable because they are using them exclusively for *their* survival. Our own adaptation is being turned against us. However, since it is natural that we have these abilities, maybe it is also natural that they be exploited and that some folks will inevitably become more skilled at the art of exploitation and manipulation than others.

However, as powerful and irresistible as buzzwords and the like are, it is sometimes possible to resist them, or at least to be aware when they are being employed—whether for better or for worse. One can at least make a decision as to whether one wants to be or will allow oneself to be manipulated and/or self-deluded, or not. There are times when a certain amount of self-delusion is "good"—when it allows us to accomplish a necessary task, or create something unlikely or new. (If I'm in the middle of writing a song I don't want blunt criticism, for example.) It might even allow us to have the nerve to speak out, and in those cases denial—of a sort that gives us hope—might be deemed worthy.

The two biggest self-deceptions of all are that life has a "meaning" and that each of us is unique. One can see that evolving a built-in obscuring mechanism for those depressing and inevitable insights might be of practical use. Okay, maybe in a sense we are unique: the huge numbers of available combinations of traits, propensities, body types, and experiences that make up each of us is unimaginably large. Our variety is immense, but still it must be restricted within certain boundaries or we wouldn't be able to recognize ourselves as types at all. What we are is somehow simultaneously "infinite," but always similarly shaped. Almost infinite variety within severely restricted limitations.

Maybe what we think of as self, of us as individuals, of each of us with unique personalities and character, also exists in dogs, and might even extend down the food chain as far as insects. Insects with character and personalities? Why not? Why stop with doggies? An insect might be just like me. I, what I call I, might not be unique after all. The range of possible combinations of character traits might extend both up and down the evolutionary tree. There might also be just as many personalities in

each species as there are among us humans. Our inner policeman says to us, "don't even think that" when we stray into a forbidden thought zone like this and begin thinking thoughts that
might drive us crazy or inhibit much-needed action—thoughts
like, Maybe I'm not unique at all. He sometimes says it for our
own good—to keep us from going insane and to allow us to do
the things we need to do. As a species we have to have our little
delusions.

The other self-deception—that life has meaning—is famously
dealt with by religions all over the world. Our susceptibility to
this comforting idea is impossible to deny. I would argue that
while religions might indeed be a lot of superstition as well as
an unfortunate excuse for violence and countless horrors, they
might also serve a purpose. It would seem that at the very least
they make it easier to go on, to function, to make and do, if one
believes that our own (human) lives have a meaning.

Remade

Though Berlin was remade after World War II had reduced
much of it to rubble, progress was hobbled by the Wall and
by the occupation on both sides of that barrier—the Soviets
in the East and the Yanks and British in the West. Vast areas
in what used to be the center were located close to the Wall
and were left as fields and vacant lots, sometimes occupied by
gypsy caravans and flea markets. It was as if they knew the
Wall would eventually come down, so these spaces were never
developed. Since 1989, with the Wall and most of the occupi-
ers gone, a strange new city has arisen. In one former prewar
center, Potsdamer Platz, the massive new edifices of the corporate state have gone up—Sony, Mercedes, Siemens, and others
have new steel-and-glass buildings there. Nearby, the new government center, rapidly relocated here from the tiny town of
Bonn, is also trying to find its place. A transportation hub has
opened that was built by moving the river and then putting it

back. None of this development is organic; it's city planning on a massive scale. It's a colossal experiment that poses the question, Can one create a (vibrant) city center from scratch?

I bike around Mitte where the galleries and cafés are now being elbowed aside by luxury boutiques, as they were in SoHo in New York. And a couple of years after I began writing this I now sense that Berlin is indeed being acclaimed as a cultural capital, perhaps even as *the* cultural capital, of Europe. Despite some areas of towering corporate glass and accompanying wastelands of concrete plazas it does indeed seem as if the impossible can happen—a once vibrant city, a center of European culture, has come back to life.

Istanbul

Ride a bike in Istanbul? Are you nuts? Yes . . . and no. The traffic here is pretty chaotic and there are a number of hills, but in recent years the streets have become so congested that on a bike I can get around the central city—in the daytime at least—faster than one can in a car. As in many other places I'm almost the only one on a bike. Again, I suspect that status might be a big reason for this—bike riding, in many countries, implies poverty. I rode around Las Vegas and was told that the only other people on bikes there were people who had lost everything, probably through gambling. They'd lost their jobs, families, houses, and, I guess—ultimate insult for an American—their cars. All they had left was a bicycle to get around on. As cheap cars become available I'm afraid lots of folks in India and China will ditch their bikes as quickly as they can so they too can be elegant modern car drivers.

I pass cafés full of people intensely playing backgammon or smoking hookahs. I get some designer knockoffs at a shoe store. The minarets of the mosques make handy landmarks. I love this city. I love its physical location—bounded by water, dispersed across three landmasses, one of which is where Asia begins. Its way of life, which seems Mediterranean, cosmopolitan, and yet tinged by the deep history of the Middle East, is intoxicating.

Mostly I stick to the many roads that run along the Bosphorus and the Marmara Sea, thus avoiding the many interior hills. Occasionally I see some old wooden houses, so one can imagine what this place must have looked like before they all collapsed or were set on fire.

Ugly Modern Buildings as Religious Icons

As I bike around I note that the old buildings—wooden houses, nineteenth-century European-style palaces, and Ottoman-era edifices—are dwindling. Everywhere I see bland concrete apartment buildings going up. I wonder how buildings and neighborhoods of such obvious character can so easily be eliminated. What is everyone thinking? I sound a bit like Prince Charles in this, but I wonder, how is it that no one can see what is happening?

Throughout the world the international style, as the Museum of Modern Art calls it, has been used as an excuse for every bunkerlike structure, atrocious housing project, lifeless office building, and ubiquitous, crumbling third-world concrete housing block and office. Crap the world over has the imprimatur of quality because it apes, albeit badly, a prestigious style. Why has this style caught on so thoroughly? Why, all over the world, are beautiful cities being turned into a giant maze of gray upturned bricks with grids of identical windows in them?

Maybe, I think to myself, these structures express something. Something more than the bottom line on a developer's budget. Maybe, besides being easy and cheaper for the developers to build, they also stand for collective desires and aspirations of some sort. Maybe they represent or symbolize, for many people, a new start, a break with all the previously built things that have surrounded the townsfolk. And, especially in old towns, new buildings represent an end to history. They declare, "We will not be like our fathers! We are not ruled by the kings, czars, emperors, shahs, or any of those idiots from our past. We, a modern people, are different. We are no longer peasants. We are no longer hicks or hillbillies. We want no part of the visual system associated with our past, however noble it might be, and of which our memories are made. The weight of our history smothers us. It is, for us, a visual and symbolic prison. We will make a fresh start, like nothing ever seen on the face of the earth. (God knows, the Chinese are doing this in leaps and bounds.) And, if we have to do some damage in the process, then so be it." At least that's the emotional logic I imagine many people here and elsewhere feel.

These new buildings may not be beautiful. They may not even be utopian, as some architectural scholars and theorists of modernism might have hoped, but they are cheap, functional, and they don't remind people of anything that went before. The walls are straight, not crooked and wobbly, with angles that are, thank God and modern engineering, at 90 degrees, and the plumbing works—for now. For better or worse, they imply a self-determination. They say, "the future will be ours." The new generations will shrug off the weight of countless millennia and symbolically declare themselves free. Wrongheaded maybe, ugly for sure, but free. And there lies the religious, ideological, and emotional element inherent in these monstrosities.

These buildings represent the triumph of both the cult of capitalism and the cult of Marxist materialism. Opposing systems have paradoxically achieved more or less the same aesthetic result. Diverging paths converge. The gods of reason triumph over beauty, whimsy, and animal instincts and our innate aesthetic sense—if one believes that people have such a thing. We associate these latter qualities with either peasants—the unsophisticated, who don't know any better than to build crooked walls and add peculiar little decorative touches—or royalty and the upper classes—our despicable former rulers with their frilly palaces, whom we can now view, in this modern world, as equals, at least on some imaginary or theoretical level.

Here is a photo of Salvador, Brazil, where a district of warehouses and colonial commercial buildings has almost been completely transformed into a bland everytown business district. A musician friend there offered that these zones, once

so full of character, should have been treated "like European cities."

A crane fell here in Manhattan today as I type this. It killed four by last count and smashed a neighboring building. Another building went down two weeks ago, and the week before that part of a Trump building collapsed and a man was beheaded.

In the guise of uplift and progress, these buildings actually dehumanize people when they don't kill them outright. Although they are all made of identical materials—reinforced concrete, glass, and steel—they don't soar and swoop like the interstate highways, dams, and bridges made of the same materials. The graceful arcs of interchanges on the expressways and autobahns are not mirrored in these condo blocks. Neither are they meant to last like those structures. The future is here, in spirit, for an instant—but it will disappear, it will crumble, before our very eyes.

So instead of a small number of really impressive "monuments" such as those that survive from the disdained historical past, our century will leave, across the planet, a sprinkling of almost identical structures. It is, in a way, one vast global conceptual monument, whose parts and pieces are spread across the world's cities and suburbs. One city, in many locations.

They're doing it in New York right now. All over town almost identical concrete and glass buildings are rising. Many are going up so quickly that one wonders if the speed of construction isn't just a way to get them up before anyone can object. Now, with the credit/economic disaster in progress, the heat is truly on to spend any previously allocated money. Some towers have the names of famous architects attached, others do not. Visually it's often hard to tell them apart—they are all, ultimately, designed by the developers, while the starchitect is simply another kind of logo that can be applied in an attempt to distinguish one building from the other.

On a previous trip to Istanbul I had been invited by a group called the Dream Design Factory to do a public art installation during the Istanbul Biennial. The biennial is fantastic. Not all of the art is great and most of the artists are new to me—many hail from Turkey, Syria, Greece, Egypt, India, Iran. Not very many artists in the big Chelsea galleries are from those places, not yet. The exhibit locations are in wonderful old structures scattered around town—factories, warehouses, and customs offices, even in the Roman cistern that lies under part of the historic district.

My piece won't be in one of those places. Instead, I'll be installing in an as-yet-unrented space in a modern shopping center that is not quite in the center of town. At least it will have lots of foot traffic. I'm a little disappointed about it not being centrally located, but it's great to be here. My show will be some bus-shelter-sized lightboxes with computer-manipulated images of personal weapons and money. They are meant to look like glitzy contemporary ads, so the shopping mall location might not be so bad after all. I stay at the Pera Palas Hotel, a slightly run-down joint that was once, in the days of the Orient Express, the height of elegance. Hemingway, Garbo, Hitchcock, and King Edward III stayed here, as did spies such as Mata Hari and Kim Philby. Atatürk stayed here too, and his room, number 101, is kept as a museum.

Pera Palas Hotel elevator, Istanbul, 1994.

Sakıp Sabancı

The next day the Dream Design team meets me at the hotel and we drive along the Bosphorus. The team is led by Arhan, who looks like a Turkish Tin Tin, with one shock of hair sticking up in front. The Dream Design Factory does graphic design as well as events, promotions, fashion shows, and raves. We are also joined by Esra, a young woman who seems to have arranged today's field trip, and Arhan's friend Saba, an elderly Turkish artist who now lives on the island of Elba, off the coast of Italy. It's raining, traffic is snarled as usual, and I've seen this route before, on my bike, so I drift off to sleep in the backseat of the car. I can hear Saba, a bit of a Marxist, announce on seeing the spate of new billboards that have sprung up: "Who owns my vision? Who owns what I see?"

The mix of Esra, a young and cosmopolitan woman, Saba,

the leftist artist, and Arhan, the designer-entrepeneur-raver makes for an interesting crew.

After a while I am awoken by Esra—"David, we're here"—to the sight of a huge white gate, which opens in front of the car. At the top of the driveway is a giant mansion overlooking the Bosphorus. On the left is a slightly smaller, more modern house on the same property. I head for the big house, still half asleep. "No, not that one, the other one," someone shouts. Passing by a massive picture window, I wave at a woman sitting on a sofa with a child in the tasteful contemporary interior.

The woman meets us at the door. Strangely, she isn't much taller than she was when we saw her sitting on the sofa—her legs are shrunken and twisted by cerebral palsy. We are soon joined by her sister and offered drinks, which a butler in a double-breasted suit hurries off to fetch. Small talk. Apologies for not making it to the opening of my exhibition here. A silent woman who is not introduced feeds a child. I walk around examining the paintings in elaborate gold frames on the walls.

Esra announces that we can see Sakıp's father's collection if we like. I don't know what kind of collection she's referring to, but I'm game. We head for the big mansion after a cell phone call to alert the staff over there. The sister, nanny, and child stay behind. Sakıp Sabancı was one of Turkey's most successful businessmen. He's also known for his philanthropy—he built hospitals and founded a university.

We're met by the same butler, who must have slipped out ahead of us. The house is a museum—in the Victorian sense. The ground floor is filled floor to ceiling with paintings, vases, period furniture, statues, and glass cases filled with silver objects. As we enter a room on the right, an announcement is made—"This is the blue room"—nothing more. Any questions about individual paintings are answered by the butler. We move through room after room. Saba, being of a certain age, recognizes the work of some fellow expatriate Turkish painters who relocated to Paris. Most of the other paintings are "Orientalist"

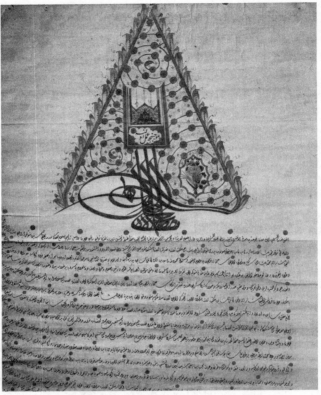

G. Dagli Orti / De Agostini Picture Library / Getty Images

in style, Ottoman-era romantic depictions of street life in Istanbul, although there are a few Russian romantic landscapes as well—sunset over the Neva and views of St. Petersburg.

The first floor, upstairs, is reserved for the amazing calligraphy collection. Ottoman-era pronouncements on law and policy, letters, and Qur'ans, of course, open to golden pages with elaborately embellished passages from the Book of Books. It's all beautiful. Interestingly, the Ottoman and Asian calligraphy pieces are much more impressive to our contemporary (Western) sensibilities than the more typically Western paintings and sculpture on the floor below. The Western and especially the

Orientalist paintings to us smack of a dated colonial romantic vision of the East that some of us would like to believe is in the past. Those paintings remind us a little too clearly of our prejudices and smugness. Whereas these calligraphic works seem, for the moment at least, perfectly in synch with contemporary Western sensibilities—text as art, the word as thought made beautifully tangible—even if they might have been oceans apart from those abstract and formal ideas at the time when they were made.

Belly Dance Party

Upon returning to the hotel, I rendezvous with a group of Turkish expatriates (who now live now in Belgium, New Jersey, and Chicago) and upon the arrival of a Kazakh gentleman, we depart for the Sulukule neighborhood to eat, drink, and be entertained by low-rent belly dancers. This gypsy neighborhood, a thousand years old, is almost all run-down houses and tea shops filled with people hanging out on the semipaved streets in the cold night air. Sadly, the whole neighborhood is threatened with demolition now, as it's coveted by real-estate developers.

Our friend from Kazakhstan knows which house we're heading for, so we ignore the kids who swarm over the car urging us to stop at their families' establishments and we proceed to "Chez Moi." We're met by more Kazakhs—bankers, they claim, although one wonders exactly what sort of "banking" these fellows do—and then a group of bleach-blond babes with rouged cheeks dressed in bulky sweaters. The house mother, a short woman in a house dress (is she pregnant?), leads us to "our" room, upstairs, where we will be entertained and, we have been forewarned, fleeced.

This is the polar opposite of Sakıp Sabancı's mansion, in the extreme. As the room is stone cold, "Mom" carries in a bucket of glowing coals from outside and plunks it down in the middle of the linoleum floor, which is pretty ripped up in spots. Our

Kazakh friend begins to negotiate while we get settled. The room is almost completely bare, except for the mismatched chairs that line the walls. A kid brings in a kind of folding card table. Four musicians (two percussionists, a tambourist, and a man with a Turkish banjo) seat themselves opposite us and begin to tune up.

The dancers, still in their winter sweaters, enter briefly and then leave. Mom takes drink orders—beer for the expats and me, roki for the Turks, and vodka for the Kazakhs. A Kurdish gentleman, who might be part of our party, sits near the musicians. He doesn't drink.

The musicians start to wail. They sound great, full of vigor and emotion that explodes in sudden bursts of intense and beautiful sadness. The sadness of the world is in this music. I don't care if they're just playing for us to make a quick buck; it's deeply moving anyway. I'm transported. A kid circulates and takes "donations." Cheese, grated carrots, and pistachios appear and eventually even a dancer, who makes the rounds before she starts asking for more donations (small bills seem to do). She takes off her sweater and plops it on a chair, revealing not a costume, but her bra and a pair of tights, rolled down just enough to reveal the arches of the top of her panties. She begins to dance. Not belly dancing really, but whatever it is, it's got some spirit. Everyone, whether from the cold, the drink, the music, or the whole situation, is in great spirits, laughing and toasting one another.

The dancer makes the rounds again, and bills are stuffed in her bra this time. Occasionally she does a sort of very basic lap dance. She sits on someone's lap (male or female, it doesn't seem to make a difference) and bounces up and down. It's more funny than it is sexy. It's all pretty tame, and it's not really belly dancing, but everyone's having a great time. Except for the man on my left, who twirls beads all night and consistently asks the girls to pass him by, most of us get up and dance at one point with the girls or with each other. Everyone laughs, fills one another's glasses, sings, shouts, and pastes dirty old bills on skin. The Kazakhs are getting pretty sloshed on their vodka, but nothing untoward ever happens. And, as the dancers don't have the requisite tummies for belly dancing, a few of the women pull off the shirts of the men, whose bellies are more than ample enough for shaking.

At one point there's a commotion outside and we discover a local TV team, led by a famous local talk show host (who resembles Fidel Castro a little—he's bearded and wearing green fatigues). The Turkish elections are about one week off, and he's polling the citizens of this poor neighborhood about their situation. He's surrounded by belly dancers on break, street kids, and the owners of the house.

I'm told that the outcome of this election, like many of the elections coming up in central Asia and in the former Russian republics, will demonstrate to what extent a sizable chunk of these populations want to return to a more stable world, whether it be based on the Communist religion or the fundamentalist sort. It is said that the fundamentalists here are very well organized, as opposed to the young secular moderns, who are largely apathetic and couldn't care less about politics. The religious party, it is rumored, is even flying in votes from the Turkish communities in Germany and Austria. They pay for the round-trip airfare, it is said, in order to guarantee another vote from the expats. Naturally, all this fervor is stronger in the eastern part of the country, far away from Istanbul, where a war with the Kurds has also been going on for years.

There is a big gap between rich and poor here, just as there is in the United States, although here in Istanbul one doesn't see, as one does in New York and other cities, the really wretched poor discarded by society. This country is truly on the border between East and West, and the conflict between westernization—the chaos of democratic liberties and heartless capitalism—and a way of life that surrenders to the righteous and sheltering arms of God and tradition may play itself out here.

The next day I ride over to the beautiful Topkapi Palace, a tourist attraction, to see its harem museum. While the proportions and scrollwork of the interior of the palace are incredible, I am more taken by the displays of religious relics. In other places, in other countries, these would be displayed in a cathedral or in a shrine of some sort—they are the holy of holies, after all—but here they are all grouped together in a museum room. A hair from the prophet, the sandal print of Muhammad, the arm bone of St. John the Baptist, and more skulls and bones are all shown in this way as if to prove how successfully Atatürk has turned the country into a secular nation.

I bike back across the Horn, over the bridge to the hotel, and in the evening I have dinner with the local concert promoter and a few of her assistants. Alev, the promoter, is a forthright, energetic thing, and her assistant Daniel (I'm sure that's not his real name; I suspect it's been anglicized), who picked me up at the airport, is a slightly effeminate immigrant from Kazakhstan arrived here via Moscow. In other words, he hasn't yet

Hairs of the prophet, Topkapi Palace, Istanbul, 1992.

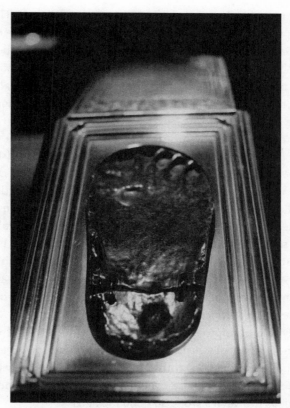

Footprint of the prophet, Topkapi Palace, Istanbul, 1992.

acquired the requisite mustache upon entry into Turkey, which I imagine makes him appear slightly less manly than the traditional men here. The ubiquitous mustaches were commented on by Alev and her staff as being indicative of a certain type of Anatolian. This view of facial hair marks my shaved friends as being somewhat more cosmopolitan, and I guess slightly more alienated—their view of mustaches might be comparable to my view of mullets, I would imagine.

In the five years of her company's existence Alev's main focus has been promoting raves and dance events (dance music events meaning house and techno parties, not ballet). The festival of which I am a part is to take place on a beach site on the Black Sea, about an hour and a half's drive from here. They call it the Alternatif Festival. There is to be a big tent, toilet facilities, all the usual Euro music festival structures, and the usual set of sponsors—a jeans company, Carlsberg beer, a radio station, and CNBC.

It turns out that the original site was near a village where some of the local "mafia" have almost completed a largish club that they soon hope to open as an attraction in that area. Having preexisting ties with the local military (the military functions as the police outside of the city municipalities here), they requested that the military make it "difficult" for this music festival to go on, or so it is claimed. The mafia, they reason, see the festival as possible future competition for their club. This all came to a head over the last few days, it seems; the military issued a directive that the festival would be unsafe, citing danger of drowning, fires from the local forest, and possible drug use.

Alev told of approaching various ministers, some of whom are fundamentalist Muslims, for help. Can you imagine . . . ? First of all they most certainly don't want to deal with a woman, and second they see these events, and Western pop music in general, as the devil's work, so good luck girl.

The Alternatif Festival folks then took their cause to the national government. It may seem a big leap, from the community folks to the federal government, but apparently local corruption runs pretty deep, so one has to leapfrog it to escape it. Our Alt Festival pals decided to link the right to hold their music festival to the pending EU membership issue—something Turkey would dearly like to have. How does accommodating raves make one more eligible for EU membership?

Turkey, as I write this, is right in the middle of applying for EU membership, and it seems they just about qualify economically. But on the human-rights and cultural fronts there are huge gaping holes. Mostly the human-rights issue, which is a bit of a Turkish cliché, as everyone thinks of the film *Midnight Express* when they think of Turkey. (Imagine if your entire country and culture was represented by one film, one which portrays your country as being a brutal cesspool. I'd pray for another successful film about anything else. A nice love story maybe.) It seems the EU also requires member nations to have a full deck of cultural institutions—historical preservation societies, support for local and regional traditions, education, and institutions focused on different socioeconomic strata of the country.

This is where we come in. Youth programs are part of the EU's cultural requirement. The other music festivals here focus on jazz, classical, and "ethnic" (i.e., world) music and are presented at prestigious venues, lavish concert halls, and the like, as are jazz festivals around the globe. Obviously these jazz festivals play to a so-called sophisticated portion of the Turkish public, with occasional demographic overlaps that include some of the hoi polloi. (I often personify that overlap at those jazz festivals.) But the Alt Festival folks hope to assert that the youth are not being served by these officially sanctioned festivals and that therefore the EU commission needs to see festivals like the Alt happen in order to be certain that all levels of the Turkish public are being catered to. It's a kind of shaky argument, it seems to me, but go for it.

There is a limited audience in this part of the world for the fringe, albeit hip, side of global pop culture, of which the other acts like Jarvis Cocker, Sneaker Pimps, and I are representative. How important it is culturally for our limited slice of the global culture pie to be presented everywhere and be supported in part by the state is debatable. Ditto, I would argue, for orchestras, jazz, and contemporary art, which have all gotten support for years. Jazz (not to mention classical music) for decades was exported by the United States and tours were funded by the U.S. State Department and even by the CIA as being representative of cool U.S. culture, which went a long way toward making that music acceptable and suitable for concert halls around the world. But that is another rant.

Alev optimistically claims that within a few years I will be able to do a circuit that includes Beirut, Cairo, Sofia, Ankara, and Tel Aviv, which sounds good to me. I've done concerts in two of those cities previously, and it would be nice to someday connect all the dots. But do these countries really *need* Western art-pop music? A cosmopolitan demographic certainly likes it, but increasingly there are homegrown acts that are just as good as anything foreign. Though, for many countries, a foreign act will usually command more respect and interest than anything homegrown—sad but true.

At present the festival is still on, but the latest word is that it will be moved to another site—possibly without the tent, but with the full stage and the other bits. Yikes. It could get a bit wobbly out there, if they've moved the stage but haven't moved all the toilets, the water trucks, and the food concessions.

I told the promoters I intend to visit the Asian side today on my bike. It's not as touristy, but I've seen the tourist stuff—the Hagia Sofia, the Blue Mosque, and the vast underground cistern that the Romans installed—on previous visits. I bike down to the water and catch a ferry, and then I pedal around the promenade that stretches along the coast on the opposite side of the Bosphorus. The ferries leave every fifteen minutes or so and I catch one that goes around the outside of Istanbul harbor and drops me near a large university on the Asian side. There's a nice green pedestrian strip along the water with scattered outdoor cafés, so it will be a pleasant ride back to the other Asian ferry terminal—the one directly across the Bosphorus from where I left.

I ride by the first train station built in the East. Trains head from there to Baghdad and points east, and near here is where the line begins, at the Bosphorus. Couples are out for a stroll, eating ice cream.

On returning I hear that the festival was denied permission

at the second site, which is not a huge surprise. Their claims that a pop music festival would do wonders for Turkey's cultural and human-rights record didn't seem to fly.

The Show Must Go On

I spend the rest of the day wandering around town on my bike and I buy some wonderful reverse bas-reliefs of Atatürk and some cool old prints of Arabic maps and medical engravings of dissected brains. I meet Daniel, Alev's Kazakh assistant, in the lobby, where I assume some journalists will join us. Instead he leads me out to the hotel garden where some tables and chairs are set up and it seems there is going to be (surprise!) a whole press conference with TVs, etc. Ah well, what can you do?

Alev then comes up to greet me and in a low voice informs me that now the festival is off entirely. I am slightly, but only slightly, shocked. Alev has arranged the press conference to announce the canceling of the festival. I sit beside her and say to the press and TV that I am saddened by what has happened as I have been very much looking forward to playing here again.

Meanwhile, all the journalists in front of me immediately get on their cell phones—it's an odd sensation to talk to an audience when they are all making calls. Alev is on and off the phone herself, and she suddenly announces that maybe there is a possibility of yet another site. This one will be smaller, and closer to town (good news, I think, that last bit, given the horrendous traffic here).

We, my band and crew, all go out to dinner, but I am first taken to a TV station, where I had agreed to put in an appearance. When we finally get there it turns out to be a sports show, and World Cup fever is rampant. Somehow they've managed to shoehorn me into the program due to the general World Cup excitement. Maybe some of the euphoria will rub off?

The next morning it seems the festival is really back on, at the new, third site. My crew head out in the morning. Although we had prepared ourselves to leave for an early-morning sound check and rehearsal, it gets pushed back twice—to two PM. Kind of a worry, that, as there are two new string players in the group and we've all been off the road for a couple of months and could use the run-throughs . . . but there's nothing to be done.

We are taken by a small bus to the park in which the concert is to be held, but the (British) driver gets lost and we somehow end up back at the hotel. Soon enough we're back in the Istanbul traffic. Other than a trolley on one boulevard and buses there is no public transportation, so at rush hour things grind to a halt.

Our soundcheck/rehearsal is pretty short—the generator is shut down just before we are to begin. But we make some progress learning "Lazy"—a live version of a remix version with strings. It's going to sound lovely—moody and orchestral in bits and driving and funky in other sections. It still needs work so we won't play it tonight, but maybe after another rehearsal.

The show goes off very well in the end. The sound is fine. The audience, while not the eight thousand they'd hoped for, is respectable and very appreciative and they love it when the strings join the rhythm section! They swoon and wave their hands around. It feels good to sing and dance. A million thoughts run through my head as I sing—personal stuff and otherwise—and they make the songs fresh for me. The two new string players do wonderfully for only having run through much of the stuff with the other strings and not the entire band. It's a short set, as it's a festival and there are other acts on after us.

Arhan is backstage. He calls Esra, who says we should come on by to where she is. She's having dinner with the minister of tourism and the minister of state at a fancy restaurant after the opening of a museum.

Esra got married a week ago in Paris to a man I'd met previously—a businessman, I think, and when we arrive I am also introduced to the various ministers and their wives or girlfriends as well as a Turkish fashion designer.

The restaurant is on a hill with a view of the Bosphorus. I am seated at the end of the table, near Esra and across from Arhan. Our table is outside, on the grass. The view is incredible. One can see the boats and ferries down below plying the Bosphorus and a steady stream of cars crossing the immense bridge to Asia. Below us are the lit-up palaces and the Kempinski Hotel along the water's edge.

Esra is, I gather, somewhat wealthy. She's charming and attractive, but not conventionally pretty. She's animated as she leans attentively toward the minister of tourism on her left—an immense man with tiny little eyes who reminds me of Mr. Creosote, the Monty Python character who eats until he explodes. When our minister leans back after making a remark his head seems like a blip on top of a mountain.

All the ministers have mustaches. All their wives or girlfriends have cleavage.

Some of the women speak English; the ministers do not, at least not to me. Conversation seems to be sporadic, and with me being a fresh new element in the mix, it starts up again—at least for a while. Eventually Arhan and I leave, as I have to pack for a drive to Belgrade in the morning.

With some of the worst traffic in the world—the city has exploded in population in recent decades—one wonders why, with its agreeable Mediterranean climate, central Istanbul hasn't embraced the bicycle as a mode of transport. Aside from the hills I come back to status as the only explanation that fits. Sure, folks will say, as they do in New York City, "It's dangerous, and where will I park my bike?" Those questions get answered and rapidly rendered moot when there is political will—or when the price of gas is five times what it is today. They are really excuses, justifications for inaction, not real questions.

Buenos Aires

I t's the Paris of the south, they say—due to its wide avenues, cafés, and nightlife. Avenida 9 de Julio is the widest avenue in the world, so there you go Mr. Haussmann. If the obelisk wasn't plunked in the middle of this boulevard you could land a 747 in the middle of the city.

Buenos Aires is far enough south to be in the temperate zone, which separates this city, and Santiago, in Chile, just across the

Angelo Cavalli / Stone / Getty Images

Andes, from their tropical neighbors just to the north. There are huge psychological separations too—the Argentines tend to see themselves as more European, and by inference, as more sophisticated, than their Brazilian neighbors. Naturally, ahem, musicians and other creative types don't carry this snobbish attitude around, but in general it is felt and seen in the architecture, cuisine, and clothing.

Though both southern Brazil and Argentina were settled by successive waves of Italians and Germans, among others, the Argentines probably deny that there are also African elements that make up their culture, while in Brazil to the north those elements are still strong and visible and the Brazilians are proud, sometimes, of their African blood and culture. In Argentina the Africans all but vanished, but in truth their influence remains, camouflaged and denied, but intact.

Built on the floodplain of La Plata River, the city is fairly flat, and with the temperate weather and the streets more or less on a grid it is perfect for cycling around. Despite this I could count on one hand the number of locals I saw on bikes. Why? Would I inevitably find out the reason no one else was pedaling around here? Was there some dark secret explanation about to pounce on me? Am I a naive fool? Is it because the driving is so reckless, the theft so rampant, the gas so cheap, and a car such a necessary symbol of status? Is it so uncool to ride a bike here that even messengers find other ways of getting around?

I don't think it is any of those reasons. I think the idea of cycling is simply off the radar here. The cycling meme hasn't been dropped into the mix, or it never took hold. I am inclined to agree with Jared Diamond, who claims in his book *Collapse* that people develop cultural affinities for certain foods, ways of getting around, clothes, and habits of being that become so ingrained that they will, in his telling, persist in maintaining their habits even to the point of driving themselves and sometimes their whole civilization to extinction. He gives a lot of historical evidence—for example, an eleventh-century Norse settlement in Greenland where the settlers persisted in farming cattle, as impractical as it was there. The cuisine or habits of the local Inuit were never adopted or adapted—their diet and ways were just not culturally acceptable—and eventually the settlers all died. This was not a quick settlement either—it lasted for over four hundred years—long enough for them to convince themselves that they were doing okay. Of course, in the era of total reliance on fossil fuels and global warming, Diamond's history lessons have a scary resonance. So, while we would like to think that people can't really be so stupid as to wipe themselves out—with the means of survival right in front of them—they can, and they certainly do.

I'm not saying cycling is a matter of survival—though it might be part of how we survive in the future—but here in Buenos Aires it seems so much a commonsense way of getting around that cultural abhorrence is the only explanation I can come up with as to why there are no other cyclists on the streets. My cycling is considered so unusual here that it is newsworthy—it is written up in the local papers.

I mainly visit this city when I am performing, though I arrange my schedule in order to have time to look around. Over the years I have become slightly familiar with some of the music and musicians here. They are some of my favorites in the world, as is this city.

Talk Backward

In the morning I decide to bike out to Tierra Santa (the Holy Land) in hopes of some photo opportunities. It's a theme park located close to the river out past the domestic airport that advertises "a day in Jerusalem in Buenos Aires." I find that it is closed today, but from outside the gate I can see "Calvary" with its three crosses poking out of the top of an artificial desert

hill. I won't get the ironic shots I might have hoped for, but the ride out was nice—from my hotel I passed through grand parks filled with professional dog walkers (none had fewer than five dogs) and then rode along a promenade that borders the river, which is so wide here that you can't see the opposite shore—one would think it is a still ocean or a giant lake.

Fishermen lean on the railing. There are kiosks at regular intervals that grill meats for truck drivers and others who want a quick lunch. Bags of charcoal piled by the sides of the kiosks will supply the heat to grill blood sausages, steaks, hamburgers, and various other cuts of the legendary Argentine flesh that sizzles during the early part of the day in anticipation of the lunch crowd. Many of the kiosks advertise *choripan*, a conjunction of chorizo (sausage) and *pan* (bread). There's another offering called *vaciopan*, which literally means empty sandwich, but it also is a cut off the cow. This is not a place for vegetarians.

The slang here, called *lunfardo,* is many-layered and inventive. There's even a genre of slang called *vesre* when you reverse the syllables—*vesre* is *reves* (reverse) with the syllables reversed. *Tango* becomes *gotán* and *café con leche* becomes *feca con chele.* Sometimes this is compounded and complicated even further when a euphemism for something—a word for marijuana or one's wife—is pronounced backward, adding yet another layer of obscurity to a slang that already approaches a separate language.

Bobo

My lovely hotel in the Palermo district is named after the book *Bobos in Paradise,* a humorous essay by the North American writer David Brooks about the gentrification and commercialization of bohemian culture, which makes it a confusing name for this hotel, as it and this neighborhood are prime examples of that process. The word also means "fool" in many languages. It is as if the Tribeca Grand had a name that poked fun at the fact that it's located in a gentrified, arty neighborhood. This hotel is located on Guatemala Street, between Jorge Luis Borges and Thames streets—the street names alone say a lot about the cultural makeup of this town, with its mixture of Latin American and European references. It reminds me of how street and town names not only commemorate dates and well-loved (by some) politicians (LaGuardia Place and the FDR drive here in New York, 9 de Julio and Avenida de Mayo here) but also express a conscious mythmaking and cultural longing—a longing for connection, historical continuity, and status. The hundreds of little U.S. towns named Paris or Madrid, the cluster of historical Greek towns in upstate New York, the *New* London, *New* Jersey, and *New* Orleans, Venice Boulevard—how a people see themselves, or how previous generations saw themselves, is embedded in these names. At a glance one can sense how the past is perceived—what people wish their history to be and what is intentionally omitted.

Mauro, who plays percussion with me, said, with a disappointed tone, that he felt Santiago, where we were earlier on this trip, was very much an "American" city (meaning North American). I can see what he means: it's pretty, it's clean, and there are lots and lots of glass office buildings and little of the messy character, charm, or funk of Mauro's native Brazil. Mauro pointed out that Chile was one of the only countries that didn't have slavery. What he might have been implying was that it was the Africans who give South American culture much of its character. Being Brazilian, he would say that. Certainly much of the unique music on this continent, and subsequently of many others these days, is a hybrid of European, indigenous, and African styles. It has been argued that even tango has some African in its family tree. Though musical roots and influences are not so hard to hear, at least to me, cultural influences extend in deeper and subtler ways—in grammar and syntax, in humor, in attitudes toward the body and sex—that are harder to tease apart from every other influence. The past is part of the weave, but often we see mainly the overall surface pattern.

Last night a small group of us were joined at dinner by Ignacio Varchausky from the local tango Orquesta El Arranque. He mentioned that numerous groups these days are trying the tango/electronic fusion, but to his mind none of them have succeeded yet—not that he doesn't think it's a worthwhile goal. Unlike lots of *tangueros* here, who tend to be fairly protective and conservative, he and the other members of El Arranque are open to collaborations and to new approaches, both from that music's past and from other foreign styles. Lately, the band members have unearthed old (1940s) handwritten tango orchestra arrangements, and some of them are surprisingly radical, he says. The orchestrations became more smoothed out since then, more conservative, and these older, wilder approaches were often swept under history's rug and forgotten. They're in the middle of completing a CD on which older tango masters, those who are still living, join them and play with the younger guys. He says this is unusual because tango is not a very collaborative or open scene.

Later that night I run into Nito, a member of the local band Los Autenticos Decadentes. They are a large band that came up in the '80s along with Los Fabulosos Cadillacs. (As one might imagine, the Cadillacs name is meant both ironically and sincerely; here one can love North American pop culture and distance oneself from it at the same time.) Both bands were initially inspired by the Two Tone bands in the UK and the ska scene there (Madness, the Specials, Selector), as were No Doubt and many other bands around the world. Those short-lived UK bands have more bastard children than is often acknowledged. Both of these Argentine bands rapidly evolved and began to incorporate local influences. Los Decadentes fell in love with regional popular styles—working-class dance music and *murga*, a kind of carnival music—to which they added contemporary lyrics, while Los Fabulosos Cadillacs incorporated more Afro Uruguayan and tango sounds and rhythms.

Nito and I had crossed paths years ago in New York City when Los Decadentes performed at a disco and I lent them an accordion. Back then the band was viewed by locals here in Buenos Aires as a kind of theatrical comedy band—a bunch of rowdy goofballs, which they more or less were at first. Musically, they weren't taken seriously, though soon enough they learned to play, stay in tune, and write amazingly catchy songs in a variety of rootsy and popular genres—if you include disco anthems as roots music, and I do, since disco pop is heard in bars everywhere alongside *rancheras* and *cumbias*. They soon had hits and became fairly popular.

I ran into Nito in Mexico City after a show I did there, and he amazed the Mexicans with his knowledge of *narco corridos,* the ballads sung in the north of that country that glamorize the exploits of drug dealers and traffickers. One could draw a parallel in contemporary rap lyrics with, for example, Ghostface Killah's song "Kilo," but these Mexican songs are performed with accordions and guitars. Nito knew the words to all of them. Now, here in BA, he's handed me a pile of CDs of Argentine and Paraguayan *cumbia* bands. I didn't know such bands existed in those countries (those rhythms are usually identified with Colombia or Mexico, not with these countries farther south). There's even a *bachata* band here, something I thought only existed on the Caribbean island of Santo Domingo. He says Paraguay is the Jamaica of South America, though what he means by that is slightly unclear. He's not referring to the dope. I think he believes they've evolved an original slant on music and have a voracious appetite for whatever they hear, from wherever. Their own popular music incorporates and absorbs a lot of music they hear, but they process it and give it their own twist, and it's hugely influential—at a grassroots level. The music these Paraguayan bands play is not sophisticated in the accepted sense. It's trashy music for the two D's—dancing and drinking—but as often happens these outsiders—the musicians from Buenos Aires—are recuperating this low-class music and re-presenting it to a new audience, the way the British appropriated U.S. blues and Detroit techno and sold it back to the United States.

Nito attempts to tell me what the various *cumbia* CDs he gave me represent. He says, "The words are deep, important, like Leonard Cohen." Somehow I doubt that it is the appropriate analogy, as this musical style is usually the favorite of poor people, and it reflects their concerns, as rap did at one time in North America. But I can see what he means. There is deep poetry here, in the way we think of blues as being deeply poetic, within its self-imposed structural and verbal parameters. Others might claim that Tupac or Biggie Smalls were likewise unacknowledged deep poets working within the parameters of vernacular speech and phrasing.

Nito said that rock and roll is now viewed as the music of the big companies, as it emanates from the large, usually northern, wealthy countries, and therefore it is no longer considered to be the voice of the people—not even of the people where it comes from. I have to agree that seen from here, contemporary rock is the product of foreign, often North American, multinationals. Their marketing muscle has made it bland, predictable, and ubiquitous. It's a corporate product that is (or was) being exported. No matter what or who the artist may be, no matter how well-intentioned someone like me might think he is, our music, when it is sold here, is invariably tainted by who is selling it and where it comes from. That said, international "rock" was an important part of the musical diet for a generation here. It's in everyone's blood. It's a lingua franca, even if places like Argentina, far from the northern "source" of rock, no longer look to the north for musical news and inspiration.

Oddly enough, when I first played here it was with a large Latin band, which must have been a bit of a shock to those expecting to hear "Psycho Killer." We did a lot of salsa, *cumbia*, and sambas. I did do "Psycho Killer," but with two *berimbaus*—a

Brazilian one-stringed "rhythm" instrument that is usually associated with the martial art/dance capoeira. I was a little shocked
when I played that concert. I thought for sure the various
grooves and flavors of Latin music would all be familiar here,
even if the current generation didn't play them, but they weren't.
I was under the mistaken impression that those infectious Latin
rhythms I hear all over New York City would be familiar all over
South America. Boy was I wrong. Although there are a few—a
very few—Latin American artists whose appeal extends across
the whole continent (and often to Europe as well) most of the
regional styles have, well, regional audiences. There's a salsa,
cumbia, bachata, and *reggaeton* audience that encompasses the
Caribbean basin along with immigrants from there who have
settled in New York, but except for a couple of artists, that music,
which was for decades a strong part of New York's musical landscape, didn't penetrate south of the equator.

So it turned out in a small way that Mr. Psycho Killer was
bringing salsa and samba to Buenos Aires! I imagined I would
be bringing coals to Newcastle (or "sand to the beach," as the
Brazilians would say). I imagined I had made a big effort to
import something that was already familiar or available in copi-
ous quantities, but it seems the world is not as simple as that.

Now many of the bands here have increasingly incorporated
local grooves and styles into what was once essentially a version, however creative, of northern rock. This, some think, may
limit their international audience (though I tend to think the
reverse is true). Nito says that he is content knowing that their
band may never be "international." He's proud that they represent the culture and identity of this region, which he knows
may limit them commercially but he feels is right and proper.

Día de los Niños

The next day during the afternoon I ride my bicycle out to a
park where I notice that there is a "shrine" that consists of a

small statue of a saint, and around him offerings of plastic bottles of water—hundreds of them—all over the place. At first glance, if one didn't know better, it almost looks like a recycling depot. But this has that distinctive, unmistakable appearance of a deliberate human act. An act of faith, a process that has created a nexus of desire and magic. The bottles have a purposeful look, not the look of a heap of rubbish. These everyday objects have been ordered and activated, given power and significance, and charged with hopes and longing. Even if one doesn't believe, one can sense that a creative and spiritual act has taken place. A transference of will from inside to outside. I take a few photos and then pedal on.

A Village of the Dead

I continue to ride around town. Some of the larger multilaned boulevards are bike challenging, so sometimes I opt for the side streets. Since each neighborhood is more or less on a grid it's not that hard to figure out how to navigate this city. Sometimes

I can even move from neighborhood to neighborhood and stay almost exclusively within elongated parks or along the riverfront promenade.

I pass through Recoleta. It's a little like the Upper East Side in Manhattan or the Sixteenth Arrondissement in Paris: elegant, older, European-style apartment buildings with ornate carvings; well-off patricians, mostly older women and gentlemen; fancy clothing boutiques; and upscale restaurants. Here is the cemetery where Evita is buried. The graves in the cemetery are mostly aboveground, as they are in New Orleans, but with a huge difference: these are big, ostentatious tombs—they could be the tombs of kings and queens. The caskets and their inhabitants are even visible through the glass doors of many of these "little palaces." For that's exactly what these are—big houses. This place is a neighborhood, a barrio, exclusively for the dead. A whole city, a necropolis. In many of the "homes" one can also see stairs going down into semidarkness where I can just make

out more shelves holding more inhabitants. This is where I presume the previous generation "lives."

In another necropolis—la Chacarita—there is the grave of Carlos Gardel, the famous tango artist who died in a plane crash. The tomb is covered in plaques commemorating his influential work and inspiring example.

There are long avenues of "buildings" in varied architectural styles—art deco, classic Greco-Roman, gothic, modern—block after block, an entire metropolis just for the dead, built on a slightly reduced scale from the real city outside the high walls that surround the cemetery. A few men sweep and clean away dead flowers, while a few visitors wander aimlessly, and a few bring fresh flowers.

Some citizens of the city are upstanding, while others are tired of living.

And some will soon be devoured by buzzards.

Musical Connections

I'm performing tonight, sitting in on a couple of songs with the local band La Portuaria, whose lead singer, Diego Frenkel, is an acquaintance of mine. Diego's wife appears in the afternoon, carrying their new baby. She was in the original company of the De La Guarda theatrical piece *Villa Villa* when that group came to New York City. When I saw that show—and was swept up into the air by a man with hairy butt cheeks—I imagined it was a kind of political allegory, a celebration of release, freedom, and anarchy after years of dictatorship—a roar of freedom, yet still an acknowledgment of the painful and terrifying past. I might have been imagining all that, projecting my own ideas about Argentine culture and memory onto a freewheeling piece of physical theater. But maybe a theatrical explosion like this happens after being bottled up?

Diego, it turns out, is also friends with Juana Molina, whom I invited to join me on my most recent U.S. tour. I'd heard Juana's second CD, *Segundo*, and loved it, though I didn't know her history at that time. Her dad, Horacio Molina, was a great musician, and when Juana was a little girl the likes of Vinicius De Moraes and Chico Buarque passed through their house. The family eventually left Argentina and spent six years exiled in Paris during the dictatorship. Later, with her siblings, she showed a gift for comedy and for inhabiting characters, so before long she had her own TV show called *Juana and Her Sisters*. She might be compared to Tracey Ullman if one needs a reference. Success proved to be wonderful but also a trap and a huge detour from the music that she had always hoped to write, so a few years ago she stopped doing the TV show and began to perform her quiet, peculiar, and wonderful songs.

The local public hated her initial foray into music. They heckled her and shouted, "Be funny!" Luckily, Ms. Molina heard that she was getting played on the influential public radio station KCRW in L.A., so she moved there and began to acquire a small following. I don't know how she is received in Buenos Aires now, but with glowing reviews from the north under her belt the locals might be ready to have another listen. Her music is serious, quiet, and experimental, for want of a better word—she didn't leave TV to be a pop star, that much is obvious.

"Maximum Effort—Minimum Results"

While in Recoleta I stop by the new contemporary art museum, MALBA, where there is a show called Los Usos de la Imagen, with works mainly borrowed from a large Mexican art collection. There are some of the usual international names, but there are also a good number of South and Central American artists represented, some of whom are new to me. One of them,

Santiago Sierra, made a video of indigenous women repeating a Spanish phrase they'd learned phonetically: "I am being paid to say something the meaning of which I ignore."

Sierra also had a photo of another indigenous group, which he had paid to dye their hair blond—a heavily loaded symbol in much of Latin America. In another piece, a truck was paid to block a highway for five minutes. People were paid to fill a room, to hold up a wall, to masturbate. I found this work disturbing. I wasn't sure if these people were simply being exploited or if the exploitation, being so obvious, was instead ironic and a criticism of the exploitation that exists all around. The ambiguity, for me, was unsettling.

Another artist, Francis Alÿs, a Belgian who now lives in Mexico, paid five hundred Peruvians to form, side by side, a huge line, and they were then instructed to shovel the sand of a massive dune that lies in the desert south of Lima as they inched forward, step-by-step, continually shoveling. Theoretically they were moving the whole dune, imperceptibly, as the massive human chain of laborers made its way across the hill. "Maximum effort—minimum results" was his catchphrase summarizing the effort.

I assume that in some way these works are a comment on both the exploitation of the local labor force and the gulf between rich and poor in many Latin American countries. The exchange of cash for absurd or loaded behavior is sort of funny, and more than a little sad. In an art context it's shocking—but one becomes used to it on the streets, where people willingly perform tedious and repetitive tasks for very little money. It reminds me a little of bum fights—a rumored L.A. practice in which young men would pay homeless guys on skid row to fight one another and then they'd circulate videos of the results. It was a debasing, disrespectful, and degrading way to treat other people. Getting cash for shoveling sand or memorizing a meaningless phrase may be disrespectful, but it's hardly as demeaning as getting punched for cash.

The "work" that these artists pay for might be absurd, but it's harmless. It's provocative in a sad, fucked-up kind of way. As a poetic response to a social and financial context, these acts seem intuitive, instinctual, but when transposed to an art fair or a shiny gallery or museum in New York City a whole other level of meaning is added. And when billionaires buy and sell art about the exploitation of the lower classes, the layers of context and meaning are maybe not exactly what the artist had in mind.

The Saint of Unemployment

I ride farther out from the center of town. I don't have a destination. I stumble upon a *feria*—a village fair—this one an outdoor festival that celebrates gaucho and country culture. It takes place in a small plaza out in the suburbs. On the way I pass a queue of people. One sees only the line, no destination or end—just people standing, patiently, and occasionally inching forward, but toward what is unclear. The line is so long that it disappears somewhere down the road, and where it ends is too far away to tell. The line snakes through a succession of neighborhoods, in and out of small town centers. It disappears from my view and then incredibly it suddenly appears again. It's four kilometers long at least. Half a million people or more, so I am told later, waiting to see San Cayetano, the patron saint of the unemployed. This is the saint that people pray to when they are in need of work, and today is his day. All the local roads in the area around the church where the saint is housed are blocked off by the police. The people come to pray for work, for employment. Some of them come carrying a few stalks of DayGlo-dyed wheat, which they will take home in remembrance, while others leave with nothing.

Being Your Own Billboard

Almost all the girls in the big cities of Argentina I visit this year wear extremely tight stretch jeans. It is as if there is a mating ritual in progress and we foreigners here are privileged to witness it. These skintight jeans constitute their courtship plumage. The local guys mostly pretend not to notice. But how can they not? It is such a blatant effort to attract their attention. Trying to be cool, the men play an elaborate game of not paying any mind. So there is this obvious signaling and pretending not to notice going on. It's beautiful, and the tension must be unbearable.

Apparently there are more women than men in Argentina, so maybe that explains part of it—with an imbalance like that, the women face more competition than they would in most other countries, so they have to try harder to attract a man's attention. At least that would explain it in Darwinian terms.

I think a similar process operates in Los Angeles, though the context there is slightly different. I don't know what the male-female balance is in L.A., but I suspect that because people in that town come into close contact with one another relatively infrequently—they are usually physically isolated at work, at home, or in their cars—they have to make an immediate and profound impression on the opposite sex and on their rivals whenever a chance presents itself. Subtlety will get you nowhere in this context.

This applies particularly in L.A. but also in much of the United States, where chances and opportunities to be seen and noticed by the opposite sex sometimes occur not just infrequently but also at some physical distance—across a parking lot, as one walks from car to building, or in a crowded mall. Therefore the signal that I am sexy, powerful, and desirable has to be broadcast at a slightly "louder" volume than in other towns where people actually come into closer contact and don't need to "shout." In L.A. one has to be one's own billboard.

Consequently in L.A. the women, on the face of it, must feel a greater need to get physically augmented, tanned, and have flowing manes of hair that can be seen from a considerable distance. Their clothes are a little (or a lot) too sexy (especially when seen up close) and to add to this effect they strike come-hither poses as they stand or walk—postures that drive the Angelino males to distraction and probably influence much of that city's creative output.

The Stolen Building

I make my way back toward the center of town, and on my way I pass by a beautiful old administration building. It is covered with different-colored ceramic tiles, and these tiles seem different from many of the others used in town. I am told later that this edifice houses the Department of Water, which is in charge of the city's water supply. The need for this department was made painfully obvious during the city's great yellow fever epidemic in 1871 when between 150 and 170 people died every day. The outbreak killed half the population of Buenos Aires, and during the height of the epidemic so many people were dying every day that the railway company laid in a temporary branch line to serve a new cemetery—special trains for the dead leading to the magnificent town for the dead.

Why, though, does this building look so different from all the other period buildings? It turns out that the tiles and ornamentation all arrived by boat from Europe and were originally intended for a building in Venezuela, but someone made a mistake, and the boat ended up in Argentina instead. The mistake was thought to be fortuitous, and rather than sending them on their way, they were used for the construction of the Water Department building.

No Encuentros

I bike through the Parque Ecológico, a park that has paths through the wetlands that border one whole side of the city. As if the New Jersey Meadowlands were attached to Manhattan and had paths winding through the acres of reeds and

marshlands. It seems the park is also a spot for secluded meetings, as there are signs advising that it is not a place for *"encuen-
tros"* (meetings) . . . meaning sexual liaisons. The reeds hide
much of the city, though it is right next door. It's a strange sort
of park. You can't leave the paths even if you want to, for to venture off the trails would be to wade into the marshy wetlands.

Mondo Cane

I stop by the waterfront to watch a group of maybe six dogs
that have gathered there. A black doggie, an outsider possibly
attempting to join the group, or wanting at least to be taken seriously, stands slightly apart from the rest of the dogs and barks,
fairly aggressively, while a large Labrador repeatedly mounts a
sad-looking female with a houndlike face. He eventually suc-
ceeds in the task, after which the two are locked together for a
few minutes.

None of the other dogs seem to pay much attention to this
sex act taking place in their midst. Barking Blackie is shooed
off by the others repeatedly, but he returns, again and again. A
twin of the Lab fucker barks, demanding to chase sticks thrown
in the water by some nearby people—he somehow seems to
miraculously ignore all the fucking and barking and growling
around him. This dog can focus! The lovers have unlocked now,
and the others pass by one after another and smell the sad gal's
pussy, but they make no attempt to mount her. The two lovers
now lick their privates . . . possibly to ease the pain of being
stuck together.

Finally, fed up with the outsider Blackie's aggressive nonstop
growling and barking, a muscular member of the group takes
the case in hand, grabs Blackie by his red collar, and, while
both dogs are knee-deep in the water, attempts to semidrown
him. Or at least that's what it looks like he's trying to do. Others
join in—one chomping down on poor Blackie's leg. A violent
scrum ensues. Blackie, the outsider, could easily be drowned as

the others thrash about and hold him down—but no—after a minute or two of violence they all let go of him and there is no blood, despite all the showing of teeth and even what seemed like real biting.

The pack seems satisfied that maybe now he will know his place. It seems they intentionally didn't hurt him. It was all for show, to demonstrate that they weren't going to put up with his noise, aggressiveness, and implied threats. The social hierarchy has been reasserted. Blackie stands up, still knee-deep in water, dripping, slightly stunned, not moving. He doesn't run away. He slowly saunters up the bank to the "protection" of some bushes. A minute or so later here he comes again for more punishment; once again throwing down his never-ending challenge.

One dog pisses on another's face. No reaction. What! The hierarchies here must be well worked out if the pissed-upon doesn't even react.

On my way biking downtown from where I live in midtown Manhattan I sometimes pass by a little dog park at Twenty-third Street and Eleventh Avenue, next to the West Side bike path. It's a triangle of man-made hillocks and humps. The dogs brought there by their owners usually each pick a hump to occupy, and there they stand—one dog on top of each mound, each a king of his own hill. Everybody's happy. Clever design for a dog park.

I imagine that if there were only one mound in that park there might be more fights—a constant and nasty struggle might ensue to see who would be top dog—but as there are quite a few options available every dog can be king, at least for a little while.

Watching dogs, it sure seems we haven't "advanced" much from the territorial and hierarchical struggles that they act out so transparently in front of our eyes. The thing about dogs is that their posturing is often just that—Blackie wasn't really hurt, no blood was shed. Actual violence is truly a last resort. We humans constantly push to see where the boundaries lie as well, but sometimes when acted out on a national or global scale, or when the posturing involves a handy gun or some tanks and cluster bombs, it's a little too easy to quickly fire off a few rounds and zap the target, knowing there will probably be no (immediate) repercussions. Rather than simply relegating an "inferior" to his or her appropriate position in the pecking order one has eliminated the person completely.

I cycle back to the hotel, where they instruct me not to bring my bike into the lobby. They suggest I ride down into the underground parking area—and from there I can use the elevator to take myself, with the bike, up to my room.

What's Going On in Your Country?

The next day I do an interview at the local radio station. The studio is filled with people engaged in mysterious activities, all of which produce various kinds of noises. This, as I can eventually see, is entirely purposeful and intentional. A man next to me casually lifts up a piece of metal on a string and strikes it—*CLAANNNGG!* A woman noisily plays with an infant on the floor. Another man casually strums an out-of-tune guitar. Papers are rustled. It is as if they are "scoring" my conversation—creating an artificial sonic ambience and an imaginary "place" in which the interview is occurring. I wonder if they have a whole set of environments and ambiences that they can re-create—offices, beaches (on the weekend), factories, forests, ranches?

On the table are some tiny books. One is no bigger than an inch from top to bottom. They are published in Peru, and contain quotations and popular wisdom. They are bite-sized. I could eat one.

It's the mid-aughts, and these days many journalists ask me, "What is going on in New York?" They mean: what is the political feeling since 9/11? I usually reply that New York, after a year or two, has more or less returned to its cosmopolitan, multicultural self, where no one thinks twice if the cab driver is wearing a turban. But the interior of the country, with access only to *USA Today* and Fox News for their information, well, they are still trembling with fear that Saddam or Osama bin Laden is going to come and steal their SUVs. The lack of information available to the populace that isn't pure propaganda, and the continual efforts of the Bush administration to keep everyone in fear, has created a nation that wants nothing more than to close its doors and hide and to have other people—the imperial troops—make whatever imagined threat there is out there simply go away. They want someone else to do whatever it takes to protect them from this weird, inscrutable, and invisible enemy that they believe wants to take their comfortable lives from them.

Most of the journalists here, as in Europe, are searching for an explanation from me as to why people in the United States continued to support Bush and Company. It's a constant puzzle to them how he could have been reelected. A puzzle to me too. As support for Bush and his policies continues in the U.S.A., the press and people here lose what is left of their admiration for the American people, whom they largely have looked up to for their spunk, imagination, freedom, business acumen, can-do spirit, and brilliant pop culture. They admire the democratic institutions of the United States too—but that's more complicated, because all these southern countries know from experience that it was the United States that helped instigate and support the dictatorships they lived under for decades. So platitudes from U.S. politicians about spreading democracy and freedom ring pretty hollow here—those phrases are recognized as a cover for spreading U.S. influence, power, and business.

I tell them that I am guardedly optimistic. In my recent touring experience in the U.S.A., lots of ordinary people, many of whom indeed voted for Bush last time around, now express feelings that he hasn't done a very good job, even if they continue to believe that, for example, the invasion of Iraq was justified. I suspect that it will be many years before we know just how bad a job he and his cronies have done. It saddens me, because, like a lot of people, I was inculcated with a kind of faith and belief that the opportunities and the system of checks and balances that the United States seemed to represent were a new political animal on the face of the earth. One that could and did influence and inspire others around the world, for good. That myth of benign and beneficial influence and inspiration to other nations and people was true, at least to some extent. The best of the United States—rock and roll, rhythm and blues, Martin Luther King, and so on—were inspirational in other completely different cultures. But eventually, as I read more accounts of recent history, I became more skeptical. I came to know about the various misadventures the United States had gotten itself into—supporting dictatorships and toppling democracies. I continued to harbor a sense that deep down a moral invisible hand—the sometimes wacky but practical and good-hearted American people—would have the sense to adjust the course and therefore continue to be an example for other nations. In the mid-aughts, I, and it seems much of the rest of world, have had serious doubts about that. Now, with the election of Barack Obama, a huge measure of hope, optimism, and respect has returned, though this poor guy has been handed a country with its economic legs cut off and mired in an expensive and never-ending occupation in Iraq and Afghanistan.

Musical Connections, Continued

In the early evening León Gieco and I stop by for tea at the apartment of Mercedes Sosa, a force in Argentine music for a number of decades. This reminds me of the human chain of connections that brought me here, to her apartment. Bernardo Palombo, an Argentine folksinger, was teaching me Spanish in the early '90s in New York. He introduced me during classes to the music of Susana Baca, Silvio Rodriguez, and others, and I would practice my still rudimentary Spanish by asking about their music and lyrics. Amelia Lafferriere, a friend of Bernardo's here in Buenos Aires, had worked with Silvio, as well as with León Gieco, a folk rock singer here. Leon is friends with Mercedes Sosa. I covered one of León's songs, "Solo le Pido a Dios," on my first tour here (I also covered one made famous by Mercedes too, "Todo Cambia") and later, in New York, he invited me to join him in a concert he did with Pete Seeger. (The connections are mind-boggling, even to me. Six degrees of musical separation, indeed.)

Mercedes is an amazing singer and a larger-than-life personality. She emerged in the mid-to-late '60s and could be considered a kind of art-folk singer, as she makes few concessions to mainstream pop tastes. In a way some of these songwriters were musically closest to the British folk models in that they looked to their own cultural and historical roots and sounds for inspiration. One might group Mercedes with the *nueva trova, nueva canción,* or new song, movement, which emerged in the '60s here and throughout Latin America, and had no equivalent up north—though there was a parallel with '60s folksingers who also included songs about politics and human rights in their repertoire. Here, however, to sing about human rights and freedom, at least at that time, was a life-and-death matter. It took a kind of passion and bravery that we musicians up north haven't had to deal with.

The Tropicálistas in Brazil were jailed or sent into exile. Here and in Chile it was a lot worse. Mercedes was arrested onstage and exiled. Victor Jara in Chile had his hands chopped off and was killed. León was also forced into exile. Mercedes fled first to Brazil, and then to Paris and Madrid, León to Ann Arbor, Michigan.

León looks a bit like Sting, if Sting drove a truck in Patagonia. León is more of a rocker than Mercedes, though they both often add and absorb elements of indigenous music—and I don't mean just tango—into their songs and recordings. This musical blending, for me, says as much about what these artists are up to as their lyrics do. Their sound says they are proud of their heritage and culture, that they don't want to simply be an imitation of the internationally popular North American models— and yet they include elements of that music in the mix as well. To me this says that they, and many others, view themselves and the present as a third stream, a hybrid that isn't exclusively one thing or the other, but can borrow from anything out there. These musicians are defining their identity in a formal way that you can hear instantly. León has also written songs that, like some of Dylan's, put into words what a lot of people felt at a particular time, and for this reason he's revered, and a lot of people know some of his songs by heart.

León was, for a time, in a band with Charly García, a classic rocker here, so from Mercedes to León to Charly there is a thread that ties a number of fairly disparate musical strands together. And, at least as far as being influenced, I guess I'm part of that chain now too, as I'm thrilled to know both of them—for their music and for what they represent, culturally and politically.

Mercedes is a large woman, and she has a booming voice that in volume could be compared to that of an opera singer. Her friendly mestizo features contain some indigenous elements—or maybe I imagine this because she often wears a poncho onstage. She and León's conversation with each other is intense and wide-ranging—from remembrances of Victor Jara to glowing admiration for David Lindley and other wacky and talented L.A. musicians with whom León has recently recorded.

It's two in the morning now, early by Buenos Aires standards, and we've moved to a Japanese restaurant in a hotel. After dinner, as we leave, a group of young girls, who were sitting on the curb waiting for a local teen idol to show up, surround Mercedes with hugs and kisses. They're more than one generation apart, but even the teen fans know who Mercedes is.

The Church of Football

The next day on TV the Mexican and Argentine players enter the field for the World Cup match that will decide which of them continues to the final rounds. The entire city has stopped for the game. Everything has come to a standstill. I'm at a sound check in a club, where I will be sitting in with La Portuaria. All the club and band technicians have stopped work and gathered around the TV. The national anthems have been sung and the players have taken the field. The streets outside are nearly deserted, the huge avenues almost clear of traffic. All shops and restaurants are closed, except a few where televisions can be seen with clumps of people huddled in front of them.

After the sound check Diego, the lead singer, and I stop at a sandwich shop for a late lunch. The café is manned entirely by women, which might explain why it remains open (the men are all glued to the TV sets). Though it isn't the center of attention there is a token tiny TV sitting on the bar, which competes with a CD of techno music. Diego mentions that he was in high school during the dictatorship. The World Cup was held here in '78—and he says that some claim it was used as a screen for many to go missing and become disappeared. The government supported the sport event massively and used it as a clever way to disappear people when few were paying attention. One can see today how easy that would be. This would be the time to invade.

Most people were then, and even now remain, in partial denial about what was going on, many claiming they saw or knew nothing—although many sensed what was happening. As a high school student Diego went to visit some friends one day and no one answered the door. It was soon apparent that the house was now vacant, and would remain so. Later his father said that maybe they had been taken. There was a general feeling of paranoia, and Diego says that for a high school kid this fear manifested itself in ways that any schoolkid of that time might worry about—that if your hair was too long you'd be in trouble or if you got caught with a joint you might be picked up. Those typical young hipster affectations could have been viewed by the state as outward signs that you might be a sympathizer with its enemies. So even though these might have been the same concerns of high school kids in many countries, here the repercussions for being picked up for being a long-haired hippie were much more ominous. Everyone was careful; political talk was hushed. Gunshots could be heard on the streets at night—the sound of the military or the police (often they were the same thing) going about their dirty business.

I remember having a similar feeling in elementary school in Baltimore, though it couldn't have been anywhere near as intense as it was down here. It was during the Cuban missile crisis, and the level of fear and paranoia in the United States must have been high. Of course as a kid you assume that everything, whether it's abnormal or not, is just the way things are. Only in retrospect do you realize how fucked up it was.

I remember walking home from school. (I would have been in fifth grade—maybe ten years old?) It was about a mile back to my home, and I would usually take a route that passed through mostly suburban neighborhoods of lawns and trees, split-level homes, and clapboard houses. I remember picturing in my mind dark-winged bombers suddenly flying overheard. (Would they be Cuban bombers? Russian?) I imagined that first their engines would be heard approaching, a low ominous hum coming from somewhere in the distance, and then they'd appear over our suburban roofs. As I walked home I would mentally plan my route to possible shelter should this happen. Block by block, I would think to myself, From this block I could make it to Dean's house, if I run—Dean's house was maybe a block or two away—then, a little farther on, I determined that at that point my friend Ricky's house would be a better bet for shelter. The way home had to be calculated, planned, measured, from one potential safe house to the next. It was a frightening passage for a kid. No wonder the movies of that time were the way they were, full of paranoia and monsters. We were all scared shitless and the monster was invisible.

Gentrification

Palermo, the district where we are now having a sandwich, used to be a quiet neighborhood with lots of pocket parks—which are still here, though it's not so quiet anymore. It got gentrified in the last few years, and now it's filled with clothing boutiques, chic eateries, and bars. Diego recently moved out of his apartment across the plaza from this sandwich shop. Their house is for sale. He asks what changes New York is going through—commenting that it now seems so clean. Same process—the artists and new arrivals seek apartments farther out as the rising rents drive them away from the center. I comment that the resulting lack of mixing of various kinds of people—artists, professionals, and working folk—is ultimately detrimental to creativity. Creativity of all kinds. With young creative types now spread out over New Jersey, the Bronx, Williamsburg, Red Hook, and elsewhere, it's harder for any kind of scene or movement to gain traction. There needs to be sufficient density for it to develop. Creativity gets a boost when people rub shoulders, when they collide in bars and cafés and have a tentative sense of community. New York, or at least Manhattan, will, on its current course, end up like Hong Kong or Singapore—a vast gleaming business and shopping center. Creativity—that indefinable quality that China, for example, probably covets—will be extinguished in New York if random and frequent social contact is eliminated.

It's often said that proximity doesn't matter so much now—that we have virtual offices and online communities and social networks, so it doesn't matter where we are physically. But I'm skeptical. I think online communities tend to group like with like, which is fine and perfect for some tasks, but sometimes inspiration comes from accidental meetings and encounters with people outside one's own demographic, and that's less likely if you only communicate with your "friends."

I have no romantic feelings for run-down neighborhoods where crack vials litter the pavement and the plumbing barely works. Granted, those neighborhoods typically offer cheap housing and a tolerance for noise and eccentricity, but to confuse the availability of space with the unfortunate circumstances that often make those spaces cheap is, well—they don't need to go hand in hand.

We walk to my hotel, a few blocks away. The streets are empty. (The football is still going on.) The rain has stopped. Diego asks about hip-hop. I reply that the beats and music are often incredibly innovative and sophisticated, but for the most part it's corporate rebellion these days. Which isn't to say there isn't a lot I like—*Trapped in the Closet* is one of the wackiest, most creative video pieces I've seen in years. Diego brings up Baile Funk—the fairly recent Brazilian evolution of 808 drum machine beats, techno, hip-hop, and funk. (Though it's more like being pummeled in a violently disorienting fairground ride than getting funky, in my opinion.) We agree it's incredibly innovative and ridiculously extreme. Diego says the lyrics in the Brazilian case are violent and rough, but unlike U.S. hip-hop the words in Baile Funk are usually from a victim's point of view.

History Told Through Nightlife

I stop by a book and record store where I select various CDs, and the clerk plays me samples from local recordings: one of solo *bandoneón* (the accordionlike instrument used in tango), one of candombe jazz (an unexpected hybrid to me, as candombe is Afro-Uruguayan carnival music), and one of a large orchestra playing old tangos. Over on a table there are numerous books detailing the history of the national rock scene and others describing the varieties of Porteño nightlife.

A history of nightlife!—what an interesting concept. A history of a people, told not through their daily travails and successive political upheavals, but via the changes in their nightly celebrations and unwindings. History is, in this telling, accompanied by a bottle of Malbec, some fine Argentine steak, tango music, dancing, and gossip. It unfolds through and alongside illicit activities that take place in the multitude of discos, dance parlors, and clubs. Its direction, the way people live, is determined on half-lit streets, in bars, and in smoky late-night restaurants. This history is inscribed in songs, on menus, via half-remembered conversations, love affairs, drunken fights, and years of drug abuse.

One wonders if the things that people do to relax—after work and after-hours—is a mirror of their inner state, and therefore a way to see unspoken hopes, fears, and desires. Views and expressions kept bottled up in public, in the daytime, and kept hidden in typical political discourse. Nightlife might be a truer and deeper view into specific historical and political moments than the usual maneuverings of politicians and oligarchs that make it into the record. Or at least they might be a parallel world, another side of the coin.

It's easy to say in retrospect that the goings-on in the Weimar cabarets prefigured World War II, or that punk rock was a dark reflection of the Reagan era, but there might be some truth to looking at all nightlife that way. Was the simultaneous flowering of both Studio 54 and CBGB, when New York City was at financial rock bottom, a coincidence? Maybe not? Will this latest economic meltdown signal a creative renaissance, a rebirth of affordable and anything-is-possible nightlife? Can one read the present or the future by looking at the dance floor, into back rooms, or at who's on the bar stools? The myriad restaurants and lounges of the past decade in New York City were often filled with hedge fund billionaires, and the rise of bottle service in discos and celebrity hangouts can now be seen as a harbinger of what was to come. But, yeah, it's easy to say that in retrospect.

City of Vampires

After the performance I go out to a club at the invitation of
Charly García, who came to the show. Charly was one of the
instigators of the rock nacional movement here, which emerged
in the '60s. Charley became more well known in the early '70s.
He was contemporaneous with the folk and *nueva trova* artists mentioned earlier, but for people like Charly, though those
others were respected, folk might also have been the style to
rebel against. He, and many others, represented sex, drugs, and
rock and roll—decadence as opposed to political causes.

The band at the club, Man Ray, had just gone on. It's two
thirty AM. The band is fronted by a woman who sometimes
sings with Charly. Socially, this town appears to be like New
York—late shows, people out till morning light—but in some
ways it's even more a late-night hang than New York is or ever
was. A vast majority of restaurants are open here till at least
four AM—many more than in New York. And the streets are
packed at three thirty! The movie theaters have regular shows
starting at one thirty AM, and these movies are not *The Rocky
Horror Picture Show,* or some typical midnight movie—even *El
Rey León* (*The Lion King*) was letting out at three AM! Then, after
the movies let out the audience inevitably goes out to eat or to
have a drink. Whole families are out strolling in the middle of
the night! When do they sleep? As in the larger cities of Spain,
people eat late—never before nine thirty—and then they might
catch a show that starts in the wee hours.

A city of vampires. Do any of them have day jobs? Do they
keep these hours all week? Are there two separate societies—
night people and day people? Two shifts, two urban populations that never meet or cross paths? Are they using coke or
massive amounts of yerba maté tea to stay up? Or, have they
snuck in a little siesta after work while the rest of us were having dinner on New York time?

I fade around four AM and go back to the hotel and crash.

Mauro and some of my road crew are out till seven AM—moving on from that rock club to another place that features music they describe as a mixture of zydeco and *cumbia*, played by DJs. They say it gets rolling around five or six AM.

Glover Gill, leader of the Austin, Texas–based Tosca Tango Orchestra, is here, as I am using his string players in my band, and they have managed to squeeze in a couple of their own dates while they are here. A group of us go to see a traditional tango group at a baroque palace, El Palacio de San Martín, as part of the World Tango Festival in progress here. The palace is an incredible edifice—there is a Beaux-Arts balcony and beyond it a stained-glass panel of St. George killing the dragon. An old-fashioned tango *orquestra* is set up on a stage and exhibition dancers perform on the dance floor before the public takes over.

The audience, except for us, are all dressed in their slinky finery—all very elegant and sexy. There are some amazing dancers, which is a little intimidating. Later on we go to La Cumparsita, a sort of tourist tango joint in the San Telmo district. There are the ubiquitous pictures of Carlos Gardel on the walls—many, many of them. I have about had it with the Gardel myth. I feel like saying, "He's been dead for a long, long time—get over it, move on!"

This morning I struggle to wake up. I pedal to Casa del Tango, which is about four kilometers away, joining the string players to observe a rehearsal by El Arranque. I sit in the dark theater seats in their rehearsal space—a modest former theater—watching as they prepare. They discuss arrangements and how to play various sections of the piece. Then they run through a few full numbers, which are amazing.

The Takeback

While Argentina was under a military dictatorship in the 1970s, the IMF and World Bank provided loans and in return demanded that Argentina's industries be opened up to foreign investors and its national industries be privatized. The country soon went heavily into debt (which is fairly typical whenever the World Bank gets involved somewhere) and unemployment rose. A lot of the country's wealth was quietly flown out, in dollars. In 2001 it all came to a head and the government closed Argentines out of their own bank accounts and food riots broke out across the country. The peso was devalued, factories were closed, and half the population fell below the poverty line.

Later that year some workers decided to restart some of the shuttered factories themselves. The owners, who had abandoned these factories, protested and took the workers to court. The owners and the banks wanted to sell off the assets—the machinery and materials—and make a quick buck. In some cases the workers won the right to keep the factories running—the judges, it seems, sometimes felt that employment was more important than a one-time profit. The factories, a few of them, are now run without bosses; they pay their property taxes, and have begun to pay off their debts. Here's a still from a documentary called *The Take*:

From *The Take*. © Andres D'Elia. All rights reserved

This might be inspiring for some U.S. businesses now: for example, newspapers that are saddled with debts due to takeovers by investment funds and forced to declare bankruptcy. One wonders if the workers in those businesses, and maybe even in Detroit, could run the factories themselves. In the 2003 elections here President Menem, who backed the factory owners, eventually dropped out of the race and Néstor Kirchner became president. The present president is Kirchner's wife, pictured here with Mercedes Sosa. Times change—as they have in the United States.

Mercedes Sosa and Cristina Fernández de Kirchner. This image is licensed under Creative Commons attribution 2.0 License. Source: Official Web site of the Presidency of Argentina

The distinct nasal twang of an "American" accent echoes through the plane as I head north. I'm flying American Airlines to Miami. The voices exude confidence, superiority. (They don't sound like they're very flexible or open-minded, and they're not.) After the gentle, sensuous vowels of Latin America, this—my language—sounds harsh, cruel, authoritarian.

Manila

This is not the most bike-friendly city in the world—even though a lot of Southeast Asian towns swarm with scooters, food delivery guys on motorcycles, and cyclo taxis. I suppose I value the perspective I get from a bike, and the freedom, more than I realize. I'm more addicted than I think. Well, I also know that this city is relatively dense—unlike L.A. or Mexico City—so though some things and certain far-flung neighborhoods might be a bit of a trek, much of the flavor will be within reach by bike. I can explore without an itinerary, though I do have research and meetings prearranged.

Two quotes encapsulate for me why I came to Manila. One is from James Hamilton-Paterson's book *America's Boy*, one of the best accounts of the Marcos era: "There are moments when it seems that the world's affairs are transacted by dreamers. There is a sadness here in the spectacle of nations, no less than individuals, helping each other along with their delusions. What is thought to be clear-sighted pragmatism may actually be shoring up a regime's ideology whose hidden purpose is itself nothing more than to assuage the pain of a single person's unhappy past."

And this, from *Imperial Grunts* by Robert D. Kaplan: "Just as the stirring poetry and novels of Rudyard Kipling celebrated the work of British Imperialism . . . the American artist Frederic Remington, in his bronze sculptures and oil paintings, would do likewise for the conquest of the Wild West. . . . 'Welcome to Injun Country' was the refrain I heard from the [U.S.] troops from Colombia to the Philippines, including Afghanistan and Iraq . . . the War on Terrorism was really about taming the frontier."

The first quote, for me, summarizes the Rosebud view of historical (and contemporary events) while the second is about the enduring power of mythology and potent image to justify, well, whatever you want it to.

I arrived in Manila over the Christmas holidays in 2005 with a pretty specific agenda. A few years earlier I had been reminded that the former first lady of the Philippines, Imelda Marcos, was a habitué of discos during the late '70s and early '80s. This would have been the era of Studio 54, Regine's, Privilege, and Le Palace (in Paris) and other velvet-rope clubs. This was also, um, the era of martial law and heavy censorship in the Philippines. Being a fan of some of the club music of that time I wondered if it might have supplied the sound track for a person in power like Imelda. Could dance music be a vehicle through which to tell a story like hers? A story of power, personal pain, love, and social class? Was the lightness, effervescence, and headiness inherent in that music—and the drugs that went along with it—similar to the feeling one gets when one is in a powerful position? And was there even a story to hang this idea on?

I also had another agenda, another reason for being attracted to a project such as this—I wanted to see if there was a way to tie a group of songs together besides the fact that they happen to be on the same CD. I wondered, in this form, would songs play off one another and receive some added weight from one another? Why not, if the same characters recur now and again? In this format, the listener would get some additional insights and progress on the characters' lives and feelings so songs would be informed by other songs. Within a song cycle like this could songs strung together become more than the sum of their parts?

I'd spent about a year reading and doing research and I soon became attracted to what I saw as a story that perfectly eluci- dated Hamilton-Paterson's proposal that politics and history are a kind of personal psychological spectacle. The Philippines is an extremely class-conscious society, and Imelda, who grew up in an unsuccessful branch of an important regional family, was, after her mother died, raised by a servant, Estrella, who was only a little older than she. Being *that close* to being socially accepted, but not quite, Imelda had a pile of psychological bag- gage to lug around from pretty early on. I saw part of a possible story being about the initial closeness of these two women and their subsequent estrangement, and also about Imelda's "class struggle"—her need to be accepted, and her working out that need in public on a grand scale. The project would be about her conflation of fantasy, personal pain, and politics, a combination that played itself out in a tragic and dramatic way in the history of that era.

I contacted Fatboy Slim, the British DJ, to cowrite songs that I felt would embody what these two women were feeling at various points in this story and that, when appropriate, would sound authentically clubby. Sometimes I used the women's own quotes, or texts from speeches or interviews, as a basis for the lyric material, which was a new experience for me. It was lib- erating to write almost exclusively from their point of view— and sometimes even use their words. Not that I hadn't written through characters before, but having their own words avail- able made it easier to find truly unique and surprising phrases that I wouldn't have come up with on my own.

One of these quotes serves, for now, as the title of this project: *Here Lies Love.* In a contemporary interview done for the Ramona Diaz documentary *Imelda,* Mrs. Marcos is quoted as wishing that her epitaph, what she wants written on her tombstone, should not be her name, but the words *here lies love.* In her view she has, in the words of a classic Filipino song, "done it all for you." The "you," from her point of view, being the Philippine people.

Tiny Doors

Once I had these songs—about twenty or so—written and demoed, I thought it might be a good idea to see firsthand the country and people I'd been reading about. Besides gathering some more research and archival material—images, video, film, and texts—I hoped that by going there I might catch and absorb some of the Philippine ethos, sensibility, and awareness—by osmosis and through conversations. I realized that this sequence was backward and so I was half prepared to discover that my previous research and assumptions might be all wrong, in which case I'd have to revise everything or scrap the project. This trip maybe should have taken place sooner, and I would soon find out if that was the case.

I believe that politics is, besides being pragmatic, social, and psychological, also an expression of a wider surrounding context. That includes everything that might affect what people feel and do—music, landscape, food, clothes, religion, weather. Politics is a reflection of the streets, the smells, what constitutes eroticism, and the routine of humdrum lives just as much as it is a result of backroom deals, ideologies, and acts of legislature. Sometimes this occurs in obvious ways. The Philippines is a Catholic country with animist roots, spread out among scattered islands the geographically isolated towns of which are distant from the capital, Manila, and those factors all contribute. Sometimes there are visual and other clues to things that influence events—attitudes expressed and made visible via posture, body language, humor. A visual and gestural language is by nature untranslatable into words, but nevertheless indicative of attitudes and even ideologies. I wanted to catch some of that, or at least as much as I could.

Just as there are elements in our genes waiting for chemical keys to allow for expression as a chicken liver or a human heart, there might also be elements in a place that trigger expression through politics, action, and culture. Much human behavior is a manifestation of these keys being inserted and turned—keys that open genetic, geographical, and cultural doors—through which the latent tendencies pass.

I was given a few contacts in Manila by friends and acquaintances in New York, and I asked a few of them if they thought it would be crazy for me to bring a bicycle in order to get around Manila. Some of them thought I was nuts or just plain obsessive but a few said, "Why not? The streets are pretty crowded and chaotic, but you could give it a try." I packed up my folding mountain bike and after a long flight I looked out the plane window at Manila and the surrounding bay and wondered what I'd gotten myself into.

Joel Torre, a local actor, generously meets me at the airport and everyone says hi to him as we walk to the car pickup area. We drive by Imelda's Cultural Center on the way to the hotel—a giant Lincoln Center–type edifice that Mrs. Marcos had built on landfill. She wanted both to put the Philippines on the world cultural map and to encourage local talent. And, especially with the film and theater schools that she established, she definitely accomplished the latter.

I've booked myself into the Aloha Hotel, a small pink building facing the bay. Some friends in New York recommended staying in Makati, the more upscale district of modern highrises, fancy hotels, and glass-walled shopping malls, but geographically this less-chic area seemed closer to the historical and political landmarks I'd been reading about.

Across from the hotel is an esplanade that borders the bay. It is lined with kiosks, vendors, and outdoor bars and cafés, some of which have either live or piped-in music. Appropriately enough, as I unpack and assemble my bike in my hotel room the disco beats from one of the cafés waft in through the window. There's no chance of taking a postflight nap with the music booming, and since there are only a few more hours of daylight I force myself to stay awake and get out and see something.

I must say, given that I'm filled with thoughts of this project, the disco music is actually inspiring rather than annoying— though I'm glad it doesn't go on all night. A song with a fairly radical synth playing a squealy pulse gives me some musical ideas. A cover version of 50 Cent's "In Da Club" is the last thing I hear as I pedal along the esplanade toward the old city center.

A Special Relationship

I pass more hotels, giant Chinese restaurants, Rizal Park— where a lot of political demonstrations and rallies that I read about took place in the '80s—and the U.S. embassy, a heavily fortified edifice that I initially mistake for a military base, which in a way I guess it is. The special relationship between the United States and the Philippines is immediately obvious. The Philippines became a U.S. colony merely a year after the United States gave assistance in the Philippine struggle for independence against their former Spanish rulers. After ousting the Spanish the helpful Yanks must have decided it was too good an opportunity to walk away from, so, under a suspicious pretense, and with the drum-beating help of the Hearst newspapers, the United States had its first real colony—though not without a long, drawn-out war that claimed at least one million lives. The Philippines only achieved independence in 1946. They like to say their history was three hundred years spent in a nunnery and one hundred years in Hollywood, as a way of explaining the wacky cultural collisions and attitudes that abound here.

Postindependence and post-World War II the United States continued to maintain a number of massive military bases just north of Manila. From here supply lines were established to what would become the Vietnam War. From the United States' point of view, any politician who ran the Philippines had to be aware of what side their bread was buttered on, so as a result there was always a tight relationship between the two nations.

Emergent Architecture

Binondo is the area I end up biking to today. Karaoke machines are everywhere. Right on the street! Even little stalls in this funky old city center have them. This is a neighborhood of winding streets and vendors, many with tiny one-table emporiums. The traffic slows to a crawl here, or is relegated to bikes and little trucks that bring supplies and goods to the vendors. Regular traffic seems to avoid these areas, as the narrow streets are too crowded with pedestrians and the overflow from the stalls inevitably slows the movement of motor vehicles. Here the custom-decorated jeepneys are the largest vehicles on the streets and even they can only inch forward while attempting to pick up passengers, but I can move faster than most of them on my bike. This area is a great place for walking too—and for buying fruits, vegetables, washcloths, bootleg CDs and DVDs, Christmas gifts (at this time of year), fresh fish, medicines— anything that can be displayed stacked in little piles on wooden tables. How many kinds of things can be stacked in little pyramid piles? Pretty much anything you can name. Here is one kind of common denominator in the world of stuff.

Why is it that all third-world markets are structurally more or less the same? I am reminded of similar ones in Kuala Lumpur, Cartagena, Marrakech, Salvador, and Oaxaca. It's almost as if these markets were all designed by the same person the world over, as they take very similar forms everywhere. The human scale and the pleasant chaos must be part of an unconscious, though thoroughly evolved, plan, as are the smells and the piles of refuse here and there. One of the stall owners sweeps the rainwater and mud out of the street with a broom. This is evidence to me of an unwritten layout, a subconscious form, and an invisible map, which extends even to an unwritten system of self-maintenance. I suppose this recurring pattern and structure emerges because human scale automatically self-regulates the manner in which similar goods are best sold, how they are most efficiently displayed, and where. It is as if some genetic architectural propensity exists in us, that guides us, subtly and invisibly, as to how to best organize first a kiosk, then a stall, and from there add incrementally as our innate instincts guide us, until soon enough there exists a whole marketplace and neighborhood. Some tiny part of our DNA tells us how to make and maintain places like this in the same way that genetic codes tell the body how to make an eye or a liver. That architect who designed all those markets the world over is us. Could it be that our genes tell us not just how to make ourselves but how to make the built external world? I'm glad the whole city hasn't been malled, as some of the guidebooks claim.

Oddly enough one could say some of the same things about the newer built-up areas of many big cities, where many of the districts of condos, glass-walled offices, and chain stores could have all been designed by the same person—a very different person—who would by definition then be the most widely hired and ubiquitous designer/architect in the world, despised by some, a source of pride for a few, envied by others. I think with modern shopping malls and glass office buildings there is a little more conscious borrowing, ego display, and one-upmanship at work than in the pleasant hodgepodge typical of the stalls and tiny shops in front of me.

Victor Gruen built the first mall in the Minneapolis suburb of Edina in 1956, and one could argue that he was more a conceptual developer than an architect. Malcolm Gladwell, in a *New Yorker* article, says that Gruen didn't just invent the mall; he invented an archetype, as so many other malls followed the exact same model as this first one. I would agree that both the mall and the souk tap into some kind of meme for social shopping that reproduces itself prolifically. A kind of self-replicating architecture.

Along the bayside walk that I take back to my hotel, there are outdoor restaurants, many of which feature cover bands. As rumored, the bands are all surprisingly good—if by good you mean amazingly faithful in their ability to reproduce well-known songs. Close your eyes and it's Seals and Crofts, or Neil Young, with an ever-so-slight accent. The singing and playing is uniformly competent and professional, though of course completely unoriginal, which is by design. One man sings on a little stage with two glowing plastic Santas on either side of him. I wonder to myself if I should consider using one of these bands or these singers for a live band for *Here Lies Love?*

Sol's History Lesson

I wash up and then bike to an apartment building a few blocks away where I meet up with a group of people I'd previously contacted via e-mail. They're all arriving at film director Antonio "Butch" Perez's apartment. Across the street from Butch's apartment is a former love hotel with a huge banner across the entrance proclaiming, Closed for the Glory of God. I am told the owner of a chain of love hotels, of which this is one, became born again and decided, being newly devout, that he of course had to close down his own establishments. Some of the other ones, I hear, are still operating, so he still has an income. He may be devout, but he's not a fool.

Butch's place is beautiful—a spacious loft apartment with tropical Zen decor and windows at one end offering a view over some tin roofs to the expanse of Manila Bay. "Not so many years ago this was one of the quietest places in town," he says, "but now there are car stereos and burglar alarms, police klaxons and sirens, open-air karaoke on the bayfront, and more scooter traffic—the noise level is so much higher." As a New Yorker I am used to the noise so it doesn't seem excessive to me.

I am joined by editor Jessica Zafra (her magazines *Flip* and *Manila Envelope,* both in English, are wonderful), poet and columnist Krip Yuson, photographer Neal Oshima, restauranteuse Susan Roxas, performance artist Carlos Celdran, adman David Guerrero . . . and eventually even more filmmakers and writers wander in.

I describe the *Here Lies Love* project to everyone as best I can, which isn't saying much, as I wasn't prepared to make a pitch. The CD of demos I brought and especially the compilation of rough edits of video footage done to the music explain the concept much better than I am able to do verbally. The videos especially are well received. They're mostly edited from stock and period news footage from the Philippines and elsewhere cut to specific songs. Some of these folks view them intently, with fascination, as if their own lives were being replayed, so theirs is hardly an objective view. Painful memories, some of them.

Sol Vanzi joins us. She lives on the same floor. She informally handles Imelda's relations with local and international media. (Imelda returned to Manila from Hawaiian exile after Marcos died. She now lives in a nice apartment in Makati.) Sol also runs a Web site that collates Philippine news: http://www.newsflash.org. She's sixty-one, she tells us, and she immediately sits down, cracks open a can of beer, and launches into a tirade during which she disputes all the conventional wisdom about the Marcos regime and Imelda. She just naturally assumes (rightly, I suspect) that she's not addressing a group of Marcos loyalists. However, most of the others here seem to know her, so her rant is mainly directed toward me.

I would have assumed that the events at that time—the era of martial law—would have split Philippine society down the middle between the loyalists and the exiled and repressed. But it seems that here everyone knows everyone else, and almost always has, and everyone crosses paths often enough for a weird tolerance to have developed. People I would have assumed to be natural sworn enemies sit down to have a drink together. Things here are not as simple as they were in my preconceived picture. I'm glad I'm here.

Sol continues her monologue directed at me. She says that she instructed a video cameraman to hide in the basement of the palace when it was being overrun—this was minutes after the Marcoses fled—with instructions to record the state of things as they were the moment the family left. She claims that this video proves that the various stories of half-eaten tubs of caviar and other evidence of extravagant excess were "urban myths," as she referred to them. It is evidence that these things were planted—by Cory Aquino and others in the opposition parties, or so she claims.

She also claims that it was the Americans who most likely killed Benigno Aquino when he returned to the Philippines to challenge Marcos in 1983. (I thought Marcos said at the time that it was the commies? Or that it was the insurgents, who were also allied with the commies?) Sol pushes on, claiming that Imelda was never poor as a child, which, to be fair, is a statement that could be seen as being relative: Imelda certainly wasn't as poor as the people living in the shanties squeezed along the riverbanks in a lot of Philippine towns.

But by all accounts she did live in a garage as a child—with a car still in it—while the children of her father's first wife continued to live in the main house. Things went downhill from there; for a while Imelda, her brother, sister, and their servant and pal Estrella lived in a nipa hut—a shack made of woven palm fronds. So, no, she maybe had had it better than many, but for someone from an important local family she was relatively

poor. One could say more psychologically poor than economically, in that she was ostracized by the more socially acceptable part of her extended family.

Sol segues into a riff on how limited class mobility is in the Philippines. How if you are from a provincial town you are automatically handicapped, even if you are from a "good" family in that town. (This mirrors Imelda's situation.) Sol implies, as do others, that it is almost impossible to rise above your station, as your class will be revealed by your accent. Even if that doesn't give you away folks will probably ask you where you're from, and then the game's over. Shades of the UK, where your regional accent can limit your chances for success in some fields.

What I am learning, despite all her endless protesting and the refuting of claims that no one has even voiced, is that things are not as black and white here as I, or many other left-leaning Westerners, might prefer to think. The Marcos regime, though corrupt from the start, was no more corrupt, at least at first, than many others. Maybe even less, at the beginning. What distinguished the couple in some ways was that they did actually build clinics, highways, roads, bridges, cultural centers, and a high school for the arts, as well as instigate a health plan and many other programs that they promised in their campaigns. (That high school of the arts produced many of the creative types who are still active—friends of people in this room.) Similar programs had been promised by other politicians every time election season came around, but Marcos actually delivered. Ferdinand and Imelda were therefore truly loved by many Filipinos—at least at the start of their tenure—and, according to some, they continue to be loved in the provinces even during their ouster, an event which somewhat baffled the country folk. At one point (in the '60s) the couple intentionally modeled their image on that of the Kennedys—posing for family snaps in Malacañang Palace wearing hand-tailored versions of native dress and generally looking young and glamorous—which they were. As was the case with the Kennedys in the United States, the public loved it. So did the international media. The Marcoses were featured in *Time, Life,* and publications around the world—they were a very photogenic couple. Everyone bought into the fantasy—just like the media bought into the Kennedy myth, which was being created at around the same time.

Of course, beginning with Marcos's 1969 reelection campaign and then when martial law was declared in 1972 the scales began to tip, and the chicanery, censorship, human-rights abuses, murder, corruption, and lies eventually outweighed the love and good works. Here lies love indeed—love was bulldozed under or sent to a Swiss bank account. At first, when their power seemed more secure just after a sweeping election victory or after martial law was declared, it must have been irresistibly tempting to put that entitlement to use—as politicians tend to do. They wouldn't need to do all that nasty, inconvenient, and time-wasting politicking anymore. One could argue that power and entitlement made things more efficient. But it seemed to me that soon enough the need to hold on to that power took precedence over almost everything else—as it usually does.

Ted Spiegel / National Geographic / Getty Images

The palace in the end became a miasma of schemes, intrigues, paranoia, and backstabbing.

Flexibility

A book I read claims that Filipino politicians don't look on politics as a means to further their or their party's ideological goals but simply as a means to hold power. Sometimes a politician will switch parties and ideologies, if he thinks he stands a better chance of winning as a candidate from the other side. Marcos made one of these moves early on in his career, and it worked. While we in the United States might think of political parties as entities with firm ideological platforms and more or less consistent policies and agendas, here they seem to be more like a temporary set of allegiances that can be remade at will. Of course I began to ask myself if elsewhere things are much the same as they are here, though most other places make more of a pretense of ideological continuity. That might explain why people who I thought should be sworn political enemies here can hang out together.

Karaoke Nation

After Sol's lecture a small group of us head out for a meal at one
of Joel's two chicken restaurants. We drive to one and a group
of us seat ourselves around a little wooden picnic table out-
doors. The restaurant used to be simply a tiny counter, a covered
cooking area, and a few tables in back, but it has become very
popular—the chicken and the livers on a stick and the garlic rice
are all delicious. There is a covered area for eating too, but the
whole thing is more like a patio with a roof than an indoor restaurant. The barbecues for cooking the birds are installed along
the nearby roadside. I guess since Joel seems to be a well-known
actor I was expecting a more pretentious place, but this is both
delicious and casual. There's a smattering of all ages, races, and
types hanging out and chatting over their drinks and chicken.
The menu consists of essentially whatever you see being cooked
in front of you. If there were additional dishes available I didn't
see evidence of them.

On the way back to the district where my hotel is, Butch says
he needs to stop at a karaoke bar to say Merry Christmas to his
production designer and erstwhile muse, Marta, who is now
"playing for the other team" and is there with her girlfriend. We
are led by an attendant down a buttery-yellow hallway past a
series of identical doors and the assistant opens one and there
are four of Butch's friends singing to a TV screen. We order
beers but lamely fail to join in the singing festivities. Someone
programs "Burning Down the House," maybe in hopes that I
will sing, but I just stare at the screen as a guy who looks like an
'80s Bon Jovi poses with a guitar while a model house burns in
an image superimposed behind him. I guess I'm a bit of a party
pooper, but this did take me by surprise. Marta, exuberant and
very pretty in plaid pants, sings along with the song, though it
seems my phrasing on that song was a little tricky.

Some claim karaoke was invented here in 1975 as the Sing
Along System by a man named Roberto del Rosario. TVK/

Video karaoke clubs are everywhere and come in all shapes and for all incomes. Maybe it's a way to allow everyone to sing. Even though I was a party pooper at the karaoke club, I know from experience that singing is therapeutic, and fun to do. They sing Western pop songs here—and some Filipino pop songs too, many of which are sung in English. For a Filipino, singing Western pop songs is not like singing a foreign song. Western pop, especially U.S. pop, is such an integrated part of Filipino culture that Filipinos feel it is their own culture too. And it is, in a way. Who, or what nation, can own the experience you have when you hear a song? There's even a karaoke TV channel. Endless cheap corny videos with music playing and scrolling lyrics. You can stay at home and sing along with your television. Like some kind of radical conceptual art piece—but unlike conceptual art it's super-popular.

Makati

The next day I bike up, or rather east and inland, to Makati, the district where Imelda lives now. It's an area of high-rises, gated

communities, and glitzy shopping malls—not really typical of the Philippines, but a source of local pride. One of these high-rise condominiums was taken over by a group of disgruntled soldiers in 2004, but they were soon ousted.

Biking here in this upscale neighborhood is not always easy—there are no bike lanes as there are along the bay area, and the fumes from the jeepneys and tricycles (a motorcycle with a sidecar that can hold maybe two passengers) are over-whelming. Foreigners notice the jeepneys right away. How can you not? They are super-colorful, freakish progeny of leftover U.S. Army jeeps that have morphed, elongated, and mutated into a kind of cheap, tricked-out form of public transport. Jeepney drivers adorn their vehicles with names and sayings: Lovely, Mama-Cita, Metal Mania, Pray For Our Way, Grandma's Pet, Reconnaissance Patrol. This one reads Simply the Best, no doubt quoting from the Tina Turner song. There is a kind of jeepney wisdom.

The traffic sometimes devolves into borderline gridlock, but mostly things move along with a chaotic grace, and I of course make better time than most of these four- or even three-wheeled vehicles.

The Philippines, for many Americans, is the land where maids and nurses come from, and that's about all they know about it. I have to admit I've seen quite a lot of men and women in medical attire. Filipinos are hopeful that Japan, for example, might employ some of their highly trained medical personnel, but the Japanese are notoriously uncomfortable dealing physically with foreigners, and the idea of being touched by one, God forbid! The Japanese instead prefer to develop robots to take care of their own mundane housekeeping and medical needs. Racism as a spur to technical innovation.

After riding around Makati, visiting a mall, and getting lost in a gated community (a white man of a certain age on a bike, like me, is naturally waved in by the security guards), I head back toward the bay to explore the landfill area where

Imelda built many of her cultural projects, one of which—the Film Center—now hosts an all-Korean cast doing an Egyptian-themed drag show. This large building is reportedly haunted, or cursed, as part of it collapsed during the rushed nonstop construction that Madame Marcos mandated, and it is rumored that some of the bodies are still in the concrete, haunting anyone who visits. I am told that Koreans don't believe in ghosts, so that's why their show is running here.

The grand Cultural Center and the Folk Arts Center are in this area as well, and those are still quite active. I visit the Cultural Center one afternoon to pore over their photo and video archives of the Marcos era. Surprisingly, there isn't all that much here—most of it is at the university archives now, or in private hands. Who owns what footage seems unclear, which is worrisome, because in a way photo, film, and video archives are recent history. In many countries videotape that was used for news reports was erased and reused over and over, to save money—which means those outlets have no record of many events in the recent past.

Mythmaking

The next day I ride my bike through a funky shopping district (Quiapo) and then through San Miguel (a downtown neighborhood where Imelda lived with her family for a while). I get a tour of the Malacañang Palace—the Manila White House. I arrive a little wet from perspiration, but the guard, after I am identified, allows me to park my bike on the grounds behind a service building and he gives me a minute to dry off and get myself composed before beginning the tour.

Inside the palace I see the chair where in 1972 Marcos signed the declaration of martial law that suspended habeas corpus, and allowed him to jail political opponents and censor the press, keeping people in the dark for more than a decade—all in the name of maintaining order and homeland security. On the walls are numerous photos commemorating People Power, the mass movement that resulted in the ouster of the Marcoses in 1986. There are images of students giving flowers to soldiers, and lots of people wearing yellow. Yellow, it turns out, was adopted as an opposition color due to the pop song "Tie a Yellow Ribbon," which was chosen and sung in anticipation of the return of Benigno Aquino, Marcos's only serious rival, to the Philippines. Surreal, these pop-music connections—who would imagine a link between Tony Orlando and Dawn and a grassroots uprising that overthrew a dictator? It makes my head spin. Unfortunately Benigno "Ninoy" Aquino was gunned down at

Portrait of Ferdinand Marcos by Betsy Westendorp. Malacañang Palace Collection, Office of the President of the Philippines

the airport as soon as he stepped from the plane . . . but Cory and her supporters stuck with the yellow from then on.

The large central room is filled with glass cases of memorabilia commemorating previous Philippine leaders—but there is a glaring absence. All the leaders are represented except for the Marcoses, who are relegated to a couple of (not insubstantial) back rooms. Their absence could be seen as a lacuna, a hole, in history, but these back rooms more than make up for it—they are stuffed with commemorative dolls, clocks, and of course paintings, many of them portraits that the couple commissioned themselves.

Looming over me are two famous paintings in which Ferdinand and Imelda had themselves depicted as the Ur couple of the Philippines—the Adam and Eve of tribal Philippine mythology, who, in the traditional legend, sprang from a piece of split bamboo, the strong man and the beautiful woman.

The idea inherent in these paintings was that the Marcoses were fulfilling destiny, facilitating a kind of rebirth and renewal of Philippine identity—symbolized by their embodiment of the primeval couple. To be fair, a rebirth did happen, to some extent, and these paintings make explicit the couple's wish to also become part of the national mythology. The desire to find a slot for oneself in the collective national psyche runs deep. George Bush and Ronald Reagan were often photographed wearing western clothes despite one being a New England WASP and the other a Hollywood movie star. If a politician appears as a fighter pilot, a cowboy, or as Adam or Eve, the attraction and potency of these images are so powerful that we often respond as desired, even if we know it's an act.

Ilocos, Land of Disco Dreams

The next day I catch a plane to the area of the country where Marcos hailed from, up at the northern end of the big island,

Portrait of Imelda Marcos by Betsy Westendorp. Malacañang
Palace Collection, Office of the Philippines

where many people still cherish his memory. His son, Bong
Bong (yes, his real name!), is now the governor of this province,
and Imee, one of his daughters, is the local congresswoman. In
my research it was said that this area, Ilocos Norte, is Philippine cowboy country—it has a somewhat harsher climate than
the more tropical south, and disagreements were, and still are,
often settled with guns. I spy on my local map a neighborhood on the outskirts of Laoag, the regional capital where I am
staying. The neighborhood is named Discolandia, which sounds
like it might be appropriate for my project, so I aim myself in
that direction. I wander through a neighborhood of houses,

roaming chickens, little bodegas. And then, just past the bus depot, sure enough, suddenly there is a whole zone of clubs. It's daytime, so there is no music or activity at the moment, except in front of one club where I see an older woman carefully painting a young girl's toenails. The door to another club is open so I ask if I can have a look. No problem—an older woman escorts me in and hollers something as she leads me farther and farther into the interior, which has a few scattered chairs on the dance floor and some Christmas lights dangling from the ceiling.

She brings me to a back room, which is fairly large, and is filled with rude wooden bunk beds, most without sheets. This is where the bar girls sleep and rest, I think to myself. She hollers again, and then, from a room farther back emerges an attractive girl in a red dress who immediately escorts me back into the club room asking me, "What would you like? You like girls?" Her face is painted white—as if she is in the middle of a facial. I remember toenail girl had this white-face thing going on as well. With her full red lips she looks like an erotic clown.

I recall that the pharmacies in town are filled with skin-whitening creams, and I've seen numerous TV ads for these products as well. Four out of ten Southeast Asian women use skin-whitening creams. In many countries a lighter complexion implies wealth and class—manual laborers have darker skin from working out in the sun. Odd that in North America and Europe a tan has become desirable, maybe because it implies the reverse—that you can afford to spend time in the sun instead of working.

But why is this girl asking me these questions? Ohhhh, now I get it! Duh. These places are all whorehouses! Why didn't I notice all the signs reading No Condom—No Sex? And there's live music and karaoke (naturally) to bide the time while you're making up your mind. Here are some choices:

I walk on. I see a few girls lazing around, some doing their washing by hand and some sitting and chatting over a soda. Signs read Check Your Firearms at the Door.

Though I doubt these places regularly cater to foreigners, the Philippines used to have a reputation as a popular sex-tourism destination. I thought the epoch of underage sex for foreigners here was over, but it seems not. There are at least two Anglo geezers in my hotel sporting young Filipinas on their arms—the girls seem to be around twenty, so maybe they're not underage. On my bike meanderings in Manila I've seen quite a few more of these May/November couples—over there is Mr. Buster Bloodvessel looking for love and farther down the street I spy the Professor out for a naughty holiday. It seems this country is still occasionally the place for a foreign man to get whatever it was he never had, or get what he craved but was discouraged from indulging in back home. Maybe here in this "western" town of Laoag one can fulfill one's lifelong dream. When it's put that way it almost sounds sweet.

I also spy some foreigners with local rent boys—one overweight limping Yank with a southern accent has two! In a restaurant he orders them around, "Salt, I need salt . . . and pepper." One of the boys dutifully goes and fetches the salt. "Toast, is that toast over there?" One of the boys fetches him three pieces of toast. He seems temporarily satisfied. One can see the temptations of power at work—the more he senses he has power the more he will flex it, to witness and enjoy it in action, to feel the pleasure of command.

"Coffee and cigarettes," he announces.

Then, "Coffee and cigarettes is my breakfast back home."

To be fair, not all western/Filipino relationships are necessarily about power or sexual fantasy. A family in the hotel restaurant here in Laoag is composed of an Australian man and his attractive Filipina wife and their kids. He grumbles and grunts in response to the kids' entreaties while she texts someone on her cell phone. Hardly a perfect relationship, but not obviously predatory either.

It's Christmas in Laoag, and in the Wild West kids are caroling on the streets just after the sun sets. I sing "Joy to the World" along with one group, and then they look at me, expecting money—and not just because I am a foreigner. As I wander off I see them going from house to house, hoping for small handouts . . . and that does not mean a hot chocolate.

I begin to take tricycles on short trips. This is not a kiddie bike but a motorcycle with a driver and sidecar-type thing attached. My bike has been left in Manila, as I want to make longer day trips using Laoag as a base. A tricycle affords a limited view, so they're not so good for sightseeing, but they are

everywhere, and hailing one only takes about a minute. And they look great.

Coupled with the ubiquitous jeepneys and the buses, which only leave from designated depots and travel mostly intercity, the tricycles make an incredibly efficient public transport system in these smaller towns and villages. They have a lot to recommend them except for the hideous pollution they generate. New York has a pretty good public transport system, one that rivals, say, Mexico City, though the New York subways are not quite as clean. But this improvised Filipino network seems much more user-friendly.

I continue by bus to Batac, a small town where Marcos lies in state (supposedly it is his real body) in a refrigerated glass casket that sinks into the floor when no one is around.

The mausoleum has piped-in liturgical Mozart music, creating a creepy haunted vibe, and in the air-conditioned chamber

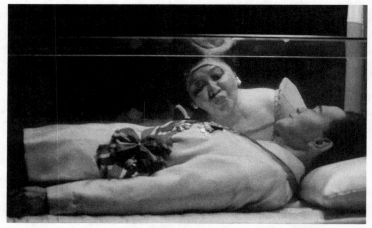

Romeo Ranoco / Reuters

there are a number of staffs on either side with sculpted metal tops featuring icons that resemble weird Masonic symbols—crescent moons, stars, spades, hammers, and some that are indecipherable. The security guy can't tell me what they all symbolize. The effect is deeply mystical, mysterious, almost Egyptian. Marcos's embalmed body sure looks more like a wax-work than the real thing. The glass coffin is bathed in an eerie blue light, and photos are strictly prohibited. Rumor has it that the *real* body lies deeper below, slowly decomposing and still denied burial among the other former presidents by order of the present rulers.

Permanent Impermanence

I travel on to Vigan, a small town that was spared the American carpet bombing at the end of World War II. Vigan is now on the UN list of important world historical sites, so although it's not on my research agenda it's close, so why not have a look?

The center of town does indeed abound in the type of old buildings of which only a few remain around Laoag and even fewer in Manila. Mostly they are wooden structures that withstand typhoons pretty well due to their flexibility, but that usually require periodic upkeep because of the tropical dampness and the termites that will destroy them after a number of years. Bit by bit, part by part, houses like these will be renovated and every wall and beam will be replaced. Impermanence is an accepted part of life in the tropics. There's a permanence embodied in the continuity of patterns and relationships, but not in physical buildings or things.

Here's one outside the town center—beautiful architecture made without architects:

The Rose of Tacloban

Imelda was born in a small town in the southern island province of Leyte and spent a good part of her formative years in Tacloban, the main city on that island. Even though she was from the less successful side of this family, their connections still counted for much. This Cinderella aspect of her past has been self-whitewashed or tweaked quite a bit; the poverty and pain part has been lessened, though she would sometimes refer to it in passing, if it was necessary to make a point. Wish we all could edit our lives so neatly. She often managed to deny the past and work it simultaneously—denying her poverty yet claiming she was once one of the poor people at the same time. Different pasts for different occasions.

In later years she built a "shrine" here in Tacloban, ostensibly to Santo Niño, the Christ child. The entrance opens into a large chapel with a wild altarpiece—the child floating, surrounded by disco lights. The shrine is mainly, however, to herself. Jeepneys heading to this destination from downtown Tacloban simply give "Imelda" as the direction on their windshields. The shrine houses lots of her furniture collection, but more important, she commissioned a series of lovely dioramas depicting her life story—or her life story as she imagined it.

Here is a nice one of her as a young girl at the shore having a family outing with an image of Marcos looming in the sky—her future husband awaiting their fateful meeting.

The rest of the "shrine" is structured as a series of "bedrooms" and "dining rooms" (in quotes because none of them were ever used for those purposes). They function more as regional theme rooms that also each contain one of the above dioramas detailing the Imelda myth. There are fifteen stations, or bedrooms, of the cross.

Back at my hotel for lunch I hear "Climb Every Mountain," possibly the version by Tom Jones, on an endless loop—for an hour! Climax after climax! Climbing that mountain over and over. Occasionally I can hear other diners quietly singing along to themselves.

Language as a Prison

The Philippines did have a written language before the Spanish colonists arrived, contrary to what many of those colonists subsequently claimed. However, it was a language that some theorists believe was mainly used as a mnemonic device for epic poems. There was simply no need for a European-style written language in a decentralized land of small seaside fishing villages that were largely self-sufficient.

One theory regarding language is that it is primarily a useful tool born out of a need for control. In this theory written language was needed once top-down administration of small towns and villages came into being. Once there were bosses there arose a need for written language. The rise of the great metropolises of Ur and Babylon made a common written language an absolute necessity—but it was only a tool for the administrators. Administrators and rulers needed to keep records and know names—who had rented which plot of land, how many crops did they sell, how many fish did they catch, how many children do they have, how many water buffalo? More important, how much then do they owe me? In this account of the rise of written language, naming and accounting seem to be language's primary "civilizing" function. Language and number are also handy for keeping track of the movement of heavenly bodies, crop yields, and flood cycles. Naturally, a version of local oral languages was eventually translated into symbols as well, and nonadministrative words, the words of epic oral poets, sort of went along for the ride, according to this version.

What's amazing to me is that if we accept this idea, then what may have begun as an instrument of social and economic control has now been internalized by us as a mark of being civilized. As if being controlled were, by inference, seen as a good thing, and to proudly wear the badge of this agent of control—to be able to read and write—makes us better, superior, more advanced. We have turned an object of our own oppression into something we now think of as virtuous. Perfect! We accept written language as something so essential to how we live and get along in the world that we feel and recognize its presence as an exclusively positive thing, a sign of enlightenment. We've come to love the chains that bind us, that control us, for we believe that they *are* us.

The Gentle People

In 1971 the discovery of a "Stone Age tribe" in a remote area of the Philippines made worldwide news. *National Geographic* ran a major piece on the gentle Tasaday, which depicted their lives as Edenic. They were portrayed as a kind of Ur people, without any of the hang-ups and baggage we carry with our fucked-up civilized lives. Shangri La was discovered to exist and it was in the Philippines.

The Marcoses in some ways were embarrassed that the world was seeing Filipinos in such unsophisticated conditions (and fifteen years later the discovery was claimed to be a fraud by the media after the Marcoses' departure). This reaction followed visits by social scientists, journalists, and film documentarians whose intrusions the government said were changing the Tasaday. So Marcos restricted the area—no visitors could disrupt the Eden

© John Nance

of the Tasaday—except for a 1976 visit by Gina Lollobrigida for a book and film, the sightseeing granddaughter of Spanish dictator Francisco Franco, and working teams of medical doctors.

Charles Lindbergh visited for several days in 1971 and '72, and his request to the government played a key part in the declaration of the protected reserve for the Tasaday, which still exists today.

Hamilton-Paterson called the Tasaday a clear-cut hoax in his Marcos book, *America's Boy,* but he retracted this a few years later in an article in the *London Review of Books,* realizing perhaps that in the Philippines things so seldom are what they seem at first, even Edens, even hoaxes.

A man named John Nance, who has had many contacts with the Tasaday, says that the claim of a hoax was the real hoax:

The Tasaday themselves are authentic, as was concluded in 1987 by a four-month-long congressional open hearing/

investigation; by the 1988 separate investigation of new president Corazon Aquino; and by the findings of eighteen social scientists—anthropologists, archeologists, linguists, ethnobotanists, and an ethnologist—made over twenty years of research in the field. Not one anthropologist who claimed the Tasaday were a hoax ever laid eyes on a single Tasaday. It has been established by the Congress and President Aquino and others that the hoax campaign was organized by loggers, miners, ranchers, local politicians, and jealous neighboring tribes who wanted to obtain the rich stands of timber and deposits of minerals on the Tasaday's ancestral homeland. Their campaign failed. Today, thirty-eight years after the first contact, the Tasaday remain on the land that still carries their name.

I see a sign on a building in Tacloban that reads: The Fraternal Order of Utopia. A man zips by on a motorcycle with a Santa hat wildly flapping.

Collective Narrative

One final, sexy fantasy image—Imelda as the nurturing mother goddess, as both a great spirit and in her earthly manifestations.

Though Ferdinand and Imelda's conflation of national mythology with their own lives to align it with their political strivings was blatant, it's also pretty obvious in the staged contrivances and the carefully managed press of many other governments. Sometimes we can only see ourselves once we step far enough back to have some perspective. The "story" of the inevitable triumph of democracy (and of messianic Christianity too) is a powerful myth that is easily sold, a grand story that the media often goes along with and accepts as right and good and as an a priori assumption. Manifest destiny, the march of progress, and the triumph of civilization are presumed to be common, universal beliefs, at least until recently. Once "stories"

Kabayanihan. © Leonardo T. Cruz

like these are in place, believed in, and accepted, one need only supply the appropriate images, news stories, and anecdotes to continually reinforce the myths and make them seem self-fulfilling and indisputable.

Living "in" a story, being part of a narrative, is much more satisfying than living without one. I don't always know what narrative it is, because I'm living my life and not always reflecting on it, but as I edit these pages I am aware that I have an urge to see my sometimes random wandering as having a plot, a purpose guided by some underlying story. I imagine that if I could step back and look at my life, I'd see that this series of meetings and events wasn't simply random, that it had to happen the way it did. As history gets rewritten over and over and over again I begin to imagine that our lives have so many possible narrative threads—all existing simultaneously like parallel universes—that the number of human histories is certainly infinite. Heroic, tragic, boring, catastrophic, ridiculous, and beautiful. We all live those stories, and often our narrative includes more than one of them.

Sydney

Sydney. Hooley freaking dooley, what a weird and gorgeous city! I bike through the downtown park—the Domain— so-called because in the late 1700s it was the private grounds of the governor. In one area of the park I see hundreds of large bats clinging to the branches of the trees. Occasionally one flexes its massive wings. During an outdoor opera recital I once attended in the park I glanced up and saw them swarming overhead at sunset, dispersing over the city in search of insects and fruit as the singers warbled arias from *La Traviata*. The juxtaposition of the Domain—a linguistic reminder of empire— and these giant slightly ominous creatures was a nice one.

Greg Wood / AFP / Getty Images

Though they've become one of the attractions of the park they weren't the intended attraction—that was the collection of tropical trees and plants in this section of the park. The bat population has grown, and they are decimating some of the trees with their climbing and guano. The trees are nice and all, but hey, giant bats! So there is now a battle between the tree people and the bats—I don't know if any organization dares stand up for the bats. The park folks have tried all sorts of vaguely humane ways to make the bats move on—I think python odor was one—but none have succeeded. This hopeless situation seems to be a metaphor for the Australian situation—man and nature on a collision course . . . but beautiful too.

The first time I went to Australia, in the early 1980s, I found it repulsive. I saw the whole place through politically correct glasses. As I saw it, here it was, the same old shit, happening all over again—the white colonials settling along the coastlines, building cottages that mimicked those of their ancestral homelands, turning a blind eye toward their systematic encroachment on and killing off of the native population. I sensed a vast continent, mostly forbidding and wild, with a smear of Eurojam along the edges. Just like North and South America once must have been.

The visual image, the incongruity as it struck me then, was jarring and disturbing. The shock in seeing suburbs consisting of cute little houses with quasi-English gardens in a land that seemed so utterly unsuited for them took me a while to get past or get over. For me, much of Southern California has the same vibe—a residential theme park in what is essentially a desert.

Here is an aerial view—much of the landscape is about as welcoming as Mars.

However, after a few more visits I began to like Australians. The folks I met were mostly unpretentious and open; the food and wine is fresh, tasty, and plentiful, and the countryside is forbidding but spectacular.

As a place for urban biking Australian towns are better than most. Sydney is a bit tough—the geography and the busy arteries that link the various neighborhoods are not very welcoming—but Melbourne, Perth, and Adelaide I find to be more accommodating. The weather is pretty near perfect—Mediterranean—and these cities, though they sprawl a bit, are in size nothing like those in the United States, so one can get from one end of town to the other reasonably quickly. There are bike paths along the rivers that flow through many Australian towns—paths that eventually lead down to the sea, and more are being added yearly.

The urban planner Jan Gehl was brought down here from Denmark some years ago and made studies of Adelaide,

Melbourne, and most recently Sydney. Gehl's reports and recommendations for Melbourne, in 1993 and 2005, were implemented, and the whole center city became a more livable place as a result. There are now 83 percent more central city residents than before. This means many people now live near where they work or where they go to school and can therefore easily accommodate most of their transport needs by bike or on foot. Parks were added, arcades and alleys revitalized, and outdoor cafés opened—about three hundred of them. Needless to say, more bike lanes were added throughout the city. (More on Gehl's philosophy later.)

Sydney is completely different. It's an odd mishmash of neighborhoods scattered fairly widely around little bays, on peninsulas, and along ancient paths. Much of the urban settlement is on the other side of the bay from Sydney proper. One has to drive over the harbor bridge or take a scenic ferry ride to reach these neighborhoods. One day I bike from the center of town to Bondi Beach, which is more or less due east of downtown on this side of the bay. The biking is, for such an incredibly beautiful city, surprisingly rough and unaccommodating. Sure enough, when I reach Bondi there are people surfing in the middle of the day, and we're still, sort of, in town.

The next day I decide to bike to the Gap, one of the rocky points to the east of the town center that encloses Sydney harbor like a pair of sandstone pincers, one from the north side of the bay and one from the south. To avoid some of the larger roads that I encountered getting to Bondi I try to stay closer to the water's edge by biking along Rose Bay and up through Vaucluse. Modest, unpretentious houses line the winding streets. I could be in a small well-to-do English town, which has somehow been airlifted and plunked down in a sunny semitropical landscape. As I reach the point, the cliffs bordering the Pacific give a spectacular view—for the dead. A cemetery occupies what seems to me the most scenic spot in the entire area.

You're Not Welcome Here

Australia is full of unpleasant reminders of nature's indifference to humans. Poisonous snakes and frogs, spiky plants, toxic spiders, rip currents, quicksand, and endless deserts abound. There's always something out there lurking, reminding you that you're just a guest here. It's almost as if the bush sits there like a croc, its jaws open and waiting for the hapless and naive to wander in. In the Australian film *Lantana* (named after a flowering plant with poisonous leaves), which follows various drifting Sydney couples, a woman's body is found within the insidious tangle of local plant life. In another film, *Picnic at Hanging Rock,* some girls on a school outing mysteriously vanish into the bush. They are never heard from again. To me, the anomie and alienation that constitute the mood of these films almost seem to be caused by the encroaching vegetation and potentially hostile landscape. The filmmakers probably see this as a metaphor for their "real" subject, but I think this *is* the real subject.

One would think that at least in a big city like Sydney one would be safe. Sydney, however, is home to one of the most dangerous critters of all—the funnel-web spider. Dealing with the urban hubbub hasn't bothered this deadly spider in the least. It loves slightly damp places, and a towel dropped poolside or in a bathroom will do nicely. In the words of climatologist and author Tim Flannery, a bite victim is "immediately plunged into excruciating pain and is soon convulsing in a lather of sweat and foaming saliva." Adult humans can stand about thirty hours of this before dying, but infants only last about an hour. To top off the insidious aspect of nature here, the venom of the funnel-web spider is more or less harmless to many animals, such as dogs and cats, but for humans it is deadly. Though the spider evolved way before people arrived here, it almost seems as though nature was merely lying in wait. Like Southern California, a place it superficially resembles, Australia is seductively beautiful, but blink and you're a goner—from either a mudslide, earthquake, bushfire, or some poisonous critter.

In New York there are raccoons in Central Park and there is rumored to be a beaver who has set up shop in the Bronx. But as far as wildlife encroaching on city dwellers it's nothing like here. In Brisbane there was recently a "wet"—a period of rain—which resulted in an infestation of both jellyfish and echidnas—a small monotreme (it's related to the duck-billed platypus) that has spikes like a hedgehog. The jellyfish here are not to be messed with. The box jellyfish is a particularly deadly little cube of aspic. According to a local source, "You have virtually no chance of surviving the venomous sting, unless treated immediately. The pain is so excruciating and overwhelming that you would most likely go into shock and drown before reaching the shore."

Around Brisbane the local dogs are reportedly becoming addicted to licking cane toads, the skins of which are poisonous, but just a little taste gets a dog high. Some unfortunate

David Gray / Reuters

dogs overdo it and end up convulsing in violent spasms, but most have learned to regulate their toad intake—and after a dose wears off they sometimes return for more.

Cane toads were introduced to Australia in 1935 in the hopes that they would eat the local cane beetle, an agricultural pest. Though omnivorous, eating both living and dead foodstuffs, the cane toads weren't interested in the cane beetles. But they do breed prodigiously and their poisonous skin kills off both local predators and pets. The would-be pest killer is now a pest. People have died from them as well, because, as with dogs, a lick of a cane toad can stimulate hallucinations that last for about an hour, and some folks aren't as smart as dogs.

The famous introduction of twenty-four rabbits to Australia in 1859 (for hunting purposes) was a similar mistake. It was an absolute ecological disaster here, as the rabbits ate every kind of vegetation and bred like . . . rabbits. They have no natural predators in Australia to control their numbers and, as a result, a fence was erected in the desert, stretching from one end of the continent to the other, in hopes of limiting their spread. In 1950 a virus was released to kill the rabbits, which it did—until they developed a resistance.

Not every native life-form here is unwelcoming. Some go out of their way to make us feel at home. The lyrebird imitates the calls of other birds—as well as other sounds it hears in its environment. In the BBC series *The Life of Birds* there is footage in which a lyrebird puts on a stellar performance, first clearing a space in the bush for its little stage and then stringing all its acoustic accomplishments together in a five-minute extravaganza of song. The song cycle is mostly a mashup of other birds' songs, but then, shockingly, this one ends with an imitation of the sound of a camera shutter, a car alarm, some loggers' footsteps, and finally the sound of the loggers' chainsaws cutting through a tree—these last few sounds were completely accurate, the mimicry impeccable, like perfect recordings!

The Peaceable Kingdom

In Pleistocene times, giant "megafauna" inhabited Australia. These animals—the great rhinoceros-like *Diprotodon*; the giant kangaroo standing three meters (ten feet) high; a giant marsupial wombat; *Megalania*, a goanna lizard six meters (twenty feet) long; *Quinkana*, a land crocodile three meters long; *Wonambi*, a python seven meters (twenty-three feet) long; the flightless birds, *Genyornis* (giant emus) and *Dromornis*, which matched the great moa in size—mysteriously disappeared from Australia about fifteen thousand years ago. People were, presumably, more or less the same puny size they are now.

Aboriginal stories, which have been recorded throughout Australia, indicate clearly that these animals were a part of the environment of early man on this continent, remembered with both fear and awe—impressions that have been passed down over eons via a unique oral tradition.

De Agostini Picture Library / Getty Images

That Aboriginal oral tradition dates back to . . . fifteen thousand years ago! A continuity that makes our own written history seem, well, not worth the papyrus it's written on. We think of our history as being more solid, more real, because it's written. But written history doesn't go back anywhere near this far. And why does it being written down make it necessarily truer or more real to us?

Adelaide is a small city on the southern rim of the continent—the last sizable town before you hit the immense deserts to the west. My favorite name for a desert—Nullarbor (zero trees)—is here. I bike down the main street of Adelaide past big old colonial buildings with grassy lawns. A cluster of Aborigines sits on the grass in a miniscule city park. A few meters away the traffic roars down the main street and pedestrians pass by. The little clump of indigenous people are like living ghosts, a reminder of the deep history of this land—a place that is now occupied by Europeans. These people are, if not the land's custodians, at least its children. They were birthed and formed by this land. They embody it, they do not manipulate it. (I admit that maybe this is my own romantic interpretation.)

The fact that they have chosen to congregate on a little patch of lawn right in the middle of town, clearly visible to all who pass by, but that they are usually ignored, invisible, is portentous, meaningful. It's a sign, a reminder, a living billboard that gives notice that all the buildings and the hustle and bustle of we who pass by are superficial. Their physical presence says that there is a deep, slow biological and geological history that this new European colonial world seeks to quietly cover over with countless new things and a frenzy of commerce in order to obliterate that history from memory. They're a living sign, a living "fuck you" to the looming office towers and manicured lawns.

I continue west and ride my bike to the beach by following a

bike path along the Torrens River that runs through the center of Adelaide. The path winds through eucalyptus groves (gum trees they are called here), where there are magpies and pelicans hanging out.

The gum trees eventually begin to thin out and soon they disappear altogether and the river empties into the sea. This is a Sunday afternoon, it's hot, but there are only six people on this part of the beach. If this beach were this close to a town of this size on other continents it would be jam-packed on a day like today. There would be hawkers selling crap and cars parked nearby. The whole country seems so new—to the European settlers anyway—that they have barely had time to encroach on much of it.

A bit farther up the beach, in the town of Charles Sturt, there are cafés and restaurants overlooking the ocean. I have a beer, some calamari, and assorted veggie dips, all delicious.

This unpretentious café food is amazing. The Mediterranean immigrants to Australia have had a positive and profound influence, not the least of which is on the food. I've had a simple octopus over greens that was much, much better than the mangy little tentacles served up in some top restaurants in New York. This was like a steak but with big suckers on the side.

Melbourne

In Melbourne I bike along the riverside and stumble upon the opening of the new downtown park. It's Australia Day, so there are lots of festivities in the park. The Aborigines see it as a day commemorating the onset of shame, horror, and degradation. I decide to pay homage to the local outlaw legend Ned Kelly, so I bike back through town to the exhibition at the jail where he was executed.

Image courtesy of State Library of Victoria, photo by Charles
Nettleton

This is a picture of Ned taken on the day he was hanged,
looking more like an elegant sadhu than an outlaw.

There seem to have been a lot of extenuating circumstances
in Kelly's story. He was Irish, and the powers that be at the time
were all English, and they viewed the Irish as dogs and referred
to them as such. He may have been treated unjustly before he
became an outlaw, which eventually led to a life on the run and
to his deadly battles with the police. In preparation for a final
standoff against them, Kelly fashioned himself a homemade
suit of armor in hopes that he might survive the imminent raid.
He also knew that he and his gang were in a hopeless position,
so part of the plan was just to take down as many of the police
as he could before a lucky shot took him. He was felled by a
man who shot him in the knees.

Image courtesy of State Library of Victoria

The Red Centre

I've been to Australia quite a few times, and the locals never fail to claim that I haven't seen their country until I've seen the interior. I decide to take up the challenge and drive around the Red Centre with a loose itinerary that will include Uluru (Ayers Rock), Alice Springs, and Kings Canyon.

Arriving in Alice Springs I see Aborigines everywhere—unlike in the coastal cities—though most in town are lounging in the parks under the few shade trees. I obtain a permit to pass through Aboriginal lands and I head west in a rental car. Shortly all traces of human presence begin to disappear, though for a while I can get a cricket game on the radio. One wonders what could be more boring than watching a cricket game? Well, here is the answer.

Soon there are no more markers, no telephone or electrical poles along the road (or visible anywhere), and no signs of human habitation as far as one can see. The cricket game fades out. Even though signs of European humanity are diminishing I am still on a paved road—for now.

I must sound like Mr. City Slicker, but even in some of the farthest reaches of the American West one can usually see high-tension power lines in the distance, aerials of some type on distant hilltops, a shack or decrepit structure. Here there is nothing. I haven't seen a car in at least an hour—and this is the main road in this region.

The traditionally nomadic Aborigines tend to leave little trace of their existence on the land—none that I can see anyway— though I occasionally spot an abandoned or burnt-out vehicle or a tire stuck in a dead tree, sometimes placed there to mark a completely invisible turnoff.

Eventually, as the road enters Aboriginal lands, it becomes a dirt track, and any traffic I'd previously seen on the paved road disappears completely. In the distance there are ranges of hills, a vaguely circular formation that, from the way it looks on the map, appears to be the far-flung remains of a massive meteor crater. A group of camels crosses the road. Camels! It seems that camels were imported, along with Afghan labor, to haul goods from Adelaide up to Alice Springs, until a rail line was completed in 1929. After they were no longer needed the camels were simply abandoned to roam, and eighty years later they're still here, wandering.

I stop and take a short walk into the desert. From the car window most of the vegetation appears to be grassy, similar to the succulent grasses in New Mexico or West Texas. I wonder, if the vegetation is similar, why isn't anyone grazing cattle out here? A few steps and I have my answer. These "grasses" are spiky, almost painful to touch or to rub against.

Whatever the camels (and kangaroos) are eating, it probably isn't this stuff.

The track dips down occasionally into what might be called arroyos—dried-up riverbeds—which in many cases are sandy. I'm glad I rented a 4-wheel drive. As I approach maybe my third one of these things I spy, as I pass over a rise, something down in the riverbed. It's a scarily sunburned family standing around their station wagon (not a 4-wheel drive) that is mired deep in the sand and is facing me. I drive through the sand to the opposite side and get out to help if I can.

They've been here for hours and I'm the first car to pass by. They're from Melbourne. Aren't they supposed to know better—being locals? Dad has the rear hatch open and as I approach he reaches into their cooler, which is stocked with beers, and hands me a cool one. A tinny, I think they're called here. VB, Melbourne's finest—though I prefer Cascade, the Tasmanian brew with the extinct Tasmanian tiger on the label.

The red family needs to get out of the sun. I suggest that if Dad wants to go forward I can push him with my car, but Dad seems worried that the push might dent his station wagon—or jostle the beers maybe. He prefers to be pulled, but neither of us has any rope. His hitch is at the back of his car, so the only way to move him will be to pull him back from where he came. I can sense that Dad doesn't really want to go backward, but it's the only way I could conceivably drag him. He produces a tarp from somewhere and says maybe if we twist it and roll it up it could work like a rope. It's worth a try. We tie the back ends of our cars together and I begin to ease forward. The tarp tightens and the knot tying it to his car slips off. But the tarp doesn't tear or break. He ties it tighter and I move even slower—and inch by inch I get his vehicle back onto solid ground.

I'm thinking, great, job well done, but Dad has a look on his face. He's pondering trying to get across this sand trap I just pulled him out of so he can move on to wherever it is he might be headed. He wants to try to get across again! I suggest that there are quite a few more of these sand traps up ahead, as I've been through them. I tell him it's his decision, but I'm not going to help him out twice and that I won't be back this way. I prepare to drive off. As I pull away I can see him contemplating whether or not to drive his family back into the sand pit.

A few days later I reach Uluru (aka Ayers Rock) and Kata Tjuta, another isolated rock formation in the middle of nowhere. These are both on Aboriginal lands, and the Aborigines co-run the park.

We, the traditional landowners of Uluru-Kata Tjuta National Park, are direct descendants of the beings who created our lands during the Tjukurpa (Creation Time). We have always been here. We call ourselves Anangu, and would like you to use that term for us.

The Anangu also prefer that people not climb the rock, as it's a sacred place for their culture, but their wishes are clearly not being honored in this case: there is a rope and other things fastened onto one of the more gentle slopes of the rock, so quite a few are making the climb. I decide to jog around the rock instead, as it's early morning and still cool out. It's about three to four kilometers around. There are numerous caves and sheltered recesses along the base of the rock, filled with Anangu paintings and drawings.

The paintings and drawings in the caves are a palimpsest: each generation seems to have had complete disregard for the work of their predecessors. They paint and draw right on top of the earlier work, not bothering to clear an area or find a clean stone surface. It makes me think that the drawings and paintings themselves possibly aren't what is valued in this case, but that the act of placing them and creating them is where the importance lies. The drawings are simply the residue of that act.

Just over the horizon from Uluru lies its twin impossibility, Kata Tjuta. This outcropping looks like humongous blobs of dough that have been left to rise and then begin to lean and sag this way and that of their own weight. This one is politically okay to hike into, though visually it's a bit like heading into a giant butt crack.

Back at the bunkerlike motel evening is approaching and I walk around the desert again. Now I can see small signs of life. Here is a shot of an ant mound, ringed with eucalyptus leaves that the colony has gathered.

For some reason, examining the ant mound, I break down and begin crying, inexplicably. I suspect that the desolate landscape and weird geography I've been passing through might have triggered something deeply personal—but I don't know what. In the end the tears are cathartic, though I don't know why, or what exactly might have been sorted out. I'd love to think I've just gone through some cosmic existential rite of

passage, triggered by an ant mound, but I suspect the explanation might be more mundane. It would be flattering to think that the dome full of stars out here and the little critters scurrying around on the ground have put me, the human ant, in my place, and I'm having an epiphany about my holy insignificance. But being that I'm mere yards from a crappy concrete-block motel room and a humming minifridge I doubt it.

London

L ondon is a city not on a grid plan, which can be both good and bad for getting around by bike. If one knows the streets well, one can, by taking a zigzag path, avoid the large, busy thoroughfares that snake through the maze of smaller streets and, by following those smaller arteries, travel more or less as the crow flies. However, not being a native, I have to consult a map fairly often, as the winding streets here can lead one astray—without realizing it, for example, I could be headed northwest rather than west, and gradually go miles out of my way.

London sprawls for an old city. Most European capitals are pretty compact, but London, being an amalgamation of former villages, has many centers, and activities can take place miles apart from one another. As a result there can be some long and strenuous pedals. These don't necessarily result in making a trip longer than it would be on the tube, but I sometimes arrive a little shiny.

I've learned after many years not to fill my travel days exclusively with work, but to give myself some free time, some breathing space, so I can manage to retain my sanity despite the feeling of dislocation that comes with the traveling. Random wandering clears the head of the worries and the concerns that might be lurking, and sometimes it's even inspiring. I lean toward contemporary art shows, as that's an area I'm involved in, but medical museums, industrial museums, and the National Museum of Roller Skating in Lincoln, Nebraska, were all equally exciting and served as destinations—though often what I passed along the way was even more interesting.

The Policeman Inside

In the morning I bike east from the hotel in Shepherd's Bush across town to the Whitechapel Gallery, where I have a meeting with Iwona Blazwick, the director, about a possible talk later in the fall. That takes me more or less in a straight line across London, west to east, staying on the north side of the Thames. I could have taken a large multilane road that runs that way (Westway to Marylebone Road to Pentonville Road—all the same road, really), but I prefer navigating by landmarks. Henriette Mortensen, who works with Gehl Architects, a Danish urban planning and advisory group, mentioned to me recently that this is a common urban instinct. She said that in parts of New York there are surprisingly few such landmarks, and therefore people sometimes lose their bearings. Not that they get hopelessly lost—though tourists might—but that our somewhat limited instinctual sense of location desires more markers in some areas.

In many cities these landmarks are famous buildings, bridges, and monuments. A triumphal arch, an old train station, or a plaza with a tower or church on it are common markers. In many towns these were all made during one prosperous era, which leads me to wonder if the steel and glass towers that are springing up everywhere now—some of them in wacky shapes like pickles and sharp-edged triangles—ever will be looked at by some future generation as the charming markers that give a city its identity. Will some funny-shaped steel and mirror-glass monolith function, in the future, in the same way the Eiffel Tower, the Zocalo, or Marble Arch do?

My route takes me by Hyde Park, Marble Arch, Buckingham Palace, Piccadilly Circus, the theater district, and Spitalfields Market. Not the most direct route to Whitechapel, but hopscotching from one marker to another feels like participating in a giant board game—it is immensely satisfying. Each marker is almost within sight of the next one, so progress toward my objective proceeds via a series of giant steps.

After I arrive we talk over tea and Iwona mentions that she was recently in Iran to visit some of the artists currently working there. She says most of them are regularly subjected to beatings by the government, and they incorporate that into their lives and dress, wearing six pairs of pants for their beating appointments.

The talk turns from there, unsurprisingly, to male-dominated societies, and she volunteers that societies that separate the sexes sometimes do so in order to encourage violence and aggression: to be more warlike.

At one point, as an example of her idea that oppressed people become oppressors, she mentions Israel's dominance over the Palestinians, and the aggressive behavior of the Israelis, as if this were a well-known fact. I don't altogether disagree, but I am surprised to hear it voiced so openly. In America, and especially in New York, there is a hidden level of not-so-subtle censorship of such statements. They are just never heard, or if they are, the speaker is often given a nasty look or accused of anti-Semitism.

I wonder how many other aspects of North American thought might be self-censored. Quite a few, I would imagine. Every culture must have its no-speak/no-tell zones. The "policeman inside," as William Burroughs called it. Though we might espouse free speech as an absolute virtue, some self-censorship might be excusable. There are plenty of times when we have nasty revenge fantasies about drivers who cut us off and what we would do to the people on the other end of rude phone conversations, but we don't always voice those feelings. Well, not seriously. Likewise, salacious thoughts about strangers might be voiced by louts, but "refined" folks, though they too might be turned on by an attractive woman's legs or a man's crotch, keep those thoughts to themselves. It's part of the social contract. It's how we get along. Self-censorship is part of being a social animal, and in that sense it's not always a bad thing.

We refrain, most of the time, from insulting or attacking our friends' religious beliefs. In fact the very subject of what religious beliefs might be held by an individual is often considered out of bounds in polite conversation. Likewise, we don't usually make fun of other people's families in front of them—their parents, children, or siblings. Only they are allowed to do that. And most of us refrain from direct criticism of people's personal appearance. We don't inform people that they are overweight, broken out, or having a bad-hair day.

But what Burroughs was referring to was more than that. He, I think rightly, realized that eventually we reach a point where the self-censorship of some ideas, not just what we might refer to as rude comments, can become internalized. At some point "bad," inappropriate, politically incorrect, or unconventional thoughts may not even arise or occur to us. If they do they are suppressed so quickly, unconsciously, that it's as though we'd never had them. Soon they appear to never arise at all. Freud noticed this and presumed that these forbidden thoughts accumulate and fester somewhere: the trash can never truly be emptied by intellectually or consciously throwing it out, according to him. For Burroughs this censorship is evidence of a kind of mind control—an instance of society limiting not just what we do and say, but what we allow ourselves to think. For him it is an example of the religious police or homeland security finally getting inside your head and installing their little cop in there. And that kind of censorship is perfect—once you self-censor certain ideas you don't need an outside agency as a monitor.

When that level of self-censorship kicks in you are unaware that it is happening. At that point, it seems to you that there is no censorship at all; it appears to you that your thoughts are actually unfettered and free. In all likelihood the outside instigator or legislator of your thoughts—the government, the media, your friends, your parents—have also convinced themselves that those thoughts are not even happening, that they don't exist. Eventually there is no more outside-the-box thinking as far as some kinds of thoughts go. Everything, even the maker of the box, is inside the box.

Country Life

On my way back to the hotel, I ride through Hyde Park. The sun is shining brightly, rare for this town. Lots of people are out walking what I must assume are upper-class dogs. Only a few limited breeds are in evidence: blond Irish setters, Scotties (mostly white), and the occasional whippet. Almost no other member of the dog world is visible at all. Ditto the people—only a few rarified breeds seem to enjoy the park.

I pass by what I assume is an upper-class matron and her kids. She is in full regalia—a green hunting jacket, beige trousers, and Wellington boots. Is she planning on off-roading it? Finding a particularly soft bit of ground here in Hyde Park and wallowing in her Wellies? Shooting a few of the local ducks or swans? (The colors she's wearing will help her blend in perfectly.) Her kids are likewise dressed for "country life." Miniature versions of Mum. Wonderful that though they're in the middle of one of the world's great cities they can pretend to themselves that they are in the Highlands. Well, not really—we know that here costume is, more than in most places, a signifier of what class you belong to.

After lunch at the hotel I go off again, this time along the promenade that borders the north side of the river until I reach Tower Bridge, crawling with tourists, and then I head south across the bridge to a small side street and the Design Museum. Tom Heatherwick curated what is called the Conran Foundation Collection show, which was beautifully installed, hilarious, and moving. The exhibit consists of thirty thousand pounds'—the show's financial budget—worth of his

© Steve Speller

favorite oddball stuff, some of it examples of high design but most of it not. Interesting that this show has nothing to do with Conran's, the store, except that Sir Conran is on the board of the museum and funds this particular design show. Of course far from being high design, many of the objects that Heatherwick has chosen are things we might easily have at home. By putting each thing in its own modular wooden vitrine, his installation allows you to consider the objects, whether high or low, one interesting item at a time: toothpaste dispensers, stylish high-tech design gadgets, plastic combs, and Cup Noodles packages.

Once upon a time it was considered radical to even show mass-produced objects in the same place as fine art—in museums with flattering lighting and little labels. Now, by implication and extension, Cup Noodles containers presented next to more expensive design objects become equals. We're being asked to see the elegance or at least innovation and cleverness in banal everyday crap that for the most part is never given a second look. Living with this kind of stuff every day, day after day, we often don't even notice it anymore. We assume it just is—unremarkable, undistinguished—and we forget that it was at some point designed by someone and may in fact be elegant, efficiently made, and even beautiful.

After viewing the show I have tea with the (now ex-) director of the Design Museum, Alice Rawsthorn, who can jump into a serious philosophical discussion faster than anyone I've ever met. She immediately asks if any of the journalists who've interviewed me lately were actually stimulating to talk to. I respond by mentioning a thought that had occurred to me regarding the perception of people who create things, especially performers like me. People tend to think that creative work is an expression of a preexisting desire or passion, a feeling made manifest, and in a way it is. As if an overwhelming anger, love, pain, or longing fills the artist or composer, as it might with any of us—the difference being that the creative artist then has no choice but to express those feelings through his or her given creative medium. I proposed that more often the work is a kind of tool that discovers and brings to light that emotional muck. Singers (and possibly listeners of music too) when they write or perform a song don't so much bring to the work already formed emotions, ideas, and feelings as much as they use the act of singing as a device that reproduces and dredges them up. The song remakes the emotion—the emotion doesn't produce the song. Well, the emotion has to have been there at some time in one's life for there to be something from which to draw. But it seems to me that a creative device—if a work can be considered a device—evokes that passion, melancholy, loneliness, or euphoria but is not itself an expression, an example, a fruit of that passion. Creative work is more accurately a machine that digs down and finds stuff, emotional stuff that will someday be raw material that can be used to produce more stuff, stuff like itself—clay to be available for future use.

Form Is Function

I head back west, this time along the pedestrian promenade that extends along the South Bank, then north across Waterloo Bridge and inland until I reach the British Museum, where there is a show of curiosity cabinets called Enlightenment. To me the collecting of "curiosities" and an enlightened view of the world somehow seem mutually exclusive, or at least one doesn't necessarily always lead and connect to the other, but here they have been shoved together, possibly because an activity and a worldview overlapped in time.

The objects in the Wunderkammer—preserved creatures, odd books and treatises, antique carvings, sacred objects from foreign lands—were often grouped, by Sir John Soane and other collectors of that period, by whatever criteria seemed appropriate, be it shape, material, or color. There would be, for example, a mass of bulbous objects from various parts of the world and then some sharp, pointy ones grouped together. Many of these objects had nothing to do with one another except for having similar shapes. Hardly what one would think of as a rigorous, enlightened scientific method of categorization. But thinking back on it, I would suggest that, yes, in a truly enlightened world all green objects are in a way related somehow, more than by just being green, and maybe they are related in a way we don't understand yet, just as all hexagonal objects might share a common trait as well. These crazy groupings might someday be seen as not completely arbitrary.

Any kind of taxonomy might be as good or valid as any other, though we might not know for sure until some time in the future when a scientific paper "discovers" that hexagonal or bulbous shapes, or similar colors or textures are functions that in some way determine content, in the way that the form of a DNA molecule defines and *is* its function. Form doesn't *follow* function in that case—form *is* function. I wonder to myself if genetics might be on the verge of some such wider revelation,

beyond our understanding of DNA, based on molecular structures that are common across life-forms and species. Temple
Grandin, in her book *Animals in Translation,* proposes that all
animals with a white patch of fur on their bodies are less likely
to be shy than their cousins. On the surface such an idea might
seem completely irrational. As if my hair color could be an
indication or even a determinant of my personality. But if such
ideas can be proven then we're not that far from pointy things
and bulbous things as legitimate classifications.

It's a bit like sympathetic magic in a way: the usual Western
presumption that "primitive" rituals mimic what they desire to
achieve—that phallic objects might be believed to increase male
potency and playacting rainfall might somehow bring it about.
I am suspicious of such obvious connections and I suspect that
the connections among things, people, and processes can be
equally irrational. I sense the world might be more dreamlike,
metaphorical, and poetic than we currently believe—but just as
irrational as sympathetic magic when looked at in a typically
scientific way. I wouldn't be surprised if poetry—poetry in the
broadest sense, in the sense of a world filled with metaphor,
rhyme, and recurring patterns, shapes, and designs—is how
the world works. The world isn't logical, it's a song.

I head back along Oxford Street, which is a handful to navigate with all its double-decker buses and cabs, and then south
through the little grid of Soho. I pause to watch a big Muslim
demonstration in Trafalgar Square with signs urging everyone
(everyone meaning Muslims and Christians) to get along and
to have some mutual understanding and respect. Lots of praying and chanting. I wonder if "respect" in this case isn't really a
code word for "enough with the nasty Danish cartoons"? Those
recent cartoons must simply confirm what Muslims already
suspect the infidels think about Islam. The subtext—that the
West thinks Muslims are mainly dirty, conniving bearded terrorists or arms dealers—can be read and inferred in so many
newspaper articles, action movies, the reporting and punditry

on Fox News, and in Western political speeches. It's not that those programs and action movies come out and say these things, but it's easy enough to read the implied message.

Back at my hotel I look around the sleek lobby. The staff seems mainly to be young Russians and Italians dressed in black. Two African businessmen in suits sit on a nearby sofa and leaf through newspapers. Waiting. A young Japanese man calls for a taxi. A few couples emerge from the elevators. Some of the couples are almost my age. (I'm in my midfifties.) They appear to be from the provinces and don't seem like lovers here for a tryst or businesspeople. What brought them here? The piped-in music from the adjoining bar and lounge is revving up to full disco level now that evening is approaching, and the lobby, all dark and moody, has transformed into something more like a club than a hotel. The couples and tourists now seem pretty out of place, as if what they thought in the afternoon was a hotel lobby had sneakily morphed into a dark nightclub while they were out sightseeing.

Reality-Based World

The *Independent* newspaper says that after World War II a number of studies and some reports by military officers estimated that only one in four soldiers had actually fired on the enemy. The others weren't psychologically ready to kill, so they simply didn't. Very annoying for the higher-ups. The ubiquitous image of soldiers rushing into battle with guns blazing simply didn't happen. A man named Dave Grossman was brought in to remedy the problem. He used "operant conditioning," a Skinnerian psychological term, combined with simulations that mimicked actual combat conditions. Previously, firearms training mainly involved shooting at distant targets and aiming carefully. Grossman's psychological conditioning techniques were further refined over the years, with the addition of simulators—devices that bore a remarkable resemblance to today's first-person shooter video games. (One wonders if the military should get some credit for designing what eventually became video-game software.) The efficiency of the soldiers trained by using these simulations was quadrupled, so it was proven to be extremely effective.

Based on this evidence Grossman wrote a book called *On Killing* and has since become a critic of the impact of commercial video games, claiming that they are in effect training young players to be killing machines. He believes that shooter video games teach adolescents (and frustrated nerds) to have the killing instinct, to quicken their reactions, and to lower their inhibitions. He has a Web site: killology.com.

This sounds awfully close to the complaints of shocked liberals when they observe their kids playing a round of Grand Theft Auto. Playing war games and mowing down zombies is pretty ubiquitous among adolescent boys, and most usually grow out of it and realize that it is playacting. But Grossman, an insider if ever there was one, seems to be claiming that some line gets crossed.

Similarly the recently deceased professor of communication George Gerbner claimed that when consumed in sufficient quantities, modern media, like television, substitute their realities for the reality out in the streets, "on the ground." He claimed that people who watch a lot of TV begin to live their lives as if the TV reality were an accurate reflection of the world outside. After a while the TV reality takes precedence over the "real" world. Given what's on TV, this televised version of reality paints a picture of the world as a dangerous place, full of crime, suspicious characters, and double-dealing—and with an inordinate portion of the population devoted to law enforcement. Cities as portrayed on TV are filled with blatantly sexy men and women, stereotypically oddball characters and disreputable agents, and the cops who are there to deal with all of them. The world is divided up into beautiful party people, lawbreakers, and enforcers. To some extent this skewed picture of the world, according to Gerbner, eventually becomes a self-fulfilling prophecy. When the TV-saturated public begins to act as if the TV reality is real and behaves accordingly—reacting fearfully and suspiciously to a world perceived as being primarily populated with drug dealers and con men, according to Gerbner's scenario—then eventually the real world begins to adjust itself to match the fiction. The fact is there are such things as cops, drug dealers, sleazy bitches, and attractive folks with ready banter and clever quips. These stereotypes are not entirely made up. Their existence can be confirmed, just not in the proportions seen in TV land. But as any marketing or advertising person will tell you, perception is all.

I wonder if this view of Gerbner's isn't too alarmist. Part of the reason there are so many gunslingers and cops on TV might be because that is the contemporary dramatic narrative context of the age-old story of the brave and questing hero. It's a conveniently available, semibelievable, and plausible setting in which to place these eternally recurring myths. Life-changing stories don't usually take place at an office desk or a computer terminal—and those banal workaday locations are not very conducive to visual media anyway. When I was growing up, TV was all westerns and cowboys. Then, a few years later, TV shows were all about spies. The cowboys had vanished. But I knew—or I think I did—that the world wasn't really ever filled with that many cowboys west of the Mississippi, or that half the men I saw in suits weren't in fact glamorous spies. The images and the emotional buttons they triggered still enthralled me, though.

Now, if we were to take what we are presented literally, the world would be made of smart-asses, cops, sexy bitches, and gangsters. But maybe they are all just a vehicle for the same old stories, stories we love and need, but don't really take seriously as a mirror of reality. No one seriously thinks that because Shakespeare mainly wrote about royalty that people thought the world was all upper class, a universe made up entirely of tragic kings and princes. The bubble universe of the royals, and that of the aristocracy, is by nature more artificial and more theatrical, and therefore easier to view as an allegory. That makes it a better setting for storytelling. Likewise cops, robbers, and sexy bitches. Maybe all those exaggerated characters always simply mirror a different kind of reality—the one inside.

What's Then Is Now

The past is not a prologue to the present; it is the present—morphed a bit, stretched, distorted, and with different emphasis. It's a structurally similar, though very much contorted, version of the present. Therefore, in a sense, time—history—can, at least in our heads, flow in either direction, because deeply, structurally nothing has really changed. We think we're going in a line through time, making progress, advancing, but we might be going in circles.

What we call history could be viewed as a record of how basic social forms have distorted or morphed. It simply changes shape, but the underlying patterns and behaviors are always there, under the surface—as they are in biological forms. Aspects, organs, limbs, and appendages swell and others contract to the point of atrophy in order to accommodate current evolutionary needs and contingencies, but they could just as well flow and shrink in the other direction, should specific needs and surroundings change. History might behave in the same way—the names and numbers change, but the underlying patterns remain.

Morning, I wake up and it's sunny! I cycle back along the South Bank promenade until I reach the Tate Modern. There, tucked away inside another exhibition, is a single room of spreads from a Russian magazine published in the 1930s called *USSR in Construction*, which was often designed by Rodchenko, El Lissitzky, and other fairly radical artists of the time. The layouts are beautiful—obviously intended as propaganda (the magazine was printed in a few languages)—sometimes corny as hell, but gorgeous.

If one didn't know anything else about the Soviet Union, one might look at these beautiful and radically innovative graphic layouts and think, Wow, what a cool place, what a hip scene it must be, and what an enlightened government they must have to produce and sponsor such an amazing magazine. (One might have said the same thing decades later about the U.S.-sponsored international shows of abstract art and state-sponsored jazz tours—which was indeed the intention.)

Here are some spreads by Rodchenko:

ОДНА ТРЕТЬ ЛЕСОВ МИРА ПРИНАДЛЕЖИТ СССР

Here is a layout featuring "illuminations" added to a tractor factory for the enjoyment and excitement of the workers—sort of workplace as pleasure palace/theme park. Google, the current hip place to work, where the workplace is hyped as a cool campus, has some catching up to do.

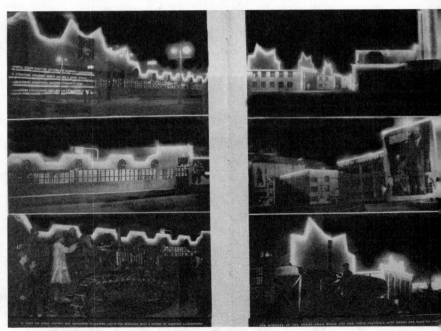

Art © Estate of Alexander Rodchenko / RAO, Moscow / VAGA, New York

Other images in this magazine feature elaborate foldouts, duotones of smiling peasants posed next to Stalin, and one incredible spread of a paratrooper—the top of the page can be unfolded to become a duotone of a parachute sail. Glorious and unsubtle propaganda. I guess all these artists were buying the party line at that point or hoping they might change things from the inside.

It's an odd sensation looking at these—both chilling and thrilling. One knows, with hindsight, what horrors Stalin would perpetrate, yet one wants to separate the innovative graphic work from the perverted version of the ideology that it was selling. It's an old question: how cool and detached can we be in appreciating design and formal innovation? It's not too hard to admire the occasionally innovative contemporary TV commercial for junk food or overpriced jeans, but lots of folks have issues with the formal and technical innovations of Albert Speer and Leni Riefenstahl.

What is often referred to as socialist realism was not exclusively a Russian movement. Propaganda murals extolling workers and industry were produced in New York and elsewhere. Bas-relief sculptures were carved on buildings in lower Manhattan depicting the press workers who labored inside. In my neighborhood there is a large bronze statue on the sidewalk of a man sitting at a machine, bent over, sewing, and another sculpture of a giant needle and button. Glorious sweatshop workers! But the cult of the living great leader didn't seem to take root here as much as it did in the East.

I head directly across the river via the pedestrian bridge to St. Paul's Cathedral (very spooky organ music is playing inside—big, ominous chords). The revolving entrance door has these words on it:

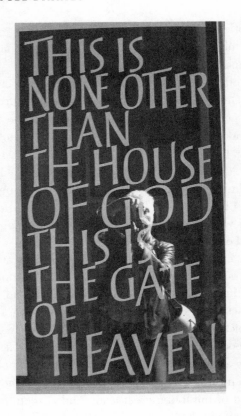

That's quite a claim for a revolving door! I guess it says it backward when you're inside.

What's Music For?

My friend C and I have lunch with two youngish guys who run an art gallery here while its owners are out of town—one is a thin German man who has just moved here a few months ago and the other is an Englishman transplanted from another local gallery. The gallery is in Mayfair, the zone of gilt-framed, stodgy landscape paintings; antiques and antiquities; luxe designer boutiques; and shops that seem peculiarly British—one is called the

Cufflink Connoisseur, while another displays polo gear and riding crops in the windows.

The gallerists ask me what I'm up to in a way that says "have you done *anything* since Talking Heads?" It's always a little weird when people obviously think I haven't done much since the hit records they remember from their childhood. The subject turns to live music we've seen or heard lately and the German man says he's only been to about five live shows in his entire life; he grew up on techno and electronic dance music and that's pretty much all he listens to—DJs. I ask what time those "shows" begin and he tells me that the big-name DJs usually don't go on before one. I feel a little old-fashioned—I'm usually in bed by then.

The Englishman comments to me that Germans are obsessed with techno, which gets a slightly puzzled and possibly annoyed look from his associate. I think to myself how very different our concepts and uses of music are, how varied they can be. I assume that for the German gentleman music is a sort of machine, a tool that facilitates dancing and some kind of release. Its function is therefore simple, clear-cut, and it either does its job or it doesn't. I imagine it's pretty context dependent too. Not too many offices have booming techno bouncing off the walls. Music, for him, will be associated with a specific place and time of day, like going to a gym or an art museum—it's not necessarily something one experiences at home. Maybe there is some social interaction at those techno clubs as well, so the music helps provide a way for that to happen too. Music, in this view, is definitely not about the words, that much is obvious.

What is music for in my case? Well, I like dancing to music too, though I find that more syncopated rhythms—funk, Latin, hip-hop, etc.—get me moving more often than the repetitive metronomic thump of house or techno. I suspect that syncopated rhythms simultaneously "activate" a variety of parts of the body (and mind) in different ways, and that the pleasure derived from this palimpsest of rhythms acts like a biological metaphor—a metaphor and mirror of social and organic rhythms and processes that we find enjoyable. I don't find this music to be context specific. I'll bop around my loft or sway to an iPod on the subway. Most often when listening and not dancing I choose music with singing as I find that the arc of a melody, combined with harmonies and a rhythmic pulse, can be incredibly emotionally involving. We call these songs. Sometimes the words help too, but I'll often put up with lame lyrics if the rest of it works.

So that's two "uses" I have for music. I also sometimes listen to sound tracks, contemporary classical music, and vaguely experimental music—usually as a background, a mood enhancer, or for atmosphere. We get doses of music this way in films and TV all the time. This is music as air-conditioning. Damn, I forgot to mention to the German gallerist my recent collaboration with Paul van Dyk, the techno master—I would have scored some points and cred if I had.

I remark that the waiter seems to be wearing eyeliner, which prompts a change in subject to the local Abercrombie & Fitch store, where I am told all the shop assistants must be (or must at least appear to be) models in order to be hired. This former bastion of WASP outdoor wear—which intentionally used to be about as sexy as the boxy Brooks Brothers look—has remade itself as a kind of homoerotic Fascist-chic outpost. Talk about a makeover! Is there a Tom of Finland lurking behind or within every buttoned-down square? Two male models stand at the entrance of the shop in hot pants, and the walls inside are plastered with photos and paintings (paintings!) of shirtless male models. The ploy has paid off handsomely; youths of all types fill the place daily. It sounds like a wonderful kitsch theme park, like a Leni Riefenstahl film or toga epic come to life. But what does it mean that gay kitsch sells clothes to straight youth? Calvin Klein has been doing it for decades. His black-and-white ads look like images from soft-core gay mags from the 1950s or '60s. Surely using this sales tool is intentional and is not just an excuse for him to meet the models. Do the straight kids who shop there, many of whom would never knowingly be associated with anything gay, think, Oh, they're just cute guys?

It's still gorgeous and sunny, so I'm off again, south, across the river, now to the Imperial War Museum, where there is a great show of camouflage that includes two of the outfits used in my film *True Stories*! Here's a ship in what was called "dazzle" camouflage:

© The Imperial War Museum, image ART2291

As my friend C says, "Where would that be camouflage? In a circus?" We think of camouflage as the ubiquitous blobby patterns that the military love to sport, whether it's practical or not, but it seems when camouflage was invented it had a wider scope. It wasn't just to blend in with the forest or desert. It was also, as it is with many insects, used to confuse front and back, shape (and therefore purpose), and size. There were examples of lovely pop-up tanks and trucks intended to increase the apparent size of convoys and regiments. Potemkin tanks and artillery, which could be collapsed and folded up. A small detachment would carry fake additional vehicles and hope that the enemy, seeing the apparent size of the opposing force, would think better of attacking.

Cultural Stereotypes 1

As I head back to the hotel, the light is fading. The winding side streets are pleasant to ride on, especially in sunny weather. This city is fairly human scale and cottagelike, as C calls it. There must be regulations limiting building height in many neighborhoods. Over the years this has forced the city to sprawl beyond reason, which has in turn increased the traffic. The buildings mostly remain under ten stories, and this scale and the architectural details tell a story about how the English see themselves as a people and as a nation. "We might be sophisticated, posh, and upper class; creative titans; world conquerors and explorers, but at bottom we are all simple country cottage folks." I'm not saying the architecture literally tells a story. I'm not talking about inscriptions engraved on the walls. It's achieved via metaphor. A story told in lintels and windowsills, through the queen—with her dowdy clothes—and the royals' country hunting costumes. The windows everywhere, with lots of little panes and mullions, are significantly more enclosing, sheltering, and comforting than giant modern picture windows. The little panes hark back to the countryside, to a mythical, simple life.

I emerge from the side streets onto big thoroughfares like Regent Street and Piccadilly, which are pretty hairy to ride on with those giant red buses and no bike lanes, but overall I've been lucky with the weather and riding.

I have drinks with Verity McArthur from the Roundhouse, a local venue recently renovated, and Matthew Byam Shaw, a producer of the play *Frost/Nixon,* among others. I meet them at a private club in Covent Garden called the Hospital, apparently thrown up recently by Dave Stewart (Eurythmics) in a former, well, hospital. Almost all the patrons have their laptops out at the lounge tables. They're socializing, e-mailing and instant messaging (I guess), and drinking, all at the same time. Maybe they're all frantically busy with social networking—trying to figure out what to do later in the evening? Or maybe interaction with live people just isn't quite stimulating enough?

The folks here love their private clubs, and they've only admitted women to some of them since the 1980s, or so I am told. The clubs must be a legacy of the class system, which lingers obstinately in so many forms. In this classist view one must separate oneself from the hoi polloi if possible—in speech, in dress, and of course where one drinks. Even if you're not upper class, you need to wall yourself off from those slightly beneath you or even those alongside you who are different in some way. Hipsters need their clubs and workingmen need theirs. Once everyone is in their place—in their appropriate drinking establishment in this case—there is order and peace in the world.

Another remnant of class and caste is the notion that everyone should stay in their place and station. To get involved in areas, jobs, and even (or especially) ideas beyond your station is bad form and is frowned upon. It is viewed as pretentious (if you're going from low to high) and inauthentic (if you're going from high to low). A film on the life of the late Joe Strummer brings out his diplomatic and vaguely upper-class upbringing and how he did a perfect job of hiding it—or at least of keeping it quiet—as it would not have sat well with the image of the anarchic justice-seeking punk hero he was to become. I always found that pure-rogue pose a little suspect regardless of anyone's upbringing, but in later years Strummer and his collaborators ventured into other musical areas that didn't require him to carry the burden of that image of a working-class hero. He seemed liberated in a way. Similarly, Prince Charles gets roasted every time he speaks out about organic farming or the evils of modern architecture and urban planning. The criticism leveled at poor Charles is usually along the lines of "royals should be seen and not heard" more than anything substantive. What difference does it make anyway where you come from? Can't you be judged by what you do, make, and say, and not by what caste you were born into?

All Happy Families Are ... Eccentric

I meet Michael Morris, of the public arts organization Artangel, at a gallery opening. There are security people at the door, and I spy someone holding a guest list. Michael e-mailed me earlier that he'd "put us on the list." For an art gallery opening? Well, lots of New York galleries now have hired security guards, just like museums, so I guess guest lists and velvet ropes are next.

It is a pretty spectacular place, this gallery—floor after floor of exhibition spaces in an industrial zone in funky Hackney, topped by a large room with one glass wall leading to a balcony that looks out over the skyline. Young women with trays offer glasses of champagne. The current show is of paintings by the late Alice Neel, a portrait painter who worked in New York for many decades. She was scorned for her old-fashioned and conservative style—painted portraits—and then, near the end of her life, she experienced a short burst of acceptance. Now, decades later, there is a new appreciation welling up again. Maybe the work looks prescient? Maybe it looks prescient every decade or so, whenever a slew of younger artists do work that is vaguely similar to hers? In that way maybe she's being used to validate the present, and in turn the present is being used to validate the past?

I am introduced to Grayson Perry, the transvestite potter who won the Turner Prize a few years ago. "It's about time a transvestite potter got this prize!" he said when he won. He also said that it was more significant that a potter got the prize than a transvestite. He's right. I have one of his pots. He covers them with images and often with rude texts. Here's one called *Boring Cool People*:

Courtesy Victoria Miro Gallery. © Grayson Perry

He is in full Victorian baby-doll little-girl drag tonight, looking like Alice in Wonderland when she suddenly got big. A blond wig, a floral pinafore frock, and bare legs ending in little pink socks with ruffles and white patent leather Mary Janes. (Where does he get this stuff in his size? Someone must make them by hand. Yes, he confirmed, and they're not cheap.)

He knows that I have one of his pieces, and he was thrilled when he heard that news years ago. I am thrilled to meet him. He is married and has a daughter—I saved a family picture that was in the UK papers when he won the Turner Prize. In the

Ian Hodgson / Reuters

picture, he stands in his dress alongside his attractive and seem-ingly ordinary wife (she's a shrink!), she giving a full-on laugh, and in front is their daughter, beaming a huge smile, obviously happy that Dad has won the most prestigious art prize in the land. Dad puts on an expression of mock horror at all the fuss, but clearly it's all in fun. If this family can be happy—if this family can even exist—then thank God for the English tolera-tion of eccentrics. In another place this lot might be miserable, oppressed, and sequestered. Not all cultural stereotypes—such as the English eccentric—are completely inaccurate or harmful.

We chat casually for a bit and then C suddenly unleashes a volley of what I think of as pretty probing questions: "Do you do a bunch of different characters?" (Yes. The little-girl character is called Claire.) "When did you first start dressing up?" (He was thirteen and he tried on his sister's ballet outfit.)

Front and Back: Cultural Stereotypes 2

Later I have dinner at a hip restaurant where I am sitting close to a largish couple from Northern Ireland, who, to be honest, don't seem to belong in such a groovy temple. (Here I go applying my own class evaluations and stereotypes—what are *they* doing in *this* place?) He's an IT functionary in town for business meetings, and she's along for the ride on the expense account, or so I would guess. They look like northerners on holiday in the big city, but they mention that they're staying next door, at the Ritz, which is more than I would imagine an ordinary regional branch manager could afford. It's way more than I can afford. They explain some of the local dishes to us. Jersey Royals are a miniscule type of potato only available at select times of year. I look over as we talk, and either from a glass of wine or some medical condition the woman has turned bright red all over—face, neck, and arms. But they're both so unassuming, easygoing, and lacking in all pretense that after a minute or two I don't even notice it.

The restaurant has doormen dressed in traditional English tails, as does our hotel. I love the juxtaposition between the two opposing poles of dress and manner: the reserved, polite, perfect, and solicitous staff in contrast with the world of theatrical shock, horror, and gross-out represented by Chapman Bros., Damien Hirst, Amy Winehouse, chavs, and football hooligans. It all has to come out, I guess—the bigger the front the bigger the back. You can't have one without the other. I'm reminded of the ads that plaster the phone booths offering spankings and humiliation. One assumes that for an upper-class type especially, keeping it all in and maintaining that reserve can get to be a bit much sometimes, so one needs to be put in one's place artificially and theatrically to somewhat redress the balance of power. I'm jumping to national stereotypes myself here.

In Venezuela there are chains of coffee shops where the clientele, almost exclusively male, is waited on by attractive women in tight outfits. The twist—what separates this chain from ordinary coffee shops—is that the interior architecture allows the female waitstaff to tower over the men. The women are positioned behind the counter on a slightly elevated platform. This means the typical Latin macho man is either being put in his place, and enjoying it, or that he is being transported back to his childhood, where his primary view is of his mother's breasts looming conveniently above him.

Toffs and Yobs: Cultural Stereotypes 3

We go for drinks at a nice place in Soho, a white tablecloth place, but nothing hoity-toity. However, after a few minutes, while we are having a drink, a couple of football louts stroll in, shoulders back, tense, tattooed, and possibly a little high. They scope out the place briefly and then begin shouting something to the effect of "come the revolution you lot will all be sorry." There is a short face-off with the poor gay maître d', who backs away—he's sure he's going to get punched—as the rest of the staff reach for their phones.

The yobs push farther into the restaurant and toss out a few more choice insults toward the worried diners. (The restaurant is next door to the Ivy, a scenester hangout. Maybe the anarchist louts got the address wrong?)

Nothing happens, and the pair wanders out. I smile at one, but he murmurs something about "yer all gonna get it," which seems bad manners, to say the least. No policeman inside these fellows.

They're gone, and the maître d' apologizes to the customers and then disappears and we never see him again.

British class antagonism lives on. It keeps the yobs in their place and makes the toffs nervously squirm in theirs. No wonder they like private clubs!

Later in the evening I dismantle my bike in the hotel room. The seat, handlebars, and wheels pop off and then it folds into a large suitcase. Time to go home to New York. Sometimes the hotel staff doesn't like me bringing a bike inside, but often it arrives hidden in its big suitcase so they haven't a clue that I'm up in the room with an Allen wrench and rubber gloves to keep the grease off my hands, assembling—or in this case, disassembling—my means of transport.

The businessman across from me in the Heathrow lounge is making baby sounds into his cell phone.

I pick up a copy of *Newsweek* on the plane and immediately notice how biased, slanted, and opinionated all the U.S. newsmagazine articles are. Not that the Euro and British press aren't biased as well—they certainly are—but living in the United States we are led to believe, and are constantly reminded, that our press is fair and free of bias. After such a short time away, I am shocked at how obviously and blatantly this lie is revealed—there is the "reporting" that is essentially parroting what the White House press secretary announces; the myriad built-in assumptions that one ceases to register after being somewhere else for a while. The myth of neutrality is an effective blanket for a host of biases.

On arriving in New York one immediately sees that the labor and service jobs are almost all being done by African Americans and recent immigrants. The first things you notice in the airport corridors are ads and banks of TVs on which CNN or Fox News is running constantly. The propaganda blast starts the minute one steps off the plane—there's no option except to be inundated.

There is, however, the almost welcome third-world aspect of New York that mitigates this obnoxious propaganda just a little bit—the clunky lopsided baggage carts you have to pay for, (despite most people not having dollars yet), the touts offering rides, and the generally aggressive chaotic hubbub—cursing, shouting, pushing, and shoving—as the exhausted foreign traveler wonders how in the world he or she is going to get home. This anarchic arrival must be frightening to a foreigner, but to me it's almost a welcome relief. It's honest, crude—the whole city as one big souk.

San Francisco

I t was raining when I arrived here last night, but today the weather has cleared up and this city sparkles with that crystalline northern Californian light that makes everything pop out from the background. All the buildings and people have hard, crisp edges. It's bucolic and hard to believe—a picture postcard, unreal. The folding bike I brought will come in handy.

San Francisco is philosophically and politically bike-friendly, but not geographically—the famous hills can make one think twice about some trips around town, even though the city proper is concentrated like Manhattan, or a European city. The local cycling organization has issued a wonderful map that shows, by the deepness of the red shading, the steepness of the streets. A street shaded light pink is a mild slope, but a dark red street is a major hill to be avoided unless you're a masochist. Luckily, this map allows one to plan a hill-free trip at a glance. I wouldn't have thought so, but one can plot a route to and from almost anywhere and avoid the worst hills—almost.

My friend Melanie C arranges a field trip to Apple headquarters in Cupertino, just south of here, and lunch with their chief designer Jonathan Ive. Ive's team designed the original iMac and its successors, the original iBook and its successors, the Power Mac, the Power Mac G4 Cube, the PowerBook, the iPod family, and more.

Ive does a brief show-and-tell with a deconstructed Power-Book, showing us how even the inside is thoughtfully and elegantly designed. He seems as proud of the intricate foldings and stampings of the invisible insides as he is of the elegant exterior. His point is that the design goes clear through: it's not merely an appliqué on the outside to make it all seem groovy, but extends into stuff most of us will never ever see. In the Bauhaus and Wiener Werkstätte circles, extraneous decoration was verboten—thought to be inessential and superfluous to the integrity of the object or architecture—and therefore it had to go. Adolf Loos famously equated decoration with the devil. Might Ive's pride at the thorough design of the PowerBooks harbor a little of that legacy?

I don't think this show-and-tell is all just ego and pride. Ive implies that the elegant insides actually make the thing work better too—that good design equals better functioning—that if the true path of good design is followed scrupulously, then not only does the thing look very cool, but it is also a better object all around. Not only has the devil of superfluous decor been banished, but there is also the implication that good design is therefore morally good too—it's on the side of the angels. It feels a little bit like he's done this presentation before, but it's a beautiful piece of work all the same. I suspect, however, that we're not going to hear him or anyone else think out loud about what they're actually working on at the moment, and say, for example, "Now if we could get all this into a phone . . ." (This was pre-iPhone, mind you.)

I mention that I am in the midst of a collaboration with Fatboy Slim (whose real name is Norman Cook) and Jonathan says he is having dinner tonight with his friend John Digweed, one of the world's top electronic DJs and a pal of Norman's. At first I am mildly surprised. I wonder if Jonathan listens to dance music as he designs? But then I see this guy in front of me with short-cropped hair and a T-shirt and realize that, yeah, he looks like a slightly older version of any British club kid. Wonder if it gets boring for him here in Cupertino?

Cupertino is south of San Francisco and west of San Jose. What little town there is lies nestled among the coastal hills and wineries. There isn't much here—some business campuses, malls, and an amazing Asian grocery store. The rolling hills to the west are home to many of the new mansions that the technocrats have built. Not so far away are Hewlett-Packard, Google, Sun Microsystems, and the other Silicon Valley companies that have turned the area that previously was known as the home of Stanford University and the sleepy little town of San Jose into a computer and IT powerhouse. The area features an intense confluence of engineers, nerds, techies, entrepreneurs, visionaries, and hangers-on.

From what I can tell, there's really not much to do around this part of the bay. I ride my bike fairly aimlessly down clean, spotless arteries and see no one around—not walking or biking anyway. All roads lead to places that are versions of what I just left. I ask if folks here go up to San Francisco to catch shows, exhibits, or to sample the wildly innovative cuisine in the San Francisco restaurants. Nope, these folks just love their work, so they stay put here in the beautiful suburbs, working late, or they take their work home.

There are massive amounts of money here. In the era of the Carnegies, Fricks, Mellons, Dukes, and Lauders, billionaires would make a visible fuss of supporting the local art museum, hospital, library, or other charitable institution or cause—as Bill Gates has done with his Gates Foundation and Paul Allen did with the Experience Music Project. But for the most part I get the feeling that this bunch prefers facing the challenges within their own chosen fields—software development, Internet technology, cool gizmos, and what happens when you bring all those together. I get the feeling that at least some of them don't really care that much about all the money they are making either—they're too busy to count it. It's all about as real as Second Life.

I remember San Francisco during the earlier dot-com boom. Back then everyone was going to start their own online business and the world was going to change overnight and investors were lining up to throw money at every geek with a vague idea, a pitch, and some programming skills. The fervor and enthusiasm at that time might have had parallels with the Manhattan Project and the zeal focused on developing the atomic bomb. That is, it was exciting and potentially world changing. But here that same missionary passion was embodied in the wacky inventor/entrepreneur. There were Web site proposals for anything and everything—services for your pets or ones that would run all your errands for you. The future seemed preordained—no one was ever going to have to leave their house ever again. Every idea was a great idea, earthshaking, revolutionary. It's no wonder the Web world is sometimes described as a legacy of the hippie era—but with more expensive toys.

It's no accident that the humble garage where Bill Hewlett and Dave Packard began their partnership in Palo Alto is an icon here. Like Sun Studio in Memphis, where rock and roll was

David Paul Morris / Getty Images

born, or Menlo Park, New Jersey, where Edison lit up the world, this funky little garage is revered partly because it's nothing special. Its ordinariness is the point. Their first product was an audio oscillator for testing sound equipment. HP refers to it as "the tone heard round the world."

The garage is considered the birthplace of Silicon Valley, which makes it the perfect visual metaphor for the anyone-can-do-it doctrine that is still alive and well around here. Start small, think big. Think out of the box. Think different.

They're all hippie sentiments, reworded.

In the first dot-com boom, real estate prices in a hemmed-in city like San Francisco (or Manhattan) naturally went through the roof. Kids just out of school who were outside the dot-com world—young artists, musicians, writers, actors, eccentrics, and bohemians, the kind of folks for which this city was previously known (and who may have been the inspiration for the dot-commers)—got pushed to the margins or over to Oakland and elsewhere.

In the late 1990s it all crashed, but the real estate prices never went back down to what they once were. The vast numbers of bohemian free spirits never moved back after they'd been displaced. The world did change quite a bit in the first dot-com revolution, but not as thoroughly, radically, and completely as some imagined. Not everyone was ready to live entirely online quite as fast as some had wagered.

Maybe with Web 2.0, with its more socially interactive and responsive commerce-based Web sites—and with WiFi and faster bandwidth more widely available—some of those imagined changes in our lives might actually occur, but not with the stuff the first revolution promised. Who wants videocassettes delivered to their house in under fifteen minutes anymore?

Paradoxically, as it does get easier and easier to marshal all sorts of services from our phones or laptops and access limitless information, the interest and demand for the stuff that can't be digitized becomes greater: live performances, face-to-face gatherings, interactions, experiences, taste, tranquility. Those who frequent social networking sites come to value authenticity as a kind of compensation, since those qualities can be faked all too easily online.

Let's Get Lost

The proselytizing and the we're-gonna-change-the-world fervor, the ardor, and the nerdy zeal of the digerati do indeed seem to have been carried over from the various streams of eccentric enthusiasms endemic to this neck of the woods.

Fringe groups have long been a tradition here. Even if it's exaggerated by those who aren't comfortable in this town (land of fruits and nuts) the Bay Area has a reputation for hosting cosmic anarchic spectacles of all types. Years ago there was the Temple of the People—not to be confused with the People's Temple and the Kool-Aid of death. This earlier temple was originally based near Pismo Beach and was mainly influenced by theosophy, a kind of ad hoc mishmash of many religions and philosophies founded by Madam Helena Blavatsky in the 1870s.

From a very different impulse and world came a not-so-dissimilar group. The Bohemian Grove encampments—rural retreats for the rich and powerful members of the San Francisco–based Bohemian Club—were also begun in the 1870s and still exist today. They feature performances and rituals in a woodland grove. Many U.S. presidents have attended these events, and the planning of the Manhattan Project began there. It's all very secretive, and although networking is strongly discouraged, it's hard to imagine that some bonds don't get cemented out among the redwoods. If you went camping with Henry Kissinger wouldn't you feel like you'd shared a common experience?

Though the Beats were largely based in New York it was in San Francisco that many of the readings and settings for their books took place—here the Wild West met the cosmic East. So

North Beach, with its Italian espresso bars and the nearby seedy dives of Broadway, is often more identified with that movement than New York is. Somehow the perception is that there was also an unbroken flow from the Beat generation straight on to the peace and love era a decade later. Neal Cassady—Jack Kerouac's model for *On the Road*'s Dean Moriarty—was indeed "on the bus" with Ken Kesey, whose legendary acid tests featured the Grateful Dead—so it's not that far-fetched an idea. The '60s here produced the psychedelic rock movement, underground comics, psychedelic posters, the *Whole Earth Catalog,* be-ins, and the anarchic camp spectaculars created by the Cockettes, a legendary drag musical theatrical troupe.

To imply that there is a link between the Cockettes and the dot-com world might seem a stretch to some, but the underlying theme of revolution for the hell of it runs straight through them all. The free-for-all of the blogosphere and the sheer nuttiness of the stuff that people post online partakes of a fair-sized hit of whatever. The sense of anarchic freedom prevails . . . and, I have to add, this bunch is okay with bicycles.

I first came out here in the early '70s, lured by the hippie eco techno worldview embodied by the *Whole Earth Catalog.* I joined a friend in an attempt to build a dome in a field up in Napa County. I eventually lost focus on the dome project and ended up busking with another friend on the streets of Berkeley—he played accordion, I played violin and ukulele and struck ironic poses. It was successful. I realized that at that time I was more interested in irony than utopia.

The Dark Heart of Peace and Love

I visit Mark Pauline at the warehouse base of his art performance organization Survival Research Laboratories. I've never managed to catch one of their public spectacles, but have read loads of interviews, watched videos, and heard accounts of awe-inspiring mayhem.

On arrival, the place looks like an ordinary urban low-industrial building with an awful lot of machinery scattered here and there outside, most of it under wraps. Mark leads me from machine to machine explaining what each one does. One shoots balls of molten copper hundreds of feet and another shoots a giant flame eighty-some feet. They're glorious and frightening. Shock and awe for the hell of it. Well, it is beautiful too.

The following comes from their Web site:

One of the main projects at SRL over the past year has been rebuilding the V-1. The V-1 was manufactured at SRL in 1990. It has served as both a high-powered, low frequency generator and a flamethrower/shockwave device in many SRL shows since that time. The design of the SRL V-1 pulsejet itself was based on dimensions gathered by

The V1. Image courtesy Survival Research Laboratories, photo by Karen Marcelo

American military and intelligence teams following WW2. It is an exact replica of the original German design.

The [SRL] makeshift assembly worked well enough, other than the unnerving fact that each time the engine was run for any length of time, several valves would break off and disappear. This would reduce the output of the machine after about 30 minutes of use—enough operating time for an SRL show, but a potential safety hazard for the audience.

These little hints about safety hazards and looming danger of course make the SRL projects all the more alluring. One unusual machine shoots a doughnut of compressed air. Mark described it as a kind of high-velocity, doughnut-shaped tornado. It can shatter glass when it hits a sheet of it flat on, but, when directed at people, Mark says it's like being hit by a pillow. Of course, after witnessing an invisible burst shatter some glass, most people are terrified of this thing, even though, not being rigid like a piece of glass, they can't be hurt.

One of the most unusual items is the pitching machine (see next page). It uses a V-8 car engine to rev up two wheels, one on top of the other, to a superhigh speed. Then two-by-fours are fed into the gap and—*wham!*—they're ejected at incredible speed. An ejected two-by-four can penetrate steel. This machine, made out of commercially available car parts, is a serious weapon.

Needless to say, not too many museums or public programs are open to the idea of hosting an SRL show these days. It probably looks to an official arts organization like something that could easily be misconstrued as a how-to manual for maniacs and terrorists. Even though they take all necessary precautions to ensure that spectators can't be hurt, the very nature of their performances are about extreme power, violence, and danger— and our attraction to those things.

San Francisco has always had its dark side. There have always been gangs, subcultures, and fringe weirdness coupled

Pitching Machine. Image courtesy Survival Research Laboratories, photo by Karen Marcelo

with a desire to flirt with the forbidden and dangerous. Sometimes this impulse was about the idea that everything and every experience should be available to be known and that nothing should be forbidden. In this view one certainly couldn't trust the government or the church to dictate what experiences might be pleasurable or useful, so best to just allow or try everything. Some experiential and psychic explorers had wonderful insights and epiphanies, and they did break through to the other side, and some ended up with Jim Jones at the People's Temple. The openness to the world of experience and to wide varieties of expression in this beautiful city can easily spill over into playing with fire—and denying that you might get seriously burned. Not that Mark and the SRL folks are dark or evil, but their machines certainly flirt with that power and mythology. It's potent stuff.

San Francisco isn't the only place where light and dark are equally alluring, but it does seem that maybe here, more than in many other places—with the bright Mediterranean light, nearby ocean, and tolerant atmosphere—those forbidden fruits really flourish. Is it the fact that this town is about as far as you can get from Europe and the East Coast and still be on the mainland that allows all those groups to be semi-accepted and tolerated? There's almost an admiration and respect for eccentricity and obsessive independent spirits here, whereas in a lot of other places independence and freedom are given lip service but that's about it.

I bike over to an alternative arts center called CELLspace where the publisher McSweeney's has organized an event. The venue is a warehouse in a neighborhood of warehouses. I read from a book I've written and show PowerPoint slides as if I am a somewhat deranged motivational or religious speaker. Afterward all the other participants and I sign our books at a table, which is a little bit of a letdown after the nuttiness of the main event. Just as I become resigned to the business of signing books, a marching band bursts through the front doors and begins to play and "parade." The Extra Action Marching Band has been at a street festival nearby and decided to stage an "intervention," as they do from time to time—bringing a pleasant dose of music, anarchy, and baton-twirling girls in skimpy outfits to random events that they have decided need enlivening. Their playing has a great groove—Brazilian, Balkan, and original tunes all mashed together. The flag girls and boys and the baton girls are all in real marching band outfits combined with sequined G-strings, and somehow their twisted and skewed take on this all-American institution brings together a natural nostalgia for the thrilling sound of marching bands and the hedonistic sensual and sexual anarchy that is endemic to the Bay Area. Before too long I end up standing on a table dancing.

After the show is over I go to the band's rehearsal/living

space in the Bernal Heights neighborhood where the Extra Action folks and their pals are having a party with live music—one band called Loop!Station consists of a guy playing cello through electronics accompanied by a young woman who manages to smile almost all the time while she sings. She says hi afterward and is still grinning. There is a genuine San Francisco light show in one room. Part of it consists of two movies projected onto the same screen on top of each other. And on another wall a projection through oil and water makes an old-school light show of blobby shapes. The Extra Action band regroup and perform another short set—how they have the energy after having played twice earlier (it is after two AM at this point) I don't know. Their music and show seem to generate energy rather than use it up.

I have the feeling I have entered a chaotic and somewhat sexy utopia. People have on all sorts of getups—Victorian hats and fake mustaches on some of the men, wigs on some of the women, and some folks wear not much at all. Haircut styles are all over the place. I am in a baby blue western jacket and golf shoes. The music is varied, and it is made with and generates sheer joy—that singer isn't the only one smiling.

Why do scenes like this develop here more than elsewhere? One of the Extra Action players has some connection with Survival Research Laboratories, which might be seen as a slightly more dangerous variation of this same impulse for release; a similar liberating, wild energy is let loose in both cases.

Machines That Deceive

Somehow, all this ecstatic anarchy leads me to wonder if the computational models of the brain have reached a stumbling block, a dead end, with recent attempts to untangle creativity. I suspect that to imagine, and thus to create, one has to envision something that doesn't exist yet. Fictionalizing is thus very close to lying—it's imagining the existence of something that isn't literally true, and writing or speaking about it as if it is real. Most fiction aims to tell us a story in a way that leads us to believe it is happening or has happened. The motivations behind storytelling and lying are different, but the creative process behind them is the same.

To have a truly creative machine we will inevitably end up with something like HAL, one that cannot only compute, calculate, and sort through a massive amount of information, but can also imagine, create, lie, and deceive. From the machine's point of view there might not be any way of telling the difference between imagining and fibbing.

We meat puppets have our morals, instincts, laws, and taboos to keep us in line, which are by nature human centered and therefore not universal. We would like to think that morals and taboos are God given and applicable to all human beings, but they really are just what's good for us as a species—or sometimes only good for our tribe, nation, or particular geographical area. Well, this creative machine will have to be endowed with some equivalent to those laws and injunctions too. In addition, if it is to create in a way that we recognize it will also need to experience fear, love, hunger, and sadness. Our instincts and impulses, our gut feelings, are all part of how we think, how we make decisions and reason. We are guided by irrational impulses and emotions just as much as by logical analysis, so for a machine to truly think like us it will have to think emotionally at least as much as it does rationally. You can probably see where this argument is going.

Machines that create might then need the whole kit and caboodle of human institutions—genetic motivations, social lives, and even a form of sex (desire, longing, mating, offspring)—in order to evolve religious and social networks that might serve, as they do for us, to temper the hatreds, deceptions, and narcissism that will inevitably emerge from this Pandora's box. These social structures would only mitigate antisocial tendencies somewhat, as those same structures do with people. We can only make creatures in our own image—we cannot do otherwise—and the shit we sometimes get up to will be passed on to these "beings" as well.

A counterargument to that sad conclusion might claim that if a bicycle is, for example, an improvement on legs, then maybe we can indeed invent some things that are better than ourselves? Well, physically, anyway. That's toolmaking, I guess. Crows and chimps both fashion devices that reach where their beaks or fingers cannot, but that's hardly godlike. For that, one would have to make a machine that is emotionally and creatively "better" than we are. If it was, if we succeeded, there's a good chance we probably wouldn't be able to recognize the improvement.

Escape from Alcatraz

I bike over to the Taqueria Cancun, which has incredible tacos and burritos. Your choice of meat fillings—carne asada, pork, or chicken, naturally, but also head, tongue, and brains. Then I put the bike onto a Muni bus, all of which have bike racks up front (!). The bus I've chosen heads across the Golden Gate Bridge to Sausalito and Marin County. There are bike trails all over the headlands and around western Marin, much of which has been left as national preserve. One can spot hawks, vultures, mountain lions, and seals. The trails swoop and drop around and over the fog-swept barren hills. Eventually most of the paths end up dipping down to some little cove or hidden beach. From inside the headland hills you can't see the city at all; even the Golden Gate Bridge is hidden.

With the brisk air and the mist it reminds me of the bleak but beautiful Scottish highlands, though the rain drizzles less often here. In Scotland, as in Iceland and Ireland, there were once forests that covered the hills, but gradually they were all cut down, leaving a beautiful and strangely otherworldly terrain. There's no denying that the legacy of man's destruction

is sometimes beautiful. Strip mines and dams are powerfully impressive. The sheep that now graze on the windswept slopes of Scotland ensure that no tree will manage to grow higher than a shoot, so even if a sapling could manage to get a grip on the boggy soil its chances of survival are slim.

Here it is not as rainy, so the hills have not turned to peat bogs, and there are clumps of trees in the valleys among the scattered bunkers—built to defend against the imminent Japanese invasion.

Inside and Outside

I bike down Mission Street into the SoMa district. It's midday and fairly warm, but passing an area of leather bars I see there

Judith Scott, *Untitled*, 2001, courtesy Creative Growth Art Center

are guys standing outside in full macho gay regalia. They must be suffering on a hot day like this, but maybe that's the point. This part of town is flat, as it was created by landfill dumped over the rotting hulls of ships, so it feels different, slightly outside of the center of town, even though it's right next to it. I stop to see an art show at the Yerba Buena Center featuring work that comes out of a place in Oakland called Creative Growth. Creative Growth is a visual arts center for people who are mentally and/or psychologically challenged. As a fan of a lot of what is often called outsider art I love some of this work.

One of these artists, Judith Scott, obsessively wrapped things in yarn and twine, creating almost life-sized cocoons that are powerful, affecting, and sort of creepy. Giant totemic objects, talismans that seem to hold some mysterious personal juju.

Another man, Dwight Mackintosh, did drawings that,

Dwight Mackintosh, *Untitled*, 1995, courtesy Creative Growth Art Center

as one studies them, are revealed to be composed of many layers of images, like stop-motion photos, all transparent and superimposed. They're like those images that we've seen in old animated cartoons when a character moves super-rapidly and you see a dozen images of the character's legs simultaneously, all overlapping to indicate speed. In Mackintosh's line drawings there are so many arms and legs overlapping it's hard at first to tell exactly what motion is being depicted or what the character is doing. Then it becomes clear—that's a hand, that's a . . . oh, it's a penis. They're all masturbating. At high speed, it seems.

The term *outsider,* as it is used in the art world, means "we are not sure this belongs in here, the artist is untrained, and maybe naive, but have a look." It also sometimes implies self-taught and probably insane or not socially functioning in the accepted sense. (That could include a lot of us.)

On a nearby wall there are a series of black-and-white photos of the Creative Growth artists. Some of these photos I find disturbing. Not having seen what the artists look like previously, just having been moved deeply by their work, I mentally place and rank them alongside the best contemporary artists practicing today. Qualitatively, objectively, I don't see any difference between their work and that of mainstream fine artists— except for the fact that there is no work here that deals with the hermetic and convoluted dramas of the art world itself. This, for me, is no great loss; in fact it's more or less a plus—though some self-reflexive art is indeed funny. Anyway, I half expect them to look "normal," or at least like other artists I know.

However, seeing the picture of Judith Scott, who has Down syndrome, makes me realize that many of these folks could never function in the gallery/museum system.

There, then, is what relegates them as outsiders. These artists may not have the perspective on their work that we expect a professional artist to have—not that most professional artists can talk lucidly about their own work either, but professionals

courtesy Leon Borensztein and Creative Growth Art Center

at least have a sense of how their work fits into the world at large, or into the art market, and can fake the talk pretty well. We presume that the work of a professional artist is slightly separate from the artist as a person—you don't have to know about Picasso's mistresses and his psychological hang-ups and obsessions to like his paintings. With the Creative Growth artists and some other outsiders, however, it seems that for many people, personal information about the artist is considered essential to judging, evaluating, and understanding her work. The fact that they are self-taught, "crazy," grew up in a swamp, or worked during the day as a janitor is somehow considered relevant. Jackson Pollock worked as a janitor at an elementary school in New York, and probably stole some paint from there too, but wall plaques in museums don't describe him as a former janitor. While professional artists distance themselves and their lives somewhat from their work, Judith obviously has an intimate relationship with hers that I imagine many professionals might envy and wish they could have.

Though some professionals claim they'd like to eliminate the gap, and work in the territory between art and life as Bob Rauschenberg once claimed, these folks have never even left that gap—for them it's not a gap but a deep chasm.

Comparisons between these artists and art professionals begs the question: what is sanity, and does being dysfunctional sometimes make you a better artist? I don't think it does, though the Van Gogh myth of the crazy (genius) artist remains alive and well. I think those questions, that dichotomy between intention and result, might be irrelevant. For me, a stain on the sidewalk or a blob of construction insulation may have an aesthetic value equal to some works by Franz West, for example. One just happens to be on a stand in a museum and the other is usually found discarded in a vacant lot. My definition of what is good art is, I'm afraid, pretty wide, and it isn't determined by the biography of its creator. Sometimes, for me, art doesn't even need an author. I don't care who or what made it. For me the art happens between the thing—any thing—and the viewer's eye (or mind). Who or what made it is irrelevant. I don't need to see their CV to like it. But I have to admit that sometimes the artist's story, if I am informed of it, adds to and affects what I see.

If you obsessively scribble on bits of paper, as hugely successful artist Louise Bourgeois does some of the time (to pick an obvious example), is your work better than some very similar work by one of the folks at Creative Growth because you have more objectivity about your own work? Is scribbling better art when it has a conscious intention? Is it better work when you're aware that you're scribbling and could do other kinds of drawing if you really wanted to? I don't think there is any way one could objectively say that of the two works one is better or worse than the other. Louise Bourgeois certainly does other kinds of work too, which might make some kind of difference, at least to some people, but the biggest difference I can come up with is that presumably she decided to make her obsessive scribbles consciously, and deliberately, and, we assume (big assumption here), wasn't simply driven to make the marks by some unconscious impulse. This is really a big assumption, especially in her case, because she makes a big deal about her fucked-up childhood, so maybe she needs to scribble just as much as the Creative Growth folks.

And the real question is, would it make any difference if she does?

Social functionality, to me, is the key word in the inside/outside dichotomy, not sanity. Many "sophisticated" and successful gallery artists are quite mad, lost in their own worlds, and often they are emotional wrecks—but they do know how to navigate the shoals and reefs of the art world. Well, a bit. They can compose themselves and posture sufficiently to get by, to talk the talk and walk the walk, though some of the successful ones might also be drooling drug addicts and conversational incompetents.

For the folks at Creative Growth making art is therapeutic. I would argue that it is equally therapeutic for the professional artist. I can personally testify that making music and performing have kept me more or less sane and allowed me a measure of social contact I might otherwise never have had. (Viewing art, however, is not therapeutic, nor does collecting art have any morally uplifting value—but that's another topic. But the act of making it is.)

I'm not sure I know anyone, anyone at all, who is completely sane. Sure, I know plenty of people who play the sanity game with skill and daring. Their masks of having it together are well secured, and they don't spit out profanities or stare googly-eyed into space. Above all they have learned to function well enough socially to be accepted as "normal." My friends are not an exclusively eccentric arty crowd either—most are what would be referred to as normal.

The poor outsiders never learned or mastered those social skills. Even a would-be self-marketer like the Reverend Howard Finster of Somerville, Georgia, never quite got that part right. Either his preaching and ranting got in the way—fire and brimstone don't mix well with white wine and cheese—or he didn't realize that in the art world, one simply can't be seen as blatantly hawking one's wares, which Howard didn't mind doing because he saw his work as serving a greater glory. He was proselytizing; he wasn't really pushing "himself."

There's an elaborate song and dance involved in passing for a professional artist. One needs to veil the sales pitch, for starters, and that protocol, those dance steps, must be mastered, as is true in any profession. But one can be mad and self-obsessed, can believe in other worlds and the influence of supernatural forces, and still be regarded as a respected, "sane" artist—no problem.

Sophisticated artists who can draw well—Klee, Basquiat, Twombly, Dubuffet—often intentionally draw in a more "primitive" manner. They are seen, partly due to the rough nature of their mark making, as tapping into something deep and profound. The crude lines imply that one is in touch with unconscious forces that won't submit to the urgings and smoothing tendencies of craft and skill. It's not an unreasonable or completely untrue idea, either; funky drawing does push some elemental buttons, and maybe the work of these artists does come from a deep and profound place that won't submit to polishing. I'm not saying they're fakers. I'm simply noting what their kind of gestures connote.

The generally accepted idea is that if it's rough, it must be more real, more authentic. Yet the poor outsiders, whose marks are very often every bit as unpolished, can't help how they draw—they couldn't make a clean line if they had to. So they are left out of the art "club." They are doing the very best they can but because their lack of exhibited drafting skill is, we believe, not their choice, they are often viewed as lesser artists. They can't help drawing crazy shit, while the sophisticated artists could, at least so we imagine, draw a nice puppy if they had to. It would seem to be all about intention. And yet, these outsider artists most certainly have intention. They know when a line is right or when it's "untrue" according to their personal standards. They have definite intentions to achieve a very specific visual look and effect—at least one would assume so given that they often labor mightily to re-create that look again and again.

This aesthetic segregation seems perverse. I enjoy much of the work of the four very successful professional artists mentioned above, but probably what moves me is when their work touches something deep that we all have in common. It is the same something that the outsiders sometimes tickle and activate in the very same way—proof that these charged marks and images can resonate with nearly anyone. They touch those same deep, dark parts of themselves and ourselves. The difference is the poor loonies can't remove themselves from the experience of communicating with extremes of dark or light and step back and away from it. To distance oneself, to feign objectivity, this, then, is the mark of a "civilized" person. It's a useful, possibly essential, social skill to have, but it's not, in my opinion, a criterion by which to judge creative work.

The great works of antiquity, the classics, could have been made by nameless (to us) skilled obsessive nutters—many of their personal stories are certainly lost to history. So maybe they could have been complete misfits too—but who cares?

On the next page is a painting made by a migraine sufferer. It depicts—so we are told—not a metaphorical interpretation of the headache but a realistic depiction of what the sufferer sees when the migraine strikes.

It makes one wonder if Braque and other cubists suffered

courtesy Migraine Action

from migraines and were painting what they actually saw. Would that make a difference? Would we think less of them as artists if that were the case?

The crossover between inside and out is not just confined to the visual arts. Beckett, Joyce, and Gertrude Stein produced obsessive and inscrutable works—but they managed to function and even won prizes for work that many still call mad. Whether something is made by a sophisticate or by a person who is functionally challenged, in recent decades it often comes out the same. And, as time passes, traditional skill and craft become less desirable qualities, and expression, truth, and emotion are deemed more important. Artists and writers are encouraged to dive into their inner depths, so it shouldn't be surprising at all if some of the same strange fish are caught. The creatures from the deep can be pretty disturbing and wacky, but we all recognize some part of ourselves in them, no matter who dragged them up.

As my friend C points out, it's fairly common for someone to attempt to denigrate someone else's creative work by claiming, "They're not a nice person." It's as if the fact that someone has a lousy personality, is a bad father, engages in phone sex, or is obsessed with little boys or little girls implies that their work is therefore less good. Does it? Surely no one cares if an artist is merely a little stingy or is gay or not anymore. Most people would say that those bits of information are often irrelevant and have no bearing on whether they like the work or not, or whether it should be taken seriously or not.

But doesn't the fact that Ezra Pound made radio broadcasts in support of the Fascists or that Neil Young was a Ronald Reagan supporter or that some composers and artists apologized for Stalin—or even for Hitler—make their work suspect, even worthless in some cases for many of us? At what point does the extra-creative activity of the person begin to make a difference in how we perceive their work? This question presumes that those political sympathies or sexual perversions actually show up in the work—and I'm not even talking about work that is blatantly propagandistic. If we opt to denigrate Speer's monumental architecture then there are a whole lot of other architects who, judging by the way their work looks, are equally "Fascist," and many of them are working today.

Where does one draw the line? Should we only judge by what is in front of us?

A History of PowerPoint

I do a talk about the computer presentation program PowerPoint at the University of California in Berkeley for an audience of IT legends and academics. I have, over a couple of years, made little "films" in this program normally used by businesspeople or academics for slide shows and presentations. In my pieces I made the graphic arrows and the corny backgrounds dissolve and change without anyone having to click on the next slide. These content-less "presentations" run by themselves. I also attached music files—sound tracks—so the pieces are like little abstract art films that play off the familiar (to some people) style of this program. I removed, or rather never included, what is usually considered "content," and what is left is the medium that delivers that content. In a situation like this one here in Berkeley one is usually asked to talk about one's work, but rather than do that I have decided to tell the history of the computer program itself. I tell who invented it and who refined it and I offer some subjective views on the program—my own and those of its critics and supporters.

I am terrified. Many of the guys that originally turned Power-Point into a software program are present. What are they going to think of what I did with their invention? Well, couldn't they just get up to talk about it? They could call me out and denounce me!

Luckily, I'm not talking about the details of the programming but about the ubiquity of the software and how, because of what it does and how it does it, it limits what can be presented—and therefore what is discussed. All media do this to some extent—they do certain things well and leave other things out altogether. This is not news, but by bringing this up, reminding everyone, I hope to help dispel the myth of neutrality that surrounds many software programs.

I also propose that a slide talk, the context in which this software is used, is a form of contemporary theater—a kind of ritual theater that has developed in boardrooms and academia rather than on the Broadway stage. No one can deny that a talk is a performance, but again there is a pervasive myth of objectivity and neutrality to deal with. There is an unspoken prejudice at work in those corporate and academic "performance spaces"—that performing is acting and therefore it's not "real." Acknowledging a talk as a performance is therefore anathema. I want to dispel this myth of authenticity somewhat, in an entertaining and gentle way.

The talk goes fine. I can relax, they're laughing. Bob Gaskins, Dennis Austin, and Peter Norvig are all here. Bob Gaskins was one of the guys who refined the original program and realized its potential. Bob declined to be introduced, so I stick with a picture of a concertina when I mention his name. (He's retired and buys and sells antique concertinas now.) That gets a laugh. He tells me afterward that he likes the PowerPoint-as-theater idea, which is a relief. I mean, there is a lot of hatred for this program out there, and a lot of people laugh at the mere mention of bullet points, so he must feel kind of vulnerable.

In working on these pieces, and others, I have become aware that there is a pyramid of control and influence that exists between text, image, and sound. I note that today we give text a preferential position: a label under an image "defines" that image even if it contradicts what we can see. I wonder, in a time before text became ubiquitous, was image (a symbol, a gesture, a sign) the most influential medium? Did sound—singing, chanting, rhythm—come in second, and text, limited as it might have been thousands of years ago, come in third? Was text once a handmaiden to image and sound and then gradually managed to usurp their places and take control? Did the pyramid of communicative power at some point become inverted?

Wittgenstein famously said, "The limits of my language are the limits of my mind. All I know is what I have words for." I am a prisoner of my language.

This presupposes that conscious thought cannot happen without verbal or written language. I disagree. I sense a lot of communication goes on nonverbally—and I don't mean winks and nods. I mean images get ahold of us, as do sounds. They grab and hold us emotionally. Smells too. They can grip in a way that is hard to elucidate verbally. But maybe for Ludwig it just wasn't happening. Or maybe because he couldn't express what sounds, smells, and images do in words he chose to ignore them, to deny that they were communicating.

Let's Open a Club!

I hail a cab and fold my bike, throw it in the trunk, and head back to San Francisco. The cabdriver would be perfect cast as Ignatius from the novel *A Confederacy of Dunces.* He's a large man wearing big shades, with a shaved head and, on this unusually hot day for San Francisco, a rolled-up, wooly winter hat. He recognizes me and tells me he knows that the lead guitarist from Talking Heads lives in Marin (he means Jerry Harrison). He also knows where Dana Carvey lives, so he proceeds to try to convince me to get together with Dana and start a club. "Nice tables, some drinks, some comedy, and good, wholesome music: how could we lose?"

Then he moves on to discuss the "negro infection," by which I think he means the lewd and violent lyrics of gangsta rap. His own musical favorite is Huey Lewis, whom he thinks needs to be played on the radio more. He suggests that maybe Huey and I could both play at the club, yeah!

At the airport, my flight is delayed, and I can hear the businessman behind me saying, "Isn't that the worst slide you've ever seen?" as he holds up a printout of a PowerPoint slide—a triangle with words on it.

New York

I ride my bike almost every day here in New York. It's getting safer to do so, but I do have to be fairly alert when riding on the streets as opposed to riding on the Hudson River bike path or similar protected lanes. The city has added a lot of bike lanes in recent years, and they claim they now have more than any other city in the United States. But sadly most of them are not safe enough that one can truly relax, as is possible on the almost completed path along the Hudson or on many European bike lanes. That's changing, bit by bit. As new lanes are added some of them are more secure, placed between the sidewalk and parked cars or protected by a concrete barrier.

Between 2007 and 2008 bike traffic in New York increased 35 percent. Hard to tell if the cart is leading the horse here—whether more lanes have inspired more bicycle usage or the other way around. I happily suspect that for the moment at least, both the Department of Transportation and New York City cyclists are on the same page. As more young creative types find themselves living in Brooklyn they bike over the bridges in increasing numbers. Manhattan Bridge bike traffic just about quadrupled last year (2008) and the bike traffic on the Williamsburg Bridge tripled. And those numbers will keep increasing as the city continues to make improvements to bike lanes and adds bike racks and other amenities. In this area the city is, to some extent, anticipating what will happen in the near future—a lot more people will use bikes for getting to work or for fun.

On a bike, being just slightly above pedestrian and car eye

level, one gets a perfect view of the goings-on in one's own town. Unlike many other U.S. cities, here in New York almost *everyone* has to step onto the sidewalk and encounter other people at least once a day—everyone makes at least one brief public appearance. I once had to swerve to avoid Paris Hilton, holding her little doggie, crossing the street against the light and looking around as if to say, "I'm Paris Hilton, don't you recognize me?" From a cyclist's point of view you pretty much see it all.

Just outside a midtown theater a man rides by on a bike—one of those lowriders. He's a grown man, who seems pretty normal in appearance, except he's got a monstrously huge boom box strapped to the front of the bike.

I ride off on my own bike and a few minutes later another boom-box biker passes by. This time it's a Jane-Austen-reading, sensible-shoe-wearing woman. She's on a regular bike, but again, with a (smaller) boom box strapped to the rear . . . I can't hear what the music is.

City Archetypes

There is a magazine in a rack at the entrance to my local Pakistani lunch counter called *InvAsian: A Journal for the Culturally Ambivalent.*

What is it about certain cities and places that fosters specific attitudes? Am I imagining that this is the case? To what extent does the infrastructure of cities shape the lives, work, and sensibilities of their inhabitants? Quite significantly, I suspect. All this talk about bike lanes, ugly buildings, and density of population isn't just about those things, it's about what kinds of people those places turn us into. I don't think I'm imagining that people who move to L.A. from elsewhere inevitably lose a lot of that elsewhere and eventually end up creating L.A.-type work and being L.A.-type people. Do creative, social, and civic attitudes change depending on where we live? Yes, I think so. How does this happen? Do they seep in surreptitiously through peer pressure and casual conversations? Is it the water, the light, the weather? Is there a Detroit sensibility? Memphis? New Orleans? (No doubt.) Austin? (Certainly.) Nashville? London? Berlin? (I would say there's a Berlin sense of humor for sure.) Düsseldorf? Vienna? (Yes.) Paris? Osaka? Melbourne? Salvador? Bahia? (Absolutely.)

I was recently in Hong Kong and a friend there commented that China doesn't have a history of civic engagement. Traditionally in China one had to accommodate two aspects of humanity—the emperor and his bureaucracy, and one's own family. And even though that family might be fairly extended it doesn't include neighbors or coworkers, so a lot of the world is left out. To hell with them. As long as the emperor or his ministers aren't after me and my family is okay then all's right with the world. I had been marveling at the rate of destruction of anything having to do with social pleasures and civic interaction in Hong Kong—funky markets, parks, waterfront promenades, bike lanes (of course)—I was amazed how anything designed for the common good is quickly bulldozed, privatized, or replaced by a condo or office tower. According to my friend civic life is just not part of the culture. So in this case at least, the city is an accurate and physical reflection of how that culture views itself. The city is a 3-D manifestation of the social, and personal—and I'm suggesting that, in turn, a city, its physical being, reinforces those ethics and re-creates them in successive generations and in those who have immigrated to the city. Cities self-perpetuate the mind-set that made them.

Maybe every city has a unique sensibility but we don't have names for what they are or haven't identified them all. We can't pinpoint exactly what makes each city's people unique yet. How long does one have to be a resident before one starts to behave and think like a local? And where does this psychological city start? Is there a spot on the map where attitudes change? And is the inverse true? Is there a place where New Yorkers suddenly become Long Islanders? Will there be freeway signs with a picture of Billy Joel that alert motorists "attention, entering New York state of mind"?

Does living in New York City foster a hard-as-nails, no-nonsense attitude? Is that how one would describe the New York state of mind? I've heard recently that Cariocas (residents of Rio) have a similar "okay, okay, get to the point" sensibility. Is that a legacy of the layers of historical happenstance that make up a particular city? Is that where it comes from? Is it a constantly morphing and slowly evolving worldview? Do the repercussions of local politics and the local laws foster how we view each other? Does it come from the socioeconomic-ethnic mix; are the proportions in the urban stew critical, like in a recipe? Does the evanescence of fame and glamour lie upon all of L.A. like whipped cream? Do the Latin and Asian populations that are fenced off from the celebrity playgrounds get mixed into this stew, resulting in a unique kind of social-psychological fusion? Does that, and the way the hazy light looks on skin, make certain kinds of work and leisure activities more appropriate there?

Maybe this is all a bit of a myth, a willful desire to give each place its own unique aura. But doesn't any collective belief eventually become a kind of truth? If enough people act as if something is true, isn't it indeed "true," not objectively, but in the sense that it will determine how they will behave? The myth of unique urban character and unique sensibilities in different cities exists because we want it to exist.

City of Little Factories—the Old Crazy New York I

I ride in the Five Boro Bike Tour this morning. Forty-two miles! That sounds like a lot to some people but it only takes a little over three hours. And there are breaks. I thought I'd be more tired than I am, as I usually just ride locally to run errands or to get to work or go out at night. Corny as it might seem, it feels like I am participating in an uplifting civic event. People in Queens, Brooklyn, and Staten Island put signs in their yards and cheer the crowds of bikers as we whiz by, like they do for the runners in the marathon—only in this tour no one is racing. No one is keeping track of who comes in first.

The organizers have closed part of the FDR Drive, the BQE, the Belt Parkway, and the Verrazano Bridge—so we participants get the thrill of riding in the middle of a highway, and of not having to stop at red lights. Gone are the worries about the ubiquitous jaywalking New York City pedestrians hell-bent on suicide missions.

There are a couple of mandatory stops—for water, free bananas, and peanut-butter crackers—in Queens and near the Brooklyn side of the Verrazano Bridge, so racing and winding your way to the front of the pack get you nothing—except maybe the best bananas.

There is lots of spandex, way too much spandex. There is a characteristic sound of spandex skidding on asphalt that I've heard a couple of times already. I guess, for some, the fun of these events, or the fun in weekend cycling, is in dressing up. A change of outfit announces, "I'm doing *this* now! I'm a biker today."

9:30 AM: The view toward Randall's Island from under a railroad bridge.

12:00 noon: I'm riding over the Verrazano Bridge, which means I'm almost done. From here it's a short ride to the Staten Island Ferry and back to Manhattan.

Of course, some guys (and gals) who join this event are a little behind on their bike manners, or maybe they are trying to prove how manly they are—both to themselves and to everyone else. There is some high-speed zooming and jockeying for those meaningless leads. I had been warned that the most danger-ous aspect of this thing would be the other cyclists—especially those who are determined to get closer to the front of the mob—wherever that is. I can't even see the front anymore. The com-pact clump at the starting area in Lower Manhattan quickly elongates by the time it leaves the island. (This is accomplished intentionally by creating a couple of bottlenecks on Sixth Ave-nue in midtown that causes the ridership to become less dense.) It's not just the hotdoggers that you have to watch out for. The fact that there are so many cyclists here who are not used to riding and certainly not used to riding en masse, scrunched together, inevitably leads to some absentminded behavior that can cause some nasty pileups.

Mostly though, there is a rare and great feeling of civic togetherness—something we New Yorkers regard as suspect, but that's what it is. We have to give in to it—the feeling generated when a mass of people do something together, energetically, en masse. Like what happens in a mosh pit or on a roller coaster—a deep biological thrill gets triggered. Unlike some crowds this is a friendly mob, happy to abide by the barriers and traffic cones (for the most part), running on banana and peanut butter crackers power.

The longest part of the route goes through the waterfront neighborhoods of Brooklyn and Queens, which gives one the pleasantly skewed impression that the old, nutty industrial city that New York once was still exists. These neighborhoods are made up of an endless series of little factories that make plastic wrap, cardboard boxes, ex-lax, coat hangers, hairbrushes, and the wooden water tanks on top of every Manhattan residential building. Sure, some neighborhoods like Williamsburg, which we riders touched the edge of, have filled up with art galleries, cafés, and wonderful bookshops, while other neighborhoods are all Hasidic or Italian, but mostly the waterfront area is still composed of funky factories. These old structures are a million miles from the industrial parks, high-tech campuses, and corporate headquarters that one sees out west (west being across the Hudson). They are small in scale, and often they are family run. These are the places that make those glue-on reinforcement rings for notebook pages and apple corers that you look at and think, Who thought of that? Who designed that? Someone actually thought that up?

A few days later I bike to East New York (a neighborhood in Brooklyn) to see one of my art chair pieces being powder coated. It is a technique used for painting industrial stuff like metal shelving and cabinets and aluminum siding, and it gives a very smooth finish—the idea being that this chair should look

like it was mass-produced in a factory. The object goes into a chamber and then the air inside the chamber is filled with powdered paint that adheres evenly to the object, with no unsightly brushstrokes or drips.

Getting to this neighborhood I ride through the various Brooklyn ghettos—Dominican, West Indian, Hasidic, and black. By ghetto I don't mean a poverty-stricken, desolate, or decaying area. I don't necessarily mean that the area is black either. Some areas that might be considered ghettos are lively and flourishing. East New York, however, is pretty dicey. A friend was mugged here recently and forced to go into a bodega and buy a man some infant formula! At its worst the neighborhood looks like some of the very bleak places I've seen in the former Soviet bloc—derelict housing surrounded by crumbling industrial superstructures. (The elevated subway line looks like it hasn't been painted in decades out here.) These signs of decay and ruin are interspersed with lots of churches, and huge temples relocated into former theaters. The official neglect is obvious and plain. We laugh at Borat, but we have our own Kazakhstan right here.

Having viewed enough stimulating squalor I decide to take the more conventionally scenic route home. I head toward the water, which is nearby, and ride along the bike path that follows the Belt Parkway along the Brooklyn waterfront. On my left are the swamps and marshes of Jamaica Bay. It's not quite Nantucket, but it's pretty damn nice—and it's surprising that it's inside the New York City limits. Today is a Saturday, and there are lots of people barbecuing. They have set up in the grassy areas at the side of the highway and even on the median strips. It would be almost lovely if the ugly highway weren't so close.

I stop for scungilli (conch cooked in red sauce) at a place in Sheepshead Bay. There are picnic tables on the sidewalk and a window where one can order clams, oysters, and various kinds of seafood. This neighborhood is named after the tasty Sheepshead fish, so they say. It was once abundant, but now it's gone from here. It was also known as sea bream.

I'm reminded that the other day I wanted to bike to Long Island City to catch an art show at PS1, but it was the day of the New York City Marathon and the Queensboro Bridge bike lane was closed (for handicapped runners they said, though it was completely empty). So I took the bike on the Roosevelt Island tram instead and rode down by the abandoned lunatic asylum on the south end of that island that sits in the middle of the East River. There was no one around. Spooky. From the tip of the island there's a great view of the UN building and of a tiny

rock island filled with cormorants—an odd thing to see in the middle of New York City.

Once I managed to get to Long Island City I stopped for a snack at a nice Hunters Point café and watched outside as the marathon cleanup crews picked up the piles of paper cups and tissues that had been handed out to the runners. The streets ran bright yellow with Gatorade—it looked like the marathoners had all peed themselves after taking lots of vitamins. A few stragglers limped and walked by. I wondered to myself if I would be privileged to see the very last person in the race—a sight rarer and much harder to establish than whoever turns out to be first. I thought I saw him. It was a man in a multicolored head wrap who had a few days' growth of beard, his marathon number was askew, and I thought he might have been smoking a cigarette as he made his way up the street, listing slightly toward the curb.

How We Doin'?

New York has a surprising number of lovely bike paths, as distinct from bike lanes. This stretch is in Upper Manhattan.

This route goes almost all the way to the top of the island, where there is a nice park on the very tip of Manhattan in the Inwood neighborhood. There's also a great route along the Staten Island boardwalk that lines that borough's Atlantic beaches. It runs for miles, from the Verrazano Bridge and Gateway Park south. There are no cars, and there are a couple of places to eat. The beaches are surprisingly clean and some are even secluded. (The secluded ones are not so clean; I guess one can't have it all.)

In Brooklyn, besides the previously mentioned path along the wetlands near East New York (which can also be ridden out to the Rockaways), there is a path along the water from Bay Ridge that leads one under the Verrazano Bridge out to Coney Island. It does, unfortunately, have a highway on one side, but the view of the harbor on the other side makes up for it. And one is rewarded with a Latin band playing on the Coney Island boardwalk on summer weekends.

The Old Crazy New York II

My friend Paul is playing bass and singing at a Village bar/pizza joint, so I stop by to say hello. Arturo's is a weird combination of two throwbacks in one: It's a jazz bar, where regulars sing standards and musicians often stop by after a recording session or a paying gig and sit in. It's also a neighborhood pizza restaurant (the pizzas are quite good) that is friendly, noisy, and slightly chaotic.

The owner, whom I've never met, fills the walls with his paintings. There are some odd-looking portraits and some typical Greenwich Village scenes of charming tree-lined streets. The owner's daughter Lisa is often there and says hello. I ask her what's up with the funky airplane models hanging from the ceiling and she says her dad decided no more paintings; he's going to do airplane models now.

Arturo's is a neighborhood joint. There are a lot of regulars. It's not the sort of place that would ever attract the attention of serious foodies or get mentioned in the new trendy guides to New York City. The piano sits smack in the middle of the front room at the end of the bar, which forces the upright bass player to squeeze into a corner. A drummer sometimes joins them on a rudimentary kit made up of a snare, a high hat, and one cymbal. He has to squeeze over on the other side of the piano and he almost blocks the entrance to the kitchen. Singers grab a hand mic that rests on top of the piano and often have to dodge waiters and customers who want to use the restroom in back, which has a bathtub in it. A big one. I wonder how many people have fallen into it, or if the staff sometimes decides to have a hot bath.

A pear-shaped woman begins to sing, to enthusiastic applause. Someone mentions to me that she is the mother of Savion Glover, the famous tap dancer. I can see the resemblance, in her face at least. Her hair is a mixture of black and gray and is wound in a tight vortex, like Kim Novak's in the movie *Vertigo*. She sings a standard, and she's great, astounding even.

She sings another song and then sits down at a nearby booth with some friends. The pianist shows Paul some chord charts then sits in the booth behind the singer, near the kitchen door. He begins furiously focusing on some music scores he has with him, spreading them out across the tabletop. He's suddenly oblivious to the scene.

A man named Jimmy takes the mic. He had introduced himself to me earlier. "I do Thursday nights," was how he put it. Jimmy's hair is hard to describe. It's like a combination of a mullet and a Mohawk, but super slicked-back. He's got on a black jacket and a tie with big yellow trumpets on it. He sings a standard (they all do, except Paul, who tends toward Stevie Wonder tunes), putting his heart and soul into it.

The audience at Arturo's, which is not a very big place, is usually a mixed bunch: some are paying attention to the singer, some are shoving food into their mouths, and some are talking to their friends. Sometimes all three at once. It's not an ideal audience for an entertainer by any means, but it doesn't seem to deter anyone here. Jimmy sings as if there is a whole theater out there, rather than people slurping down a slice. He's singing to the back row, projecting; it's incredible.

Jimmy disappears for a second. He has an Asian pianist who has his eyes closed, so maybe he doesn't notice Jimmy's absence. Jimmy reappears in a cream-colored jacket carrying a matching cream-colored umbrella. He immediately launches into "Pennies from Heaven," and one gathers these are the props he keeps on hand somewhere in the back of the restaurant specifically for this number. "Ev'ry time it rains, it rains . . . pennies from heaven" and up goes the umbrella, in the middle of this crowded room! Pizza is being served up, and folks are ordering wine using hand gestures, as the waiters can't hear above Jimmy's singing. No one here seems fazed or the least bit surprised by the corny umbrella gag. Jimmy's jazzing up the song now, scatting and improvising—the tune is almost unrecognizable at times. He sometimes acts out the lyrics as he sings them, holding his hands in a praying gesture or grabbing Mrs. Glover to dance a step or two. They make an improbable couple. Now he's got a little black hat on too. At one point his singing is so impassioned that he abandons the mic on the piano near the tip jar and begins hopping, really hopping, around the room singing at the top of his lungs.

A Blackout

Yesterday, at four thirty, while I was recording a vocal on my computer here at home, I sensed something had shut off unexpectedly. My musical and recording gear is all plugged into a kind of large battery that is designed to keep everything running on a concert stage for about twenty minutes if there is a power fluctuation or outage, so, despite the fact that all of New York City has just gone down, I am still working for a few minutes more, oblivious to what has happened. I shut my stuff down properly, leave my recording area, and check to see what made the odd sound. I soon realize the power is off, and looking outside the window I can see that it seems to be off everywhere—it's a blackout all right. I fill up some containers with water, as the building's pump won't be filling the water tower on this or any other of these buildings until this is over.

All the clocks—the ones with dials that is—on the nearby buildings now say four thirty. The digital ones are dark. By late afternoon there are traffic jams everywhere, and since I live near a tunnel entrance the traffic around here is stuck for hours. A few cabs roam around picking up people, but most eventually head home. It's unexpectedly noisy. There are alarms going off everywhere. They started hooting right after the power went out.

I ride my bike downtown to see if my office is okay. A Mexican kid on a bike asks me how to get to the Brooklyn Bridge—I guess he is going home and usually takes the train. I talk to him in Spanish and he says he is surprised, judging by my face, that I know some Spanish.

My office had cleared out in a flash, they were pretty weirded out—memories of 9/11, I guess.

After the sun goes down I ride my bike through Times Square, which is dark except for police vehicles. The great signs and the intense glow that can usually be seen for blocks have been shut down. The signs are just abstract shapes now. It's even hard to make out what some of them are selling. The area is strangely crowded with people. The tourists are all still here, but don't know what to do. Black shapes, moving in clumps. Thousands and thousands of people. Many are just hanging out. Maybe they can't get home. An Irish bar on West Forty-fifth Street is open, and the crowd of drinkers spills out, filling the entire street.

Hundreds of people are waiting at every bus stop—all hoping to get home to Queens, the Bronx, Brooklyn, or uptown. They too spill out into the streets, in clusters that surround the bus stop signs, or they just sit on the curbs, as bus service, though continuing, is slow and intermittent, due to there being no traffic lights. All traffic is moving slowly, tentatively creeping along in the almost total darkness, like you do when you walk around the house with all the lights off. When a bus comes it is a large, looming shape with two blinding lights in front. They emerge slowly from the darkness, like bioluminescent deep-sea creatures.

People are all walking out in the streets, and they're hard to see in some parts of town. There is a fat man at the intersection of Sixth Avenue and Twelfth Street directing traffic. He is using a sign—a piece of white cardboard on which he has scrawled "Stop." At another intersection farther uptown a kid in baggy pants is also directing traffic, wildly, energetically; he's having a great time. There's no looting. It's calm. People are helping one another out, and there are spontaneous parties.

The stairway in my building is getting dark (the elevator doesn't work, of course), and, one by one, the emergency lights in the stair shaft are failing. Flashlight beams now move erratically in the darkness as tenants look for their floors. Most of the tenants are now on the roof, drinking. I join them, briefly. We can see a financial brokerage building a block away. It's lit up inside—bright as day—though there's no one in it. We can see desks covered with paperwork, abandoned. I guess they have their own generator. Not much else for me to do now but go to sleep.

In the morning I wake up and sense that it's starting to get a little stuffy in here. Last night it was still cooler inside than outside—a remnant of yesterday's air-conditioning—but that temperature difference won't last long. It's August, so having no AC it will take its toll. I heat up some leftovers for breakfast before they all spoil. The water pressure is down to a dribble. I have a jar of water in the fridge, but that won't last long. Many shops and delis were open last night, selling their remaining stocks of sodas, snacks, and water out of dimly lit doorways. Sometimes they lit candles and scattered them on shelves. The candles made the delis all look like little shrines. There were long lines at hardware stores—for flashlights and D batteries. (I've got both.) Can't get phone calls. (Though by using an old landline phone I have lying around I manage to call out.) Cell phone service isn't working. Gas is working. I'm making coffee this morning.

The traffic is noisy outside. What are they all doing out there? Where are they going? I notice that there are some scallops defrosting rapidly in the freezer, so I cook them for lunch.

I go downtown again to my office and the power comes back on at around three PM.

Kara, my Australian assistant, is moving back there with her boyfriend soon, and they'd scheduled a good-bye party for tonight in Greenpoint where they live. I assume that the party is still on, so as it gets dark I bike over the Williamsburg Bridge. The bridges are full of cyclists, as the subway and bus service is still intermittent, and from this vantage point I can see that not all the neighborhoods got their power back when the Village and SoHo did. Parts of the East Village are still dark, as is most of the Lower East Side. Uptown is all sparkling with lights. Parts of Brooklyn have power, and halfway across the bridge, where the lamps are being fed by Brooklyn, suddenly there is light. So, electrical power is political. I shouldn't be surprised.

E. B. White, Death, and Hope

I read E. B. White's skinny little book *Here Is New York,* which was written in 1948 as an assignment for *Holiday* magazine. I'm not sure many travel and leisure mags would accept a piece like this these days—it concludes with some very prescient meditations on death and war.

When he wrote this essay, a few years after World War II, the UN building had either just been completed or was still being built. He points out that after that war all cities, New York being a prime example, were standing opportunities for massive carnage and destruction on a scale not hitherto imagined: "A single flight of planes no bigger than a wedge of geese can quickly end this island fantasy, burn the towers, crumble the bridges, turn the underground passages into lethal passages, cremate the millions."

Whether because they were walled, like medieval ones, or because of the sheer numbers they harbored, cities once were secure refuges for their citizens. They were places where people not only met and haggled, but were also, to a degree, protected. Now, with the atomic bomb especially, as White points out, that protective aspect of what a city is has been turned upside down.

But, he notes, just as this shadow begins to loom over great mixtures of humanity like New York, an institution, the UN, is rising to attempt to put an end to this threat. Death and hope simultaneously, as always.

That the United States has clearly and brazenly taken an anti-UN stance in recent years—failed to pay their UN dues and often initiated acts in defiance of UN resolutions and principles—is a bad sign. The United States is not the only country to have done so, but it's the biggest kid on the block and it sends a signal to all the other kids that such behavior is acceptable, a sign that death and fear is sometimes more powerful than hope, temporarily. The UN is far from perfect. Self-interested parties and nations skew its abilities to perform its mission—its members are human, after all. But the fact that that little ray of hope still exists, right here in mean, jaded New York, and that it cannot be corrupted by corporate lobbyists, religious demagogues, and crooked election rigging—well, there's something to be said for that.

The new World Trade Center is being built atop a thirty-story concrete windowless bunker. A monument to fear—a symbolic return to a medieval mind-set and walled cities. Even though we are united and connected in so many new ways, some are still building massive walls and fortifications that won't really protect us from anyone determined and clever enough. Walls and concrete barricades aren't really an effective means of protection these days—nothing is, really. All that interconnectedness that facilitated much of the explosion of megawealth over the last decade also facilitated the interpenetration of everything, so no one or no building is truly isolated and "safe" anymore. Safety is in getting along.

I bike up to check out a show at the Studio Museum of Harlem. I follow the improved bike path north along the Hudson. It gets less crowded above 100th Street. I turn right on 125th and head east past churches and fried chicken joints, and I run smack into the African American Day parade on Adam Clayton Powell Boulevard. T-shirts are being sold that say I "heart" My Nose (or My Lips or My Hair). Shocking that this affirmation is still needed—that the models of beauty presented to us don't include a lot of us—and it takes T-shirt slogans to attempt to correct things.

On my way back home I see a nun on Rollerblades going up the Hudson River Park bike path, rosary flying behind her.

How New Yorkers Ride Bikes

There are more New Yorkers riding bikes than ever. And not just messengers. Significantly, a lot of young hip folks don't seem to regard cycling as totally uncool anymore, which was definitely the case when I began to ride around in the late seventies and early eighties. I sense that we might be approaching a tipping point, to invoke that now clichéd term. New Yorkers are at the stage where they might, given the chance and the opportunity, consider a bicycle as a valid means of transportation—if not for themselves, then at least they will tolerate it as a reasonable means of transport for other New Yorkers. They might eventually try it themselves, and certainly they will accommodate it. They might even support and encourage it.

So, with some tenuous optimism, I decide it might be time to try to give the biking-as-means-of-transport idea a little nudge by organizing some kind of public forum on the subject. I end up spending about a year trying to get a bike-related event off the ground, and am just about to give up when, through a connection with another project, the *New Yorker* magazine offers to sponsor the event at Town Hall. It is the perfect venue for something like this, having been historically a place where the issues of the day were aired and debated. Race (with Langston Hughes in 1945), birth control (with Margaret Sanger in 1921), and the establishment of the Jewish state of Israel (also in 1945) all were discussed on its stage.

I imagine the event as an evening centered around a meeting, a forum, made up of ordinary people, biking advocates, and city reps from the departments of transportation, parks, health, and urban planning, as well as the police department. Interspersed with this forum would be bike-related entertainment—music, funny bits, and ironic slide lectures. Part of my personal reason for attempting this event is to ask the theatrical question of whether civic engagement, improvement, discussion, and action can be successfully combined with art and entertainment—if culture, humor, and politics can mix, and if making our city a better place to live can be fun. That idea is, for me, almost as important as this bike advocacy business. If the advocacy is going to be boring, then forget about it.

Time passes; there are meetings with city agencies and with Yves Behar and fuseproject, his design company. In one part of the event Yves and his partner Josh will present a new kind of cool bike helmet, something nonsporty types might wear. Yves and company are intrigued by that idea, as is the Department of Health, of all agencies. Why the Department of Health and bike helmets? Well, getting your brains spread out on the street is pretty unhealthy. The Department of Health did a condom giveaway in New York City that fuseproject designed, and they've installed dispensers for free condoms in clubs, restaurants, and bars around town (placed near the bathrooms, I imagine). So there's a preestablished relationship there. Should (corporate) funding materialize they'd love to do a massive helmet or even a bike giveaway—but that's in the future.

The fuseproject helmet prototype consists of a protective hard shell that can be slipped in and out of various skins—a warm woolen skin with earflaps for cold winters, a porous mesh skin for hot summer days. A very digital-technology kind of idea, variable skins. The idea is that third-party developers— fashion brands, sports gear brands, or anyone who wants yet another advertising platform—might eventually make their own skins and sell or fund them. This design also allows the commuter to lock the shell to the bike and stow the skin—the only part that touches one's own skin—discreetly in one's brief-case or handbag.

As good as this is I personally sense that helmets might be an interim step toward integrated urban biking. Although they might always be a good idea, the wearing of helmets implies that cycling is dangerous, which at present it often is in cities

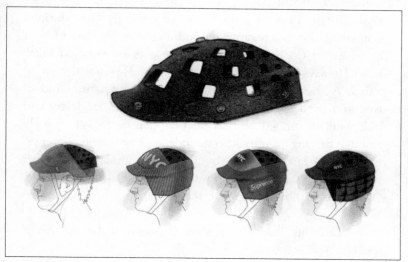

courtesy fuseproject

like New York and London. But in other cities like Amsterdam, Copenhagen, Berlin, and Reggio Emilia in Italy, the bike paths and lanes are so safe the riders don't feel the need to protect themselves. Cyclists in these places—kids, young creative types, businesspeople, seniors—also tend to ride upright with an elegant bearing; they're well dressed, and even sexy. It's a different attitude than the New York City head-down-into-battle approach.

Maybe, for some, part of the thrill would go away if urban cycling became safe. But that might be the price to pay if it means more people will start using bikes to get around. That thrill isn't really an appropriate thing to oblige schoolkids and seniors to be burdened with. Living in New York used to be a lot more dangerous in general, but that's hardly something to get all nostalgic about. So, while we might need a cool, stylish helmet to be available right now, for everyone in a more perfect world it might be optional.

Through Transportation Alternatives, a local advocacy organization, I am introduced to Jan Gehl, a visionary yet practical urban planner who has successfully transformed Copenhagen into a pedestrian- and bike-friendly city. At least one-third of Copenhagen's workforce gets to work on bikes now! He says it will approach half soon. He's not dreaming either. We here in New York might think that's natural and all well and good for the Danes, but New Yorkers are feisty and independent minded, so that can't happen here. (Why people feel that driving a car makes one independent minded is a mystery to me.) But Gehl reveals that his proposals initially met with exactly that kind of opposition over there: the locals said, "We Danes will never agree to this—Danish people won't ride bikes."

In one of his slide talks he shows before-and-after images of a street. Here is the after:

© 2009 Gehl & Gemzøe

Previously, the area bordering this canal had been used for parking; cars would drive along it looking for parking slots. This lovely spot was, not too long ago, primarily an ugly parking lot and a thoroughfare. Now it's a destination. Cars are still allowed to drive here, but not park. And from that one small change the area exploded as a pleasant gathering place and even as a tourist destination. Expensive "improvements" by the city weren't even necessary to allow this to happen. The customers and local businesses did the improvements—putting out chairs and installing awnings—though many of them initially complained that if people couldn't park in front of their establishments their businesses would suffer. That seems to be how Gehl works, making fairly small incremental changes over many years, here and there, that eventually transform the whole city and make it a more livable place.

Gehl has agreed to join the Town Hall event and give a short talk! He has recently been hired as an adviser by the city of

New York and has made studies of situations in other cities—
Amsterdam, Melbourne, Sydney, and London—in addition to
the one he did in his native Copenhagen. The Department of
Transportation here in New York has now asked his office for
further recommendations. Whether they and the city listen is
another matter, but it's a heartening move.

For the Town Hall event I now can move on and begin to
focus on securing the more obviously entertaining parts of the
proposed event. I contact the Young@Heart Chorus. They're a
choir based in Northampton, Massachusetts, and their young-
est member is in his midseventies. They sing songs by Sonic
Youth, the Ramones, Flaming Lips, and Talking Heads. (That's

© 2009 Ken Kern

how we made contact.) Needless to say, "Road to Nowhere" takes on added meaning when sung by this bunch. I ask them if they would sing the Queen song "Bicycle Race" at this event—and a few more songs, as I expect they'll be well received. They've never performed in New York City before, which is a surprise, as they're almost a staple on the European arts festival circuit. They agree to participate, but will require nap time and sufficient toilets for thirty people.

I recall that I have seen various Puerto Rican and Dominican groups around town who trick out antique Schwinn bikes, often adding giant boom boxes as well. The boom boxes mean that when the group becomes mobile they bring their own salsa or merengue sound track. I approach one group, Eddie Gonzalez and the Classic Riders, and get their card—they have a business card! I invite them to show their bikes onstage and explain briefly what they do. (Their stage entrance ends up being them playing their amazing array of customized horns to a Hector Lavoe tune.)

© 2008 Daniel Barlow

I'd seen a British Web site, the Warrington Cycle Campaign, that has a section called "Facility of the Month" with wonderful deadpan captions for photos of local bike lanes that lead into oncoming traffic or dead-end into phone booths. A representative of that group agrees to give a short tongue-in-cheek slide show.

The caption on their Web site reads: "After watching an episode of *Star Trek*, the forward-looking traffic planners of Oxford were thinking about how transport infrastructure would work in the middle of the next century. Boldly predicting that by then bicycles would be equipped with teleportation devices they realized that they could save a lot of paint by designing intermittent cycle paths, with cyclists able to beam themselves from one stretch to the next."

Hal, who repairs bikes at Bicycle Habitat on Lafayette Street, also has a more unusual job there: as new locks come into the store his job is to determine how long it takes to crack each one. Some locks he can break in a second, with a snip of some wire cutters he carries in his back pocket. Others require more elaborate tools. Hal agrees to break some locks onstage.

Rhonda Sherman from the *New Yorker* suggests adding some culture. In *New Yorker* speak this means some bike-related writing. Calvin Trillin will read a piece he's written about riding in New York, and Buck Henry will read an excerpt from a Beckett piece about a bicycle. Rhonda arranges for Mengfan Wu to edit together a touching four-minute film montage of bikes in movies—from Butch Cassidy to Kermit the Frog to a scene from the TV series *Flight of the Conchords*. Theater director Greg Mosher is contacted and coordinates the evening, and he helps everything move at a good pace and takes an incredible weight off my shoulders.

Transportation Alternatives has come up with the idea to provide valet parking for bikes at the event (!), as there is almost nowhere to lock up around Town Hall and lots of cyclists will be expected to attend.

We're almost ready. I've never done anything like this before—being an impresario rather than performing myself. I'm a little anxious. In the end, I have to modify some of my ideas for the event. It becomes obvious that a panel discussion involving numerous entities and city agencies could be a recipe for tedium and speechifying, so I give up on the idea that some consensus or compromise will be reached among all those folks in the course of one evening. It is decided that the agencies and the organizations will only present what they are actually going to do in the near future—not vague ideas but concrete plans. Naturally, this makes for shorter presentations.

On the night of the event I arrive with a bike cam attached to my helmet—well, the footage and my voice-over were actually shot the previous day but it looks like it is live. The camera shows my POV as I negotiate the Forty-second Street traffic and make my way to the theater, all the while providing a running commentary of tips for riding in New York traffic ("watch out for town cars and people with New Jersey plates"). Because a wide-angle lens is used it makes everything look slightly scarier than it is—cars and people loom suddenly into the frame— which makes it funnier, but probably doesn't do much to encourage ridership.

I have come to accept that things aren't going to change overnight, but that this event might be more about bringing a lot of disparate folks together at an opportune moment. It might serve as a kind of tacit encouragement, a visible acknowledgment that change is possible, maybe even likely, and that bike riding as a means of transport in New York City might be okay—if not now, then certainly in the very near future.

In the end, the event, which took place in October 2007, was successful, though I think it ran a little too long. We erred on the side of caution and maybe had more "acts" than we needed, as we were worried that we might not have enough content. We had plenty. It moved along fine but once in a while even I wanted to hit the fast forward button.

Rules of the Road

I might be unrealistic, but I think that if bikers want to be treated better by motorists and pedestrians then they have to obey the traffic laws just as much as they expect cars to, which isn't saying much in New York. Bikes should have to stop at red lights and stop signs. Certainly if cars are expected to, then cyclists should too. Bikes should ride *with* the flow of traffic, not against it. And if there is a bike lane, the cyclists should stay in it and not ride in the middle of the street or on the sidewalk. How does one modify New York cyclists' behavior? How does one modify any public behavior? Does modification require enforcement? The laws for such moving violations are already on the books, and I wonder, if they were enforced, would that work? Ideally, though, it would be great if there were a way to make this happen without requiring more cops or harsher penalties. Positive reinforcement works best, or so I have been told.

Likewise—now don't laugh—cars and trucks should view the bike lanes as if they are sacrosanct. A driver would never think of riding up on a sidewalk. Most drivers, anyway. Hell, there are strollers and little old ladies up there! It would be unthinkable, except in action movies. A driver would get a serious fine or maybe even get locked up. Everyone around would wonder who that asshole was. Well, bike lanes should be treated the same way. You wouldn't park your car or pull over for a stop on the sidewalk, would you? Well then, don't park in the bike lanes either—that forces cyclists into traffic where poor little meat puppets don't stand a chance.

Same with pedestrians—who in New York famously saunter out into traffic wherever they see a little gap. They've got enough brains not to walk in front of a truck, but they'll step right into the path of a cyclist, thereby initiating a game of urban chicken. The cyclists then have to slam on their brakes to avoid Mr. BlackBerry or Ms. Check-Me-Out.

As I write this in 2009, Janette Sadik-Khan, the new transportation commissioner, and others have made some changes and are initiating a host of improvements that are nudging New York in a new direction—toward being a more livable and sustainable city. In the summer of 2008 the city instituted Summer Streets, a series of car-free days in the summer during which Park Avenue and other streets that connect Central Park to the Williamsburg Bridge were all closed to automobile traffic. A significant new bike lane seems to be added almost monthly—one amazing stretch on Broadway with outdoor seating goes from Forty-second Street to Thirty-fourth. Prince Street now has a bike lane its entire length, but Grand Street has one that has met with some local resistance.

I ask Janette where she sees New York as far as transportation in ten years.

If the city continues on the path that it is on now, with attention to sustainability and transportation balance, in ten years we will have a good network of rapid bus routes that reaches all five boroughs, we will have many more bicycles on the streets (perhaps more than we can imagine if Albany fails to finance public transit!), and they will be fully integrated into the traffic system and the places that are now overpaved will have been turned into neighborhood plazas or more room for pedestrians. The city will be even safer as it continues to eliminate hot spots and redesign streets with traffic safety as the top priority. Times and Herald squares will take their places among the best and most-visited public squares in the world. There will be less motor vehicle traffic overall because we will have some form of congestion pricing or toll cordon around Manhattan—if only because it is so badly needed to help fund mass transit. Cities across America will be moving in this direction as well as they take their cues from a greater, greener New York.

Then I ask her to extend that to one hundred years . . . according to Enrique Peñalosa, ex-mayor of Bogotá, thinking long term frees us from our habitual cynical instincts.

Certainly there will be many forks in the road and choices the city will make over the next century, and technological leaps are hard to predict, but I think we can be sure that information technology will be fully built into the transportation system, so that the full array of one's travel choices at any given moment from bus arrivals to parking availability will be accessible and clear from one's home, workplace, mobile device, screen on your handlebars, chip in your head, or whatever is in use in this regard in 2109. Appropriate technology will have fully taken hold, so bicycles will be pretty standard for short trips and the zoning change that will be approved this year will mean that bike parking and accessibility will have been built directly into the city's building stock. Cars will be more like today's smart cars in scale but zero-emission and with collision avoidance systems built in, and the city will have addressed its problems with the movement of goods as population and overall trade grow—more of our stuff will be moved on trains and by water routes. So too, our crowded skies and airports will see some relief because the short- and perhaps medium-haul air markets will have yielded to far more convenient high-speed rail.

But, I wonder, sensing an uphill battle in some sectors, how does one balance the interests of business, the ordinary citizen, and I guess what might be called "quality of life"?

The answer for largely postindustrial cities like New York is that it is not that difficult, because the quality of life is an important part of the business climate. In a knowledge-based economy, people can live almost any-where and many can pick up and settle in another part of the world with increasing ease. New York has a huge amount to offer but with population growth and devel-opment pressure (which will return before long) we still have work to do regarding open space, opportunities for recreation, easing traffic and noise in neighborhoods, transportation choices, crowding on public transit, and so on. The business community in NYC largely sees opportunity when new parks open, when we propose new pedestrian areas in Times Square and even in plans like congestion pricing.

And ultimately what makes a city a place where one would want to live? For decades they were places that the middle class fled.

A lot of it has to do with opportunity, choice and the inten-sive and incredibly varied social and cultural life of a place like New York. Cities have always had that attraction for certain types of people and, as U.S. cities have become less edgy since the 1970s, more and more people want to par-take in them. Now the same people who value these things want to raise kids and grow old here and that means rein-forcing or adding in the conditions for neighborhoods, open spaces, safer streets, and places to have fun (and not just in clubs and bars) to thrive. The fact that I am transportation commissioner and with my team have the opportunity to create those sorts of conditions with bike-ways, new plazas, traffic calming, and so forth is another one of the great, amazing things about New York.

When I'm feeling optimistic I believe that the exhilaration, freedom, and convenience I experience as I ride around will be discovered by more and more people. The secret will be out and the streets of New York will be even more the place for social interaction and interplay that they are already famous for. As others have mentioned, the economic collapse of 2008 might be a godsend. A window has opened and people might be willing to rethink the balance of quality of life.

Epilogue: The Future of Getting Around

In a recent *New Yorker* article ("There and Back Again") I read that one out of every six American workers commutes more than forty-five minutes to work, each way. A growing number spends even more time—ninety minutes is not that unusual for a commute these days. Though some of these folks use public transportation—commuter trains and subways—there's a good percentage of solo car riders in there too. It's unsustainable. Unsustainable means that eventually the behavior will inevitably be changed or modified, either thoughtfully and voluntarily, or as a result of tragic consequences. Either way it will not go on as it is for very much longer.

The fact is that in the twentieth century the automobile was subsidized on a massive scale. The nicely paved roads that go to the tiniest little towns and obscure regions in the United States weren't built and maintained by GM and Ford—or even by Mobil and Esso. Those corporations benefited enormously from that system. Rail routes to small towns were allowed to wither and die and trucking became, for most goods, the cheapest and sometimes the only way to get products from place to place.

Now I have to admit it's nice to motor around a continent and stop wherever and whenever one pleases. The romance of being "on the road" is pretty heady, but a cross-country ramble is a sometime thing. It isn't a daily commute, a way of living, or even the best way to get from point A to point B. In Spain the new high-speed train can get you from Madrid to Barcelona in two and a half hours. By road it takes at least six. If the Spanish government had poured all that money into more freeways you still wouldn't be able to get there any faster.

In the UK newspaper the *Guardian* I read that the Pentagon sent a report to the Bush administration in 2004 informing them that climate change is real and that it is more of a threat than terrorism, and will—not might—have massive global political repercussions. They predict a worldwide scramble for survival and for resources that will inevitably result in an almost constant state of war around the globe. Sounds cheery. This came from the Pentagon, not the Environmental Protection Agency!

Riding a bike won't stop that or many other dire predictions from happening in our lifetimes, but maybe if some cities face the climate, energy, and transportation realities now they might survive, or even prosper—although the idea of prospering seems almost morbid, given that so many unsustainable cities will inevitably flounder through droughts, floods, unemployment, and lack of power. I expect some of the cities I've ridden around to more or less disappear within my lifetime—they're resource hogs and the rest of the continent and world won't put up with it for long. I don't ride my bike all over the place because it's ecological or worthy. I mainly do it for the sense of freedom and exhilaration. I realize that soon I might have a lot more company than I have had in the past, and that some cities are preparing for these inevitable changes and are benefiting as a result.

I recently attended a short talk by Peter Newman, an Australian professor and urban ecologist, who originally coined the phrase "automobile dependency." He presented a scary graph that showed energy consumption—mainly used in getting around—in many of the world's large cities. The United States uses the most, with Atlanta—which has sprawled incredibly in recent decades—heading the list. Australia came next, followed by Europe and, at the very bottom, Asia. I would have thought, having seen photos of the massive pollution that has accompanied the Asian economic boom, that Asia would be higher on the list for energy use, but the density of a city—and those cities are very dense—often means that its citizens use less energy in getting around, as well as less energy for heating, cooling, and waste disposal. For that reason New York is actually greener than a lot of cities that, from the look of them at least, with their extensive trees and backyards, appear to be more bucolic and might therefore be assumed to be greener. But a golf course is not green.

The Chinese also ride bikes, or used to, anyway, which kept their energy use down. And they can't afford central heating or AC. But that's all changing now as cheap cars are being introduced there and in India—a trend that doesn't bode well in the long run. It seems unfair to expect the Chinese and the Indians to be smarter about their carbon footprint and pollution than we in the West are, but the fact is if they approach our levels of car use and fossil-fuel consumption the whole planet will become unsustainable.

Why do people do things that seem to be not in their own best interests? Not just the Chinese—all of us. Well, for status, for starters. From a genetic point of view a step up the status ladder is worth more than just about anything else. Think about the mantis who gets eaten immediately after depositing his sperm—genetically he's actually done okay. The male mantis, the delivery vehicle, is expendable from this point of view—at least if he has done his job. From this perspective, if owning a car improves your image and status, and therefore your mating chances, then the sacrifice—so our built-in instincts tell us—is absolutely worth it. Not really, not ultimately, but that might be what our compasses tell us. And, if an even bigger car proffers even greater status, then sure, get an SUV, or one of those new stretch armored tank-type things.

New York City is making some headway in dealing with traffic congestion, though it is hardly a model city in this respect. A number of European cities—Copenhagen, Berlin, Amsterdam, and Paris—are much further along. But I live here, so I am curious about how big bad New York will deal with this elephant.

The Department of Transportation (DOT) has been adding bike lanes here and there over the last decade. Up till now most of them have been helpful, but many of them are far from what they need to be. In most cases the lanes consist of some white lines between the parked cars and the moving traffic, so vehicles are constantly moving in and out of the bike lanes. In addition, being next to the traffic means that every once in a while, fairly regularly in fact, drivers swerve into the bike lane to stop, unload, or park—or, without signaling, cross it as they turn a corner. One has to be constantly on the alert. I wouldn't want my kid riding in those lanes.

Adding more bike lanes like those I describe is somewhat perverse because it makes a show of responding to the problem but in a way that, in my opinion, is ultimately destined to fail. Sadik-Khan and others seem to be recognizing this, as the new bike lanes they've been adding on Ninth Avenue, Broadway, and down on Grand Street are either completely protected by a concrete curb or are next to the sidewalk, with the parked cars allotted the lane between the bike lane and the moving traffic.

In the words of Enrique Peñalosa, who instituted bike and pedestrian streets and rapid transit in Bogotá when he was mayor, if a bike lane isn't safe for an eight-year-old child, it isn't really a bike lane. I tried to get my daughter to ride her bike a little in New York when she was in high school, but it didn't take—partly for this reason and partly maybe because it wasn't cool.

When I head downtown on the new Ninth Avenue bike lanes, as I do fairly often, I notice the difference. I instantly feel as if a weight has been lifted. I no longer feel that I have to be quite as paranoid. I'm not afraid that a driver might swerve into "my" lane, and to some extent the usual adrenalized state I get into when negotiating the New York City streets almost dissipates, for a few blocks anyway. I move faster too—there's no jockeying around double-parked cars, pedestrians, delivery vans, and cabs picking up or discharging fares.

After the Town Hall event the Department of Transportation approached me about judging a contest to design new bike parking for New York City. I agreed, and suggested that though we need more individual racks here and there, it is in places where people congregate—or will congregate in the future—that the issue most urgently needs to be addressed. Movie multiplexes, music clubs, schools, greenmarkets, and parks where New Yorkers sunbathe and cruise each other need lots of bike parking, not just a couple of racks. In Williamsburg a parking spot alongside the Bedford Avenue L-train station—the main subway station funneling hipsters to and from Manhattan— was taken over by the DOT and built out to make a bike parking area the size of a car space. Quite a number of bikes can fit in here, and it's chockablock most of the time. Trading a parking spot here and there for bike parking real estate seems practical—there's nowhere else to put a sizable rack, unless a nearby building has a plaza.

In Tokyo I rode to a complex that includes movie theaters, restaurants, a museum, and high-end shops. It had a room devoted to bike parking with contraptions enabling double-decker stacking. And it was free. To some extent that room was built to prevent people like me locking up to railings and posts—places that might cause pedestrian bottlenecks. So it's not just 100 percent altruistic—it's practical too.

When I agreed to co-judge the rack designs I sketched out some amusing smaller bike rack ideas of my own, each for a specific New York City neighborhood, and passed them on to the DOT. They were not meant as serious proposals, but as an incentive to loosen up. To my surprise the DOT responded, "Let's do these! If someone pays for fabrication we'll put them up." There is a dollar-sign-shaped rack for Wall Street, a high-heeled-shoe-shaped rack for upper Fifth Avenue, a doggie-shaped rack for the Village, an abstract shape for MoMA, etc. Because these are for specific neighborhoods they're not made to be mass-produced—hence the DOT asking for someone else to cover fabrication costs.

Here is my drawing of one called *The Olde Times Square*:

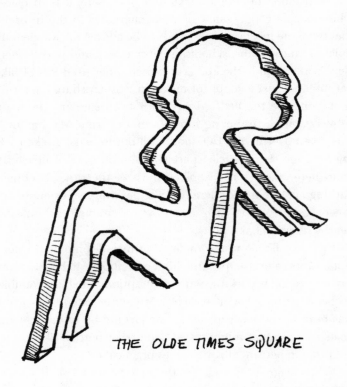

THE OLDE TIMES SQUARE

Here is the one in front of the luxury department store Bergdorf Goodman:

courtesy PaceWildenstein, New York, photo by Kerry Ryan McFate

Because these racks are one of a kind they really aren't offered as a solution to the bike-parking problem. But they did draw some attention to the issue. Some months later the real winner was chosen—an elegant and practical wheel-shaped design (see following page).

Last year Transportation Alternatives invited me to a meeting organized by the Manhattan borough president about transportation issues in New York City, which was held at Columbia University. I was not able to stay for the whole thing, but was excited to meet Enrique Peñalosa, and to hear him speak.

Peñalosa's innovations had the effect of relieving congestion, boosting the economy, and making Bogotá and the surrounding suburbs a better place to live. Some credit should also go to Jaime Lerner, the former mayor of Curitiba, a Brazilian city that made some of these changes previously and that serves as an

© 2009 Danielle Spencer

inspirational and ongoing example for clever and inexpensive urban planning. In the '70s Lerner proposed a bus-based rapid-transit system for that booming city, which is now used by 85 percent of the people living there. It works by treating buses as if they are trains or subways, with dedicated roads—a little like train tracks—and tube-shaped stations where passengers prepay, so boarding is rapid, the way it is at a train or a subway station.

The system proved to be very successful and became a model for other cities around the world. Though not as clean and permanent as rail, it is cheaper and can be implemented quickly. (Rail has the added advantage of stations that are fixed, so shops and businesses spring up around them knowing that these station hubs will be around for a while). Unfortunately, Curitiba is still, to me, a pretty boring town, but these changes have made it much more livable for the residents.

Peñalosa implemented a similar plan in Bogotá, as well as

© 2009 Carlos E. Restrepo

creating the longest pedestrian (and bike) street in the world—twenty kilometers. He began by closing select streets on weekends, and then gradually, as businesses realized that this actually increased sales and improved the general mood, he added more days and closed more streets. It transformed the life of the city. Needless to say, it reduced the congestion as well. People came in contact with each other more often, went strolling, and enjoyed their city. Peñalosa had to fight an alternative plan that was already on the table—a $600 million highway project that would have both destroyed large parts of the city and not solved the problem, like what Robert Moses did to New York City.

Here are more of Peñalosa's thoughts, from a piece he wrote called "The Politics of Happiness":

One common measure of how clean a mountain stream is is to look for trout. If you find the trout, the habitat is healthy. It's the same way with children in a city. Children are a kind of indicator species. If we can build a successful city for children, we will have a successful city for all people. . . .

All this pedestrian infrastructure shows respect for human dignity. We're telling people, "You are important—not because you're rich or because you have a Ph.D., but because you are human." If people are treated as special, as sacred even, they behave that way. This creates a different kind of society.

While at Columbia University I am introduced to some of the local New York political players: the head of the Taxi and Limousine Commission, someone from the Department of Transportation, a rep from the borough president's office. It's another world for me, not really one I feel that comfortable in. Peñalosa takes the stage and shows some slides of Bogotá and talks about what he did there. Among the things he says:

- Traffic jams are not always bad. The priority should not always be to relieve them. They will force people to use public transportation.
- Transportation is not an end—it is a means to having a better life, a more enjoyable life—the real goal is not [just] to improve transportation but to improve the quality of life.
- A place without sidewalks privileges the automobile, and therefore the richer people in cars have more rights; this is undemocratic.

Peñalosa tends to link equality, in all its forms, with democracy—a connection that is anathema to many in the United States. In his words, "In developing-world cities, the majority of people don't have cars, so I will say, when you construct a good sidewalk, you are constructing democracy. A sidewalk is a symbol of equality. . . . If democracy is to prevail, public good must prevail over private interests."

He goes on to say, "Since we took these steps [in Bogotá], we've seen a reduction in crime and a change in attitude toward the city." I can see why. When there are constantly people on the streets the streets are automatically safer. The late Jane Jacobs made a big point of this in her famous book, *The Life and Death of Great American Cities.* In healthy neighborhoods people watch out for one another. Being in a car may feel safer, but when *everyone* drives it actually makes a city less safe.

For New York, Peñalosa recommended first imagining what a city could be, what would one wish for, what could be achieved, in a hundred or more years. As with the great Gothic cathedrals one has to imagine something that one will not see in one's lifetime, but something one's children or grandchildren may experience. This also frees one from quickly dismissing an idea as too idealistic or as pragmatically improbable. Of course, like dealing with global warming, long-range planning needs political will, which is something that ebbs and flows, rises and falls. We can be guardedly optimistic, because if there is precious little of that will at times, it doesn't mean that there will never be any.

He asked that we imagine Broadway, the longest street in the United States, as a pedestrian street. He asked that we imagine reclaiming contact with the East River and dismantling the FDR Drive. And, as an interim measure, he suggests we might begin slowly, by turning one long street, like Broadway or Fifth Avenue, into a pedestrian street just on Sunday afternoons. (The fact that New York City businesses don't rely much on car access and don't have massive parking lots out front like shops in the suburbs makes this all within the realm of possibility.) Well, Sadik-Khan took his advice on that last bit, and the Park Avenue closings in the summer of 2008 were a step in this direction.

In my opinion, Forty-second Street could easily be a pedestrian street—well, it almost is now, with all the stalled traffic, picture taking, and jaywalking. Imagine it as an elongated plaza, with theaters, restaurants, trees, and, in the middle of the street, seating and outdoor cafés . . . and free WiFi.

Since the onslaught of the automobile in the middle of the last century, and the efforts of its enablers, like Robert Moses in New York, the accepted response to congestion has been to build more roads, especially roads that are high speed and with limited access. Eventually it became clear that building more roads doesn't actually relieve congestion—ever. More cars simply appear to fill these new roads and more folks imagine that their errands and commutes might be accomplished more easily on these new expressways. Yeah, right. People end up driving more, so instead of the existing traffic levels remaining constant and becoming dispersed on the new ribbons of concrete, the traffic simply increases until those too are filled. That's what New York and a lot of other cities are realizing now. The old paradigm is finally being abandoned.

In Lyon, a bike loan system was initiated some years ago that has now been introduced in Paris. As I mentioned in this book's preface, in this system, called Vélib' (velo=bike, lib=free/freedom) a subscriber swipes a credit card at one of many stations to obtain a bike. The bike is then released, and the first half hour is free. The credit card swipe is mainly for security: if you steal it, you bought it.

There are stations all over Paris—most are not more than three hundred meters from each other—so your bike can be deposited at or very near your destination. If you go for a longer ride, longer than thirty minutes, then you are charged, and the cost ramps up steeply, discouraging long excursions. So, if you just go on short trips—to meet a friend for dinner or lunch or go to the movies or to get some bread or milk—it's virtually free, as the subscription fee is minimal.

Boris Horvat / AFP / Getty Images

The Vélib' system was partly funded by a deal made with an outdoor display company—JCDecaux. The company paid for the right to sell display space on city structures, like public restrooms (which the company builds), bus stops, and newsstands, and in return they funded the Vélib' system. This deal actually generates money for the city, as well as having revolutionized the way Parisians get around.

Not only how they get around, but what other kinds of choices they make as city dwellers and how they feel about their city. In the past one's activities might have been considered and limited by Métro schedules and routes, taxi availability, and other factors like parking and traffic. The bikes liberate one from all those concerns, as well as create a mood of conviviality and social comfort—as in Bogotá.

Rumor is this system will be tested on Governors Island just off the southern tip of Manhattan—to see if the credit card technology works, I guess. Then I hear it will be tried out in a limited area like the Lower East Side or the East Village, which would seem appropriate, as a lot of people go to events and work in that area and never leave it.

In a way, these folks who are working to reinvigorate their cities all owe a debt to Jane Jacobs, who in 1968 fought Robert Moses's plan to run a highway through downtown New York City. It was previously thought that Moses was unstoppable. He managed to make it seem that he was the voice of inevitable progress and that wiping out neighborhoods to get closer to Le Corbusier's or General Motors' vision of the futuristic Radiant City was the voice of reason. Jacobs, besides elucidating what made some

Jane Jacobs at White Horse Tavern. © 2009 Cervin Robinson.

neighborhoods work and others not, made a case for cities being places where a good and stimulating life could be had.

This was news to many. In those days—the late 1960s and early '70s—a lot of people in the United States seemed to believe that cities were soon to be things of the past, that modern life could only be properly lived in a suburban house with a yard, linked to the urban workplace—a clump of high-rise office buildings—by a network of highways. One place for working, another for living. L.A. and other similar cities were the wave of the future, and New York, to survive, would be forced to emulate their example. Or so it was thought.

As it turned out, most people are now leaning more toward Jacobs's realization that the formula of separating living and working inevitably results in little actual life taking place in either area. The suburbs became weird quiet bedroom communities where kids are bored out of their skulls. Their parents only sleep or shop there, so for them it doesn't matter—until junior gets into drugs or massacres his classmates.

Jacobs famously called what happened daily on her block in Greenwich Village a "sidewalk ballet."

"I make my own first entrance into it a little after 8 when I put out the garbage can. . . . Soon after . . . well-dressed and even elegant men and women with briefcases emerge from doorways and side streets, and simultaneously, numbers of women in housedresses have emerged and as they crisscross with one another they pause for quick conversations that sound with either laughter or joint indignation, never, it seems, anything in between."

She realized that mixed use was key. That when a street or park is used by different kinds of people at different times of the day it stays economically and socially healthy, and is safer. You don't need more cops and harsh laws to make a neighborhood safe. You need to not suck the life out of it. Jacobs saw that what *feeds into* a park or a street affects the health of that street as much as what is actually on that street. Nothing in a city is isolated, and no part remains unaffected by the life (or the non-life) of the blocks surrounding it. All these organic structures and processes that she noticed and elucidated were, of course, not dictated from above. There was no urban planner who had designed these healthy lively neighborhoods as I somewhat implied in the Manila chapter. Instead of destroying them planners could and did learn from neighborhoods.

Ultimately, Jacobs realized that invisible forces—laws that govern mortgage payments, house loans, and, of course, zoning—could create, enliven, preserve, or eviscerate a neighborhood. Black urban American neighborhoods never had a chance, as hard as their citizens worked—since home lending laws were stacked against them. These arcane laws have huge and visible effects. The Garment District—where I live now—is going through a radical transformation as a result of legal changes of this latter type. About five years ago it was forbidden to build big apartment buildings and condos around there. The point was to preserve the light-manufacturing base that makes the Garment District work as a creative and vibrant manufacturing area—at least in the daytime.

The area developed over decades to be a home to light manufacturers, fashion designers, button and zipper wholesalers, pattern cutters, fabric wholesalers, and other small trades that feed the needs of the garment and fashion industries. If a designer needed a pattern cut or wanted to use a weird type of button, well, most likely it was made and would be available within a couple of blocks, so creative needs and impulses went hand in hand with the flourishing of these small businesses. It was all pretty efficient. In an effort to protect this synergy, laws limited who could build, own, or rent in this area. Someone realized that all these businesses worked because they existed in proximity to one another. They couldn't exist in isolation. You can't e-mail a button. Density is critical.

When real estate values skyrocketed (this was before the recent mortgage/credit crisis) developers began eyeing the area.

Not surprisingly it was eventually rezoned so that residential buildings could be planned, built, and rented. The inevitable result is that the small garment industries are getting pushed out. Some of the garment business had already moved to New Jersey or offshore. When the density declines to a certain level it will no longer function.

I'm not saying this is all bad. Possibly the fact that this area had developed into a single-use neighborhood helped make it so nefarious and dangerous at night. Hell's Kitchen. Until recently the west side of my neighborhood was notorious for junkies and hookers, mainly transvestites. (The poor transvestites are always getting shoved from one neglected zone to another.)

Now there are towering condos going up on every block. The neighborhood has become safer, but sadly other little businesses are leaving as well—one by one. There were two fishmongers nearby on Ninth Avenue until a few months ago. Now there's just one. There were still two butcher shops until recently, but one of those has just closed. The fruit and vegetable market run by a Latino family closed last year and another Thai restaurant took its place. There are now three Thai restaurants in a two-block area.

I suspect that many of these changes—not all of them for the worse in the case of my area—are mainly the result of those legal and zoning changes, invisible top-down decisions that over time have sweeping effects. We're not even aware of some of them unless we attend local meetings, so it's a little hard to see how they are going to affect the city. But many of us instinctively recognize the things that are worth fighting for and when we see them getting wiped out then we react—hoping it's not too late.

So, though I didn't plan to, I've become a bit of an advocate. I agree with Jan Gehl: Though I ride on them, the New York streets are not ready this year for everyone to deal with, not just yet. New York shouldn't be flooded with cyclists overnight. My recommendations to friends of where to ride in New York are limited to the streets, parks, and promenades where it does work. And there are more and more of them.

I'm in my midfifties, so I can testify that biking as a way of getting around is not something only for the young and energetic. You don't really need the spandex, and unless you want it to be, biking is not necessarily all that strenuous. It's the liberating feeling—the physical and psychological sensation—that is more persuasive than any practical argument. Seeing things from a point of view that is close enough to pedestrians, vendors, and storefronts combined with getting around in a way that doesn't feel completely divorced from the life that occurs on the streets is pure pleasure.

Observing and engaging in a city's life—even for a reticent and often shy person like me—is one of life's great joys. Being a social creature—it is part of what it means to be human.

Appendix

Security Tips

Hal from Bicycle Habitat demonstrated for an audience at Town Hall how easy it is to cut a cable (five seconds) or saw through a U-lock (a minute) or break a chain with a grinder (four minutes). Who carries grinders with them and where would they plug them in, you might ask? It happens. Not as much as it used to, but it does. Hal's advice is to use as much security (more than one type of lock if possible, then they'll have to have multiple tools) as you can bear and ride as crappy a bike as you can—if you're going to lock it up outside.

I think he's right, but maybe two locks is a little extreme. I got some security bolts recently that require specific tools to unscrew. The bolts replace the wheel quick releases and the seat release and they seem to work—neither my wheels nor my seat have been stolen in a while. A few companies make these. You get a special key-type thing and the bolts are really hard to undo without the key. The drawback is if you need to take your wheel off for repairs, well, you need to have the key with you.

As far as locks go, one bike store here recommends a stubby U-lock as opposed to the long ones, as they say it's hard to get a pipe in the tiny gap left by the short ones to leverage and break the lock. That's working pretty well so far.

Maintenance

I once got a really good bike, with expensive gears and brakes—the whole deal. But keeping it in tune and running smoothly was such a never-ending process that when it was eventually stolen (actually only the front half was stolen) I didn't bother to replace it. It was like a purebred animal: it needed constant care and was very finicky. If you're a foreign sports car guy who loves tinkering in the garage, then you'll love those high-end bikes.

Helmets and Clothing

Helmets are notoriously uncool-looking. I've tried different things as helmets. English riding helmets seem pretty safe (lots of Styrofoam padding) and they are very stylish (they're velvet covered and have a satin bow in the back!) but they have zero ventilation. God knows what those ladies' and gentlemen's hair looks like when they get back from the hunt! Ewww.

I tried a (baseball) batter's helmet once too— that covers one ear (the ear facing the pitcher). They stay on without a strap (by hugging your head tightly), which works for batters, as they toss them off after three minutes at the plate, but riding in one for even a short while gave me a splitting headache.

I tried decorating my helmets too. One year I saw a Puerto Rican man selling raccoon tails out of a shopping cart. I bought one and tied it to the back of my helmet. Davy Crockett! King of the Wild Frontier! That helmet got stolen really quickly.

In the winter and on cold days I wear a skateboard helmet. They cover a lot of your head and they don't have holes in them so they're warm. When the weather gets milder I wear a more expensive racing model with a lot of holes in it, which doesn't prevent helmet hair, but allows my scalp to breathe a little. My friend C just got a collapsible helmet in Japan—leather strips filled with tough cushion material that flattens out when it's not on your head.

Spandex—I've never tried it. I do have one pair of semi-baggy sports shorts with a crotch pad. We guys have read about bikes and the prostate. I only wear those if I know I'm going on a really long or strenuous ride. Only once in a rare while have I had numb nuts. It's a freaky feeling, and the pad prevents that from happening.

I find that unless it's really hot out I can dress pretty normally, which often means long pants and a shirt with a collar. If I relax and don't push the speed then I don't turn into a fountain—and can attend meetings, concerts, and social events without worrying too much. (I did have a shower installed at my office/studio—in case I arrive there drenched in sweat and have to look nice for a meeting. I had to clear it with the buildings department, as it's a commercial building and they thought I might be constructing a secret rental apartment. I actually haven't used it much—you can ask the folks in the office if that's been a problem.) I do stick to the bike paths along the river as much as I can, as it's maybe ten degrees cooler away from the traffic. Yup, traffic not only pollutes, it also makes our cities hotter. Not everyone can ride along a river, but riding close to trees does much the same thing.

In the spring and fall I can even wear a suit or a jacket if the event requires it. If I don't do any strenuous pedaling then I am just fine. I do either roll up my right trouser leg or throw a trouser clip on it, as not all bikes have those guards to keep the chain grease off your pants leg on that side.

Finally, I know it's even more nerdy than riding a bike, but I got a removable basket and it has really worked out. I can pick up groceries on the way home, toss my bag or backpack in there if I'm carrying a laptop or something semiheavy like that. Besides taking the weight off my body it means I don't get a sweaty back from wearing a backpack.

Travel

I have tried a few different folding bikes, but I haven't tried them all, so this is not a consumer report. I have a prejudice against the folding ones with little wheels, though I began my music touring with a small folding Peugeot with little wheels and it held up for many years. I now mainly use full-sized folding bikes that feature some form of suspension—either in the front fork or the seat. I once got really sore wrists and I think it was from riding a lot on cobblestones in SoHo without suspension. For a guitar player this was worrying. Montague and Dahon both make folding bikes with full-sized wheels. Brompton, Birdy, Moulton, and Dahon all make folding bikes with small wheels.

The full-sized bikes fold into a large suitcase with wheels (that also has room for a helmet), which can be checked as a second piece of luggage. Once upon a time you were allowed two pieces of luggage with no extra charge—that's rare now. I've gotten stuck with $125 sports-equipment charges (I think this charge was meant for skis or golf bags), so I'd think twice about throwing in the bike for a short trip these days. If I'm going to be somewhere for a week it is not only practical and fun but also economical, even with the baggage charge.

An alternative to all this luggage and packing is to rent a bike when you get to where you're going. It's getting easier to do this locally. I recently rented a bike in Berlin for a week and in Salvador, Brazil, for two days.

Organizations and Links

Transportation Alternatives
http://www.transalt.org

Gehl Architects
http://www.gehlarchitects.com

EMBARQ The WRI Center for Sustainable Transport
http://embarq.wri.org/en/index.aspx

Institute for Transportation & Development Policy
http://itdp.org

New York City Department of Transportation
http://www.nyc.gov/html/dot/html/home/home.shtml

Institute for Sustainability and Technology Policy
http://www.istp.murdoch.edu.au

Additional New York City Bike Rack Designs by David Byrne

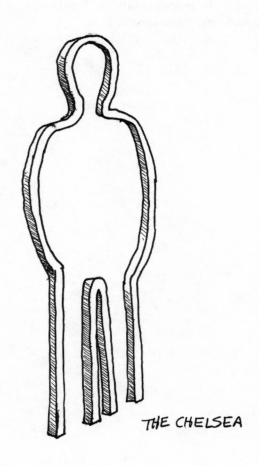

THE CHELSEA

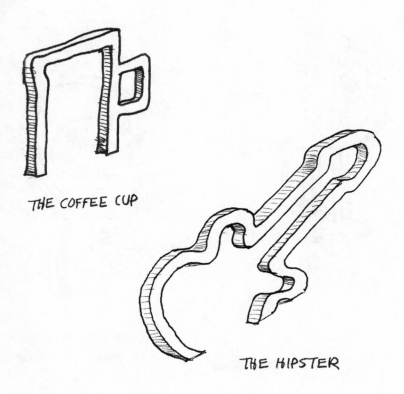

THE COFFEE CUP

THE HIPSTER

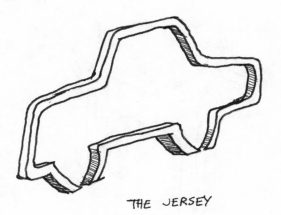

THE JERSEY

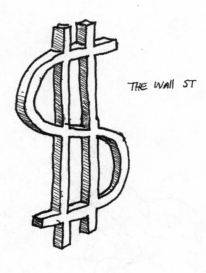

THE WALL ST

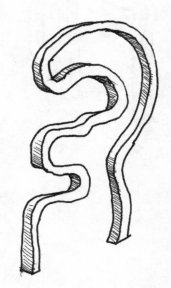

THE MOMA

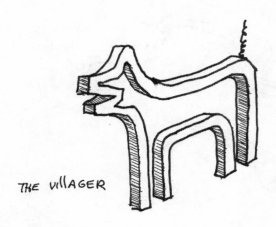

THE VILLAGER